Beyond representation

D1494753

Beyond representation

Television drama and the politics and aesthetics of identity

GERALDINE HARRIS

Manchester University Press
Manchester and New York

distributed exclusively in the USA by Palgrave

Published by Manchester University Press
Oxford Road, Manchester M13 9NR, UK
and Room 400, 175 Fifth Avenue, New York, NY 10010, USA
www.manchesteruniversitypress.co.uk

Distributed in the United States exclusively by
Palgrave Macmillan, 175 Fifth Avenue,
New York, NY 10010, USA

Distributed in Canada exclusively by
UBC Press, University of British Columbia, 2029 West Mall,
Vancouver, BC, Canada V6T 1Z2

British Library Cataloguing-in-Publication Data is available

Library of Congress Cataloging-in-Publication Data is available

ISBN 978 0 7190 7459 2 paperback

First published by Manchester University Press in hardback 2006

This paperback edition first published 2011

The publisher has no responsibility for the persistence or accuracy of URLs for any external or third-party internet websites referred to in this book, and does not guarantee that any content on such websites is, or will remain, accurate or appropriate.

Printed by Lightning Source

For Colin Knapp (who else?)

Contents

Acknowledgements   ix

Introduction: beyond the politics of identity?   1

1 Beyond realism? Modes of reading in Marxist-socialist
and post-Marxist-socialist television drama criticism   9

2 The end(s) of feminism(s)? From *Madonna* to *Ally McBeal*   34

3 Divided duties: diasporic subjectivities and 'race relations'
dramas (*Supply and Demand, The Bill, Second Generation*)   66

4 The world of enterprise: myths of the global and global
myths (*Star Trek*)   99

5 Only human nature after all? Romantic attractions and
queer dilemmas (*Queer as Folk*)   138

Conclusion: beyond (simple) representation? *Metrosexuality*
and *The Murder of Stephen Lawrence*   169

References   191
Index   203

Acknowledgements

This book was completed with the support of the Arts and Humanities Research Board in the form of a research leave grant. My gratitude is also due to Manchester University Press for their patience and support. Similarly to my colleagues and ex-colleagues in Theatre Studies at Lancaster University, Nigel Stewart, Kate Newey, Gabriella Giannachi, Karen Juers-Mumby, Chris Roberts. Special thanks to Dr Alice Booth for her help on the manuscript and for intellectual crossfertilisation. Very special thanks to Elaine Aston for Sea World, Dostoevsky's hat and so much more, and to Andrew Quick, who would like it to be known that the money he owed me was a mere pittance and was repaid long ago, unlike my greater, more abstract, debt to him. Thanks also to Mike Bowen, Dave Blacow and Andy Sellars in the Lancaster University Television Unit and to all the students over the years who have taken the TV drama course. Finally thanks to colleagues in Cultural Studies and Women's Studies, and in particular to Sara Ahmed, whose work so clearly inspires much of this book.

Introduction: beyond the politics of identity?

The title for this book is inspired by a 1998 radio interview in which Michael Jackson, then controller of Channel 4, was asked about the company's current position on its policy of catering for 'minority' or 'special interest' groups, established as part of its original charter in the 1980s. Taking the series *Queer as Folk* (1998) as an example, Jackson stated that it is now possible to go beyond 'simple, positive representations' of such groups to provide more complex characters and dramatic narratives. On a basic level, these comments indicate something of the terrain of this project, in so far as it is largely concerned with analysing the representation of so-called minority or 'marginalised' groups within various television dramas including *Queer as Folk*, with specific reference to the portrayal of character and dramatic narratives. However, what struck me about this comment was that it implied a 'narrative of progress' in the representation of these groups, which may be part of a broader social and political context but which in terms of the televisual is signified through reference to aesthetics.

There is no question that twentieth-century movements such as feminism, anti-racism, and gay and lesbian or queer liberation have had significant, albeit varying, degrees of impact across a wide range of different institutions in both Britain and North America, including those of television and of the academy. Yet in an essay evaluating the 'progress/progressiveness' of gendering within recent television drama with reference to *The X-Files* (1994–2000) and the British crime drama *Silent Witness* (1996–), Robin Nelson concludes by asking whether, in these and other recent dramas, there has been a 'fundamental change in the language of representation' or simply a process of inversions of binaries and 'role reversals' which actually leaves the foundations of the sex/gender system intact (Nelson,

2000: 72–3). This question also forms the core of my project but I want to extend Nelson's enquiry to consider the 'progress/progressiveness' of representations of ethnicity and sexuality, as well as of gender, within recent television drama. However, I also intend to turn Nelson's question back on the academic theories that inform his perspective and which appear to have created an expectation in the late twentieth century that there could or should have been a fundamental change in the language of representation of minority groups on television, *beyond* Jackson's notion of more complex characters and dramatic narratives. This means I will explore the thinking around subjectivity and identity and the relationship of these things to aesthetics that have emerged from poststructuralism, postmodernism, and most especially from 'postmodern' feminism, anti-racism, postcolonialism and queer theory. This thinking is sometimes represented as a fundamental change in perception and my concern is to examine how far, and in what ways, these ideas can and have been appropriated and deployed as part of a process of inversions, reversals and substitutions that leaves the systems they critique intact.

None of this is intended as a negative critique either of television criticism, or the theories of subjectivity and identity that may have informed it, since many of the ideas I am questioning continue to inform my own argument. Nevertheless, I am concerned with the way that, in the aftermath of the poststructuralist/postmodern theory explosion, notions of subjectivity based on principles of difference and on the fluidity and instability of meanings, have hardened and come to be taken for granted within the academy as part of what is, in effect, a metanarrative of progress/progressiveness. This metanarrative often embraces a sense of having gone 'beyond' identity politics, even as events in the world of the social have continued, repeatedly and violently, to place them back on the agenda.

Television drama provides a particularly fruitful site to consider gaps and differences, as well as concordances, between academic theories and public practices. This is not least because, due to its increasing ubiquity and importance as a medium across the globe, television is now understood as an important site for the discursive construction and production of identities. As a result, in the latter part of the twentieth century it has been a focal point for the articulation of both celebratory and pessimistic understandings of what was generally defined as postmodernity, in ways that have gone far beyond issues of 'simple' representation. Within this context it is my aim to navigate between 'high theory' and television practice, in a manner that interrogates both fields, so as to revisit and reopen certain issues as *debates* around the modern and the postmodern, still relevant to the twenty-first century.

At the risk of stating the obvious, all of the above signals that this book, like most works dealing with television, is very much an interdisciplinary project and this tendency to interdisciplinarity, in itself, can be understood as one of the effects of the impact of poststructuralist/postmodern theory within the academy. In so far as it is associated with deconstructive methodologies and the challenging of tradition, interdisciplinarity is also sometimes taken as a signifier of progressiveness. As part of my interrogation of narratives of progress/progressiveness, then, I should perhaps acknowledge some of the limitations as well as the opportunities of my own work as an interdisciplinary undertaking. One of the points I constantly re-visit in this book relates to how, within some postmodern thought, *any* confusion of boundaries produced through the play of repetition and difference in the process of making meanings comes to be perceived as inherently progressive. In fact, as Jean Baudrillard pointed out, such confusions can lead to 'indeterminacy' or pure relativism, whereby differences are embraced to the point and in a fashion that reduces them to the same (see Baudrillard, 1988 and 1993). In this sense, the term postmodern is of course profoundly problematic, in that it can not only refer to a period and an aesthetic but also functions as a catch-all term encompassing a diverse, sometimes completely opposing, set of post, anti and anti-posthumanist theories. As such, the use of this term can confuse boundaries in ways that actually obscure and suppress differences, and within the academy, detract from the specificity of the object of study and its location within particular traditions and histories.

I am not arrogant enough to suggest that I can manage to avoid these pitfalls in this book. I am attempting to work a pathway through a complex interdisciplinary terrain and this inevitably involves the reduction of profuse fields to a series of narratives of similarity and difference that entail exclusions, compromises and generalisations. However, I make no apology for the fact that in the course of developing my argument in this book, I start each chapter by reiterating some key points of 'classic' debates in the field(s).

While these earlier sections of chapters are especially useful for those less well versed in either the history of television criticism and/or theories of subjectivity and identity, they may be frustrating for readers already familiar with the terrain, who may therefore prefer to start reading at the points where I start to break into less worked-over ground. However, one of the critiques of postmodernity has been the way that this 'sensibility' has encouraged a 'forgetting of history', through a favouring of the (apparently) 'new', as part of a process of commodification that declares objects and ideas to be obsolete, long before they have outworn their potential use value or been fully explored and assimilated. Moreover, to problematise a narrative it is always necessary to repeat it and, for me, reflecting back on the history of some influential ideas in these fields is crucial to understanding and questioning the ways and means by which, in recent years, certain formal strategies and modes of representation on television have come to be perceived as either progressive or conservative. Further, my intention in this reiteration is to point up issues that may have been acknowledged in the past but sometimes get overlooked in the rush towards the future. In rehearsing these narratives, I do sometimes employ the term postmodern as a catch-all for the sake of brevity and convenience and because this is how it has frequently been used in both the public and academic realms. At the same time, a large part of this book consists of exploring strands of thought that are sometimes subsumed within the postmodern, so as to remark their distinctiveness as well as their commonalities.

The same principles apply to my approach to the television drama texts I consider. I am not attempting to survey or comment on the *whole* field of television drama and there is no intention that my examples could or should stand for the whole. In fact, I would argue that now that television is established enough to have a 'history', has achieved the status of a global medium, and the means of disseminating programmes has become so diffuse and diverse, as a whole field television drama is 'beyond' simple representation. In practical terms, at any one moment there is just too much of it being disseminated, by too many different providers, for any one person to monitor, not least because as well as current production there is a significant 'back catalogue' of television drama now available on video and DVD through the internet.[1] As I point out in my discussion of narratives of globalisation and of *Star Trek* (Chapter 4), the more there is of something the more it is possible to find numerous examples, on the level of the local and specific, to support opposing views and conflicting arguments.

Yet because television is still a relatively new medium and a commercial one, in some ways it is fairly slow moving and conservative, so that it is possible when the focus is limited to English-language, terrestrial television in Britain and the US, to identify some 'trends' in terms of form, genre and programme format and even to some extent on the level of representation. Yet even on this point it is worth noting that in all these areas there are differences between television drama in Britain and North America, which sometimes get overlooked in television criticism.

I have to admit that all this means that my choice of which television drama texts to discuss is opportunistic but not random. The shows I consider have either caused debate in relation to issues of subjectivity and identity, or refer to key debates around these issues. Nevertheless, if they are not intended to exemplify the whole field of television drama neither are they simply employed to exemplify particular theories. My 'home' discipline is Theatre Studies and as such, like Robin Nelson, I gently but firmly insist on the television text as a 'useful analytical category' and on paying attention to the specificity of the 'languages of representation' within which television texts operate (Nelson, 1997: 2). My methodology in this book is concerned to allow concrete instances of television practice to interrogate abstract theory as much as vice versa, in ways that cannot be conclusive but which do raise questions as part of a debate about the progress/progressiveness of both.

Chapter 1 starts by summarising some well-rehearsed debates from the early to mid-twentieth century, concerning realism and naturalism in television drama and the impact on those debates of poststructuralist and postmodern theory. This lays the ground for a more complex discussion of the assumptions about form, subjectivity and identity, production and reception that were produced on the way. Such issues help identify limitations and problems within the postmodern, 'post-Marxist' approaches that often dominated television criticism in the 1990s. Discussion of these establishes the discursive context(s) within which ideas examined in later chapters appear and opens up the key questions and issues for the book as a whole. This chapter is almost exclusively theoretical but this is 'balanced' by the concluding chapter of the book, which mainly offers a detailed discussion of two television drama texts.

Chapter 2 uses the debates produced around the first three seasons of *Ally McBeal* as a starting point to explore the complexities of the relationship between the 'feminine', feminism, postfeminism and postmodern feminism, in both the academic and the public spheres. In the process I map out the differences and similarities between a 'resistant feminine aesthetic', as developed within feminist theory of the 1970s and 1980s, the formal strategies associated with postmodern feminism in the 1990s and a more general 'postmodern aesthetic'. I argue that because all of these are defined in opposition to a monolithic notion of 'realism' and in relation to one another, a collapse can occur in which 'the feminine', as both a subject position and an aesthetic, becomes characterised as 'inherently' resistant and subversive. As such, it is easily appropriated to a discourse of a postmodern 'feminisation' of culture, which may in effect be a reversal and substitution rather than a displacement of the dominant norms of enlightenment subjectivity. This discourse can also represent a trivialisation of the feminist debate. This discussion is pursued with reference to developments within feminist television criticism, and to the representation of feminism in two British dramas, *Two Golden Balls* (1994) and *Big Women* (1998), before focusing in detail on *Ally McBeal* (1997–2002).

The starting point for Chapter 3 is Jim Pines's essay which asks whether or not British television crime drama could be said to be 'inherently racist' on the level of form as well as representation (Pines, 1995). In the light of the Macpherson Report on the inquiry into the murder of Stephen Lawrence (1999),[2] this question is extended to raise some more general issues concerning 'institutional' racism within television. However, this chapter opens with a consideration of the problematic concept of 'race' itself and an exploration of developments in thinking around issues of representation within anti-racist and postcolonial theory. This covers the rejection of realism as part of an attempt to get beyond simple positive or negative representations of subaltern groups, and the subsequent development of theories of cultural hybridity and diaspora aesthetics. In examining these latter concepts, I explore their potential recuperation and depoliticisation as part of a more generalised and abstracted postmodern aesthetic, within which repetition and assimilation can win out over subversion and transformation. The second part of the chapter returns to Pines's essay and offers a comparison of two British crime dramas, *Supply and Demand* (1996) and a post-Macpherson episode of *The Bill* (2000), so as to consider whether there has been any fundamental progress in the representation of 'race' and ethnicity in British crime drama since the early 1990s. The chapter concludes with a brief evaluation of some twenty-first-century British television dramas that might be said to show evidence of a diaspora aesthetic.

Chapter 4 explores various accounts of the role television is thought to play in the processes of globalisation with particular reference to the issue of 'cultural imperialism'. In doing so it questions the manner in which the postcolonial theories of cultural hybridity and diaspora discussed in Chapter 3 can function within postmodern narratives of globalisation to produce a generalised concept of 'new global subjectivity', which depends on a relativism that conceals a return to the white, western status quo by other means. The second part of the chapter pursues these ideas in relation to an examination of the status of *Star Trek* as a 'franchise' owned by a giant trans-national corporation, as a myth of the global and global myth and as a metanarrative no more or less 'imaginary' or 'performative' than many academic accounts. This moves through a discussion of the impact of a 'postmodern aesthetic' on the late 1990s series *Voyager* and *Deep Space Nine* and then to an analysis of the first season of *Enterprise* (2000) as a nostalgic and conservative postmodern return to the style and period of *Star Trek: The Original Series* (1966–69).

Chapter 5 opens with a discussion of conflicting and competing definitions of 'queer' in the public and academic realms. This includes a consideration of the concept of a queer or 'camp' aesthetic and of the practice of 'queer reading' in general but also specifically in relation to television. My main concern in this section is to examine how queer is thought to have become depoliticised on the one hand, through its articulation within high theory, and on the other, through its appropriation and commodification within main-stream heterosexual culture. In either case, there is a danger that a queer or camp aesthetic becomes indistinguishable from a gener-alised postmodern one, in ways that once again can lead to either pure relativism or a return to status quo by other means. The latter part of this chapter offers an analysis of *Queer as Folk* (1998) which argues that if this drama can be considered 'progressive', this is not simply a matter of its use of a postmodern and/or camp aesthetic but of interplay between the formal devices associated with these 'sensibilities' and a certain level of referential realism.

The conclusion takes a comment by Russell T. Davis, the writer of *Queer as Folk* to touch on the problematic relationship between notions of 'good television drama' and those of 'political correctness'. This is pursued through a discussion of two dramas, *Metrosexuality* (2000) and *The Murder of Stephen Lawrence* (1999), not in an attempt to establish a 'model' for politically progressive drama but as a means of reflecting back on the questions around aesthetics and the politics of subjectivity and identity raised in the course of the book.

Notes

1 The Internet Movie Database, for instance, provides full production details for a large number of television drama programmes, including most of those cited in this book. It also provides details of where videos or DVDs of these shows can be obtained commercially on the web. In the instance of recent and very popular programmes, these details are available from the numerous 'official' websites. For these reasons, in this book I am only giving specific production details as relevant to the discussion.
2 Black British teenager Stephen Lawrence was brutally murdered in Eltham, South London in a racist attack in 1993. Despite available evidence and a long campaign by his family and anti-racist support groups, no one has ever been successfully prosecuted for his murder. Concerns about the handling of the case by the Metropolitan Police Service eventually led to the Home Secretary, Jack Straw, establishing an official inquiry led by Sir William MacPherson in 1997. The inquiry report, published in 1999, concluded that the police investigation had been affected by 'institutional racism' within the police service. This report prompted widespread discussion of institutional racism across a range of public services in Britain. For further information see for example www.archive.official-documents.co.uk/document/CM42/4246/sli-0htm.

1

Beyond realism? Modes of reading in Marxist-socialist and post-Marxist-socialist Television drama criticism

The 'back story': the critique of realism and the turn to form

In the context of mid- to late twentieth-century British television drama criticism, the relationship between politics and aesthetics was most often defined through reference to the Marxist-socialist tradition and more specifically to the work of theatre practitioner and theorist Bertolt Brecht.

Brecht famously developed a critique of what he termed 'Aristotelian' or 'dramatic theatre', which he defined as offering an illusion of reality that conformed to the ideology of the 'parasitic bourgeoisie' (Brecht, 1987: 160–1). Usually understood as an attack on naturalism and/or realism, Brecht's analysis of this aesthetic embraced all aspects of production including illusionist staging, linear narratives, psychologically motivated characterisation and naturalistic acting. He argued that these characteristics operate together to passively 'implicate the audience in the stage situation' by means of an emotional identification with the characters and with their situation, as if these represented universal truths (37). For Brecht, this type of theatre 'takes the human being for granted' as a product of 'evolutionary determinism' and therefore as 'unaltering and unalterable' (37). In its stead, he posited a model of politically progressive 'epic' theatre, based on characters represented as contradictory 'social types', episodic and dialectical narrative structures and various other anti-illusionistic 'alienation effects' which draw attention to the theatrical 'means of production'. According to Brecht, this form would produce an active spectator, a 'rational' observer who remains detached from the action within which the human being is constructed as 'the object of inquiry', as altering and alterable, or as he puts it 'man [*sic*] as process' (37).

As Elizabeth Wright pointed out in 1989, there is already something more than a little 'postmodern' about Brecht's ideas. Nevertheless, his approach did not constitute a rejection of the ideas of a radical *realist* aesthetic, nor of the possibility of representing the 'truth' of the human subject. Rather, he acknowledged that each era has its own mode, or rather modes, of representing reality and he offers up epic theatre as a form of *socialist* realism, designed to reveal the truth of the class struggle in 'the scientific age', as a contribution to the inevitable triumph of Marxist-socialism (Brecht, 1987: 107–12). In his theatre, then, notions of the human subject and reality may be portrayed as altering and alterable but in an already determined direction.

For various obvious historical and political reasons there has been little explicit evidence of the influence of these ideas within mainstream North American television and television criticism. However, in Britain between the 1960s and the late 1980s, many television scholars, playwrights and producers, including Raymond Williams, Trevor Griffiths, John MacGrath, Jeremy Sanford, Jim Allen, Ken Loach, Troy Kennedy-Martin and Alan Bleasdale, were allied with socialism, and as a result this perspective dominated debates over aesthetics and political progressiveness in television drama. For instance, as a Marxist-socialist Trevor Griffiths was often called on to defend the use of television naturalism within his screenplays. He did so on the grounds of accessibility to a popular audience but also asserted that rather than naturalism, which he defined as un-self-reflexive, he actually employed a type of 'critical realism', which he placed firmly within a Marxist-socialist literary tradition (see Griffiths, 1986 and Poole and Wyver, 1984).

As this suggests, the definition of realism and naturalism and of the differences between them was a matter of dispute. In 1977, Raymond Williams argued that naturalism merely produced the 'flat external appearance of reality' and as an expression of a 'doctrine of character formed by environment' had a 'certain static quality', so that it emerges as a 'passive form' (Williams, 1977: 65). By contrast, realism, which like Griffiths he associated with Marxism, was 'active' and 'went below this surface to the essential historical movements, to the dynamic quality of environments' and the possibility of intervention to change them (69). Yet on purely *formal* grounds, if the nineteenth-century work of Henrik Ibsen on the one hand and that of Anton Chekhov on the other were used as models, some of Trevor Griffiths' television works such as *Country* (1982) could be placed somewhere *between* realism and naturalism, albeit rearticulated *through* the Marxist tradition. As this suggests and as Brecht himself asserted, the exact difference between realism(s) and naturalism(s) cannot necessarily be decided on the basis of aesthetics alone (see Brecht, 1987: 105).

Even so, the focus on the question of form in politically progressive drama continued, as was evident in contributions to this debate from theatre playwright David Edgar (Edgar, 1979) and television and theatre writer John McGrath (1977), and in the famous exchange in *Screen* around Ken Loach's and Jim Allen's British television documentary drama *Days of Hope* (1976). In response to an article on this text by Colin MacArthur, Colin MacCabe critiqued it as being definable as a 'classic-realist text' that ensures the position of the subject in relation to dominant norms of 'specularity' or looking relations (MacCabe, 1981: 316). Replying to MacCabe, John Caughie pointed out that *two* sorts of 'looks' were operating in *Days of Hope*, making a distinction between naturalism, which he associated with what he terms the 'documentary look', and 'classic' or 'Hollywood realism' or the 'dramatic look' (Caughie, 1981: 341–2). According to Caughie, the documentary look, which has the appearance of being unplanned and chaotic, 'constructs the social space' of the fiction, while the dramatic look invites an emphatic identification with the characters as 'psychologically motivated individuals' (342–6). While he allows that the documentary look has progressive potential, in so far as it draws attention to the camera and therefore to the 'means of production', it also fixes its objects as 'static victims' who are 'looked at and looked on' (346). In any case, he concludes that the dramatic look 'will impose its resolutions on the documentary disorder' and the drama will end up 'being about the privileged centred individuals, rather than an analysis of the document, thereby defusing any progressiveness' (346). Ultimately, then, like others such as Edgar and McGrath, Caughie argues for a model for progressive television drama closer to a Brechtian 'epic' form (351). Within these structuralist debates about realism and naturalism on television, the distinction between the two can become confused in terms of *affect*, and Brecht's notion of realisms collapses into a single and apparently stable form, designated by critics as Hollywood or classic realism.

From the 1970s, if not before, a similar collapse was occurring in parallel discussions about politics and aesthetics amongst feminist, gay and lesbian and anti-racist practitioners, activists and academics – voices that were still rare in television and television criticism. Within each of these political movements and across a wide range of cultural production, there was a search for alternative, 'oppositional' forms *other* to realism, which was characterised as the dominant mode of mainstream culture. In some instances these alternative forms borrowed from Brecht but in others the aim was to discover 'new' forms and/or to *re*discover and reclaim in positive terms what were perceived as 'authentically' black, female or gay and lesbian forms and historical cultural practices, previously lost or marginalised.

From structuralism to poststructuralism and the impact of deconstruction

The concern for the relationship between aesthetics and the politics of identity was further strengthened under the influence of poststructuralist linguistic theory within the academy, evinced, for example, by Laura Mulvey's seminal feminist essay of 1975, 'Visual Pleasure and Narrative Cinema'. First published in *Screen*, this article also prefigured MacCabe's later focus on 'dominant specularity' and Caughie's on 'looks' in drama documentary. Mulvey argues that within Hollywood realism the 'looks' of the camera and of the male protagonist operate together in 'looking at and looking on' the female characters, so as to construct them and by extension the female viewer who identifies with them as passive objects of the patriarchal male gaze. Mulvey's essay draws on the poststructuralist, psychoanalytical linguistic theories of Jacques Lacan, but also recalls Franz Fanon's influential work of the 1950s on 'race', fetishism and the politics of looking. Fanon's influence, reworked through Lacan, is also directly in evidence in Homi Bhahba's 1983 essay, 'The Other Question', and Robert Stam and Luise Spence's 1983 essay in *Screen* on colonisation, racism and representation, both of which mounted a critique against 'classic' Hollywood realism in similar terms to Mulvey, but in relation to black subjects (see Stam and Spence, 1985 and Bhabha, 1986). As Lola Young points out, all these works can be seen as attempting to move debates about marginalised identity categories beyond issues of simple positive or negative representation (Young, 1996: 8). This same drive is evident in feminist television criticism of the 1970s and 1980s, within which the aesthetic qualities of soap opera as a 'feminine' narrative form began to be discussed in positive terms (see Modleski, 1997: 45).

In this context, in 1981 when a television programme dealing with racism in Britain was critiqued on the grounds of its use of realism, Stuart Hall was moved to point out that too great an emphasis on aesthetics in oppositional politics can prove a distraction. As he put it, 'the social division of labour', or the oppressions of gender, sexuality and race, 'cannot be simply overcome by a few typographical or stylistic devices' and he also warned against reducing all types of realism and naturalism to a 'single monolith' (Hall, 1981: 51 and 49–50). In fact, what was tending to happen as a result of all these interventions was that classic realism was being reduced to a monolith that was perceived as naturalising the ideological perspective not only of Brecht's culturally and socially dominant 'parasitic' bourgeois subject but of a white, western, heterosexual, masculine, parasitic, bourgeois subject. Attempts to challenge, resist and overturn this form were then perceived as an important part of the process of 'decentring' and/or deconstructing the enlightenment subject that is often linked to a particular theoretical moment in the 1970s and specifically to Lyotard's 1979 work *The Postmodern Condition: A Report on Knowledge*.

However, like Brecht, many feminist, anti-racist and gay and lesbian thinkers of the 1960s and 1970s maintained a notion of a subject and of objective reality *outside* of representation, to which representation refers. By contrast, in principle, the concept of subjectivity and of identity that begins to inform the ideas concerning the relationship between aesthetics and politics in the 1980s and 1990s is one that is the product *of* representation, or rather, an effect of language, discourse or symbolic systems. Influenced by ideas from Derrida and Foucault but developed by a wide range of feminist, postcolonial and queer theorists, in this paradigm (contrary to some interpretations), the existence of the 'real', of nature, or of a biological or metaphysical essence of human subjectivity is not denied. Rather it is posited that there is no access to reality, nature or subjectivity except *through* linguistic and discursive systems, which are demonstrably historical social and cultural constructs. Produced within and by these systems, subjectivity is perceived as operating in the same fashion as they do. In brief, this means that subjective identity is structured around a series of interdependent binary oppositions, and is produced through the play of repetition and difference, which produces multiple, shifting and often contradictory meanings and identities. Subjectivity and identity are therefore in 'process', and if like some meanings they give the *appearance* of being single, stable and universal, this is because the binary oppositions that structure the system are hierarchical. This means that one term or position has been traditionally (historically and socially) valued over the other in western thought and perceived as the 'first' or original term, to which the other positions or other terms are understood to refer back. Any 'differences' from the 'original' are then constructed as 'imitations' or 'poor copies' (see Derrida, 1978 and 1981). Hence, for example, femininity and homosexuality are defined not in 'positive' terms in and of themselves but negatively in terms of their difference and implied 'inferiority' to masculinity and heterosexuality.

The first stage of deconstruction is a reversal that reinscribes in positive terms the traditionally 'inferior' term(s) in any given binary opposition, including and indeed *specifically* in the oppositions between the real and representation and, in terms of subjectivity, between 'original' and imitation or poor copy. In the second stage, the relationship between opposing terms is 'suspended' so as to put it radically into question, so that the reversal is never a permanent *fait accompli*. In theory, this should eventually lead to a 'third stage' of deconstruction, which achieves the dissolution of the stable and singular enlightenment subjectivity into subjectivities and an endless proliferation of shifting identity categories, to the point that the concept of such categorisation becomes utterly meaningless (see Derrida, 1981). However, this stage has not actually been reached in most theory and certainly not in the practice of everyday life. This is mainly because deconstruction itself is not a single act but a long-term process or rather a set of processes which recognises the impossibility of transcending deeply entrenched systems of thought and behaviour at one go. As such, deconstruction recognises the necessity of 'working within' the system of hierarchical binary oppositions it describes, and like this system operates through *both* repetition *and* difference, difference *and* repetition. The alternative models of subjectivity that emerge from deconstruction *might* therefore be politically more progressive than that posited by enlightenment subjectivity, but are in effect reversals of it, defined in relation to and dependent on it, repeating as well as differing from it and by the same token repeating and differing from each other.

These processes of reversal and repetition, added to the difficulties of achieving a suspension of meaning outside of strictly limited contexts, mean that there is always the possibility that these alternative modes of subjectivity and identity can be recuperated back into the system. In short, they can be appropriated to a single, dominant model, which claims the 'truth' of subjectivity and identity as *essentially* multiple, contradictory and shifting, and which therefore simply *replaces* the 'old' enlightenment model, rather than *displacing* the binary structures of thought which produced it. This model may then appear to embrace and celebrate differences while actually reducing them to the same, in ways that, as Sarah Ahmed points out, universalise and privilege 'a certain kind of Western subject, the subject of and in [postmodern] theory' (Ahmed, 2000: 83).

'The' postmodern aesthetic and the postmodern as a model of reading

On the same principle, these modes of thinking can produce a singular 'dominant' postmodern aesthetic. As part of the process of reversing and suspending the traditional relationship between the real and representation, deconstruction has tended to focus on the textual and linguistic as opposed to the material and the embodied. As a result, much of this theory, including that produced from within postmodern feminism, postcolonial and queer theory, has been expounded through 'close readings' of literary texts or cultural artefacts. Within such readings, emphasis is often placed on how particular aesthetic strategies, defined in 'opposition' to realism and naturalism and historically associated either with the avant-garde or with specific marginalised groups, can be seen to undermine, resist or subvert enlightenment subjectivity, or rather its naturalisation within realism and naturalism. These strategies therefore come to be defined and privileged as progressive, primarily in so far as they *differ* from classic realism. Under these terms, in the abstract, divorced from situated social and historical contexts and embodied practices, they can easily become confused with one another and cohere into a single generalised postmodern aesthetic, understood as expressive of a single postmodern subjectivity. If and when, as argued above, this mode of subjectivity is either implicitly or explicitly constructed as the 'dominant' mode of subjectivity and identity, this postmodern aesthetic is then in effect simply the latest form of realism. Yet both this subjectivity and this aesthetic often retain an aura of political progressiveness by dint of their earlier association with subaltern modes of identity and with practices that oppose classic realism.

In his groundbreaking *What is Postmodernism?* (1986), Charles Jenks attempts to identify and define postmodern aesthetics in visual art and architecture, but this is achieved through providing concrete and carefully located examples of *different* articulations and styles of both modernism and postmodernism. Nevertheless, some of the characteristics Jenks identifies, such as double coding or hybridity, the combination of elite and popular forms, old and new traditions, hyperconsciousness or self-reflexivity, pluralism, irony, parody, displacement, complexity and eclecticism, were rapidly taken up as standard, *general* descriptors of a *single* postmodern aesthetic (Jenks, 1986: 10–14). This, despite the fact that Jenks asserts that many of these features indicate the retention of a modern 'sensibility' within the postmodern, and he includes realism in this list (14).

According to Sara Ahmed, this reductive collapse of *both* realism and postmodernism into single and opposing monoliths can be traced back to Lyotard's *The Postmodern Condition*, which defines the postmodern as the radical or progressive 'working within' modernism (Lyotard, 1984: 79). However, Ahmed argues that Lyotard presents a postmodern aesthetic as a 'totalisation and negation of realism', in ways that allow later literary theorists to construct 'a progressive shift from realism through modernism and on to postmodernism' and to produce 'postmodernism as a model of reading' (Ahmed, 1998: 146). As she points out, this narrative of progress depends on the assumption that realism is 'necessarily a tool of the dominant culture' and that it is *successful* in implicating the reader passively into a particular ideology and subject position (147). A postmodern aesthetic is then defined as *overcoming* this realism, by producing a plurality of meanings through its anti-linear narrative strategies and contradictory characters, and above all by drawing attention to its own constructedness, so that as Linda Hutcheon states, it 'displays its own conventionality' and 'explicitly lays bare its conditions of artifice' (cited in Ahmed, 1998: 149). As with Brechtian alienation, these strategies are thought to produce 'active readers' and distance them from 'any self-conscious identifications on the level of character and plot' (Ahmed, 1998: 149).

Ahmed argues that this model of reading assumes in advance that readers' identifications are 'dependent on a text repressing its own fictional status', a theory not proven, for example, in the case of the reception of Brecht's work. This is because the model presupposes that the politics of a text is reducible to its literary form and excludes consideration of 'the *particularity* of representations' (149, my italics). Ahmed then goes on to discuss the representation of gender in number of avant-garde literary and cinematic texts by (white, western, middle-class) male authors, which might be otherwise read as misogynistic but where, within postmodern criticism, the question of sexual difference is assumed to be 'cancelled out' or negated by the form of the text (150).

If Ahmed points to the dangers of postmodernism as a 'model of reading' in relation to Lyotard, a similar operation can be seen in play in the work of Jean Baudrillard, who rather than a narrative of political progress, presents the shift from realism to modernism to postmodernism as one of reaction and decline. While Lyotard, like many other literary theorists who follow him, focuses his analyses on works of the experimental avant-garde, Baudrillard concentrates on popular culture and the mass media – especially television. Indeed, Baudrillard understands television as a postmodern medium that *as a whole* displays the qualities of a postmodern aesthetic, characterised primarily by the suspension of all reference to any reality outside of itself. For Baudrillard, this aesthetic is indeed a new form of realism, or rather 'hyperrealism' that reflects and expresses the triumph of the ideology of late postindustrial capitalism and signals the end or death of the social and the political (see Baudrillard, 1988). In this model of reading, viewers are figured in advance as passive consumers of endlessly proliferating, self-reflexive signs or images, which have lost all connection to value, truth or reality, producing a subjectivity and a hyperreality based on indifference or pure relativism (see Baudrillard, 1988: 207–19). Significantly, Baudrillard's position can be seen as a response to the failure of the Marxist-socialist metanarrative, which is also one of the starting points for Lyotard's discussion in *The*

Postmodern Condition. As such, both are strictly speaking post-Marxists but whereas Baudrillard assumes this failure as allowing for the uncontested and uncontestable triumph of capitalism, Lyotard's interest in aesthetics relates to the search for other, yet to be thought, models for politics.

The limitations of post-Marxist television criticism (John Fiske)

Much television criticism of the late 1980s and early 1990s tended to be reluctant to embrace both Lyotard's and Baudrillard's formalism but was especially wary of the latter's sweeping and pessimistic conclusions. While Baudrillard's ideas frequently informed discussions of television as a commercial institution and/or as part of the mass media, most critics strongly rejected his figuration of 'the masses' as manipulated by the media or as resistant only in terms of a passive and silent refusal of meaning (Baudrillard, 1988: 217–18). Instead, there was a preference for Foucault's challenge to Marxist paradigms of 'top down' models of power as determining social and cultural relations and for his conceptualisation of a more complex and localised networks of force, within which the exercise of power is understood not only to produce but also to enable resistance (see Foucault, 1979). This influence, along with that of Derridian deconstruction, can be seen in Stuart Hall's 1981 essay 'Notes on Deconstructing the Popular', in which he insists that people are not passive 'cultural dopes', that there is a 'double movement of containment and resistance within popular culture' and that its relationship to 'tradition' renders it a significant 'site of struggle' (see Hall, 1994: 456, 459 and 465).

John Fiske's argument in his book *Television Culture*, first published in 1987, works within similar terrain with additional inspiration from other sources, such as Roland Barthes's essay 'The Death of the Author' (1977) and feminism. However, his initial point of reference is to Althusser's theory of interpellation, which he uses to describe how popular television texts 'hail' or address viewers, creating a 'preferred reading position', which conforms to the ideologically 'dominant discourse or subject position' (Fiske, 1991: 40). He then goes on to argue that such textual address can be resisted, evaded or negotiated with, in varying degrees by differently situated readers, so that 'reading a television text is a negotiation between an existing social subject position and the one proposed by the text itself', which produces 'gaps' and contradictions and allows for 'multiple' readings of the text (41). However, he goes on to assert that 'in this negotiation the balance of power lies with the *reader*', since 'The meanings found in the text shift towards the subject position of the reader, more than the reader's subjectivity is subjected to the ideological power of the text' (66, my italics).

To some extent, then, in this paradigm all readers are understood in advance as 'active' and Fiske proceeds to describe popular television texts as 'activated' and therefore as *promoting* and *provoking* a multiplicity of different interpretations. The logic of this argument is that, in order to be popular, television must appeal to a diverse range of viewers and therefore 'provide space' for a diverse range of meanings and pleasures to be articulated in relation to their differing 'social interests' (73, 88 and 92). While he argues that the television text exists in a state of tension between 'closure' and 'openness' of meaning (84), he simultaneously describes it as operating through a 'producerly' aesthetic, borrowing from Umberto Eco's notion of the 'open' text and Roland Barthes' concept of 'writerly' texts. These both refer to a type of text that is multiple and full of contradictions, foregrounds its own nature as discourse, resists closure, coherence or unity, refuses a hierarchy of discourses and replaces the concepts of 'product' and 'structure' with those of process and segmentation (94). Fiske also suggests that the producerly text has similarities to Anne. E. Kaplan's definition of 'radical' texts (95). In short, the producerly text operates as something very like the postmodern aesthetic, as discussed by Ahmed above.

As Fiske acknowledges, both Barthes and Eco actually define the writerly or open text in terms of 'avant-garde highbrow ones with minority appeal', in *opposition* to the readerly text, which 'approximates to what MacCabe calls the "classic realist text" and which for Eco are those characteristically produced by the mass media' (Fiske, 1991: 94). For Fiske, the difference between the avant-garde writerly and/or radical text and the popular producerly television text is that the latter does not work with 'an authorial voice', or 'shock' the reader into recognition of the text's discursive structure, and does not require new discursive competencies. Instead, it relies on existing discursive competencies but 'requires that they are used in a self-interested and productive way', treating its readers as 'members of a semiotic democracy' who are 'motivated by pleasure to want to participate' in the process of making meanings (95).

It is not clear how the form of a text, however pleasurable, can *require* an audience to use their discursive competencies in a *self-interested* and *productive* way. It is also difficult to grasp how 'readerly' realist television texts can be redefined as 'writerly' in one fell swoop. In fact, when Fiske cites 'the' television text, he is often referring to the qualities of television as a *medium* and it is the qualities of the whole that he claims ensures its 'producerliness' and openness. This point is not always clear because he constantly moves between discussing the medium, *specific* television texts, the conditions of reception and the subjectivity of those who receive them, always emphasising the similarities between these things.

Hence the properties of the medium, on the micro level of editing and the macro level of programming, advertising and scheduling *and* the conditions of its reception, mean that for Fiske, television as a whole is a 'rapid succession of compressed vivid segments where the principle of cause and effect is subordinated to that of association and consequence to sequence'. Further, its 'movement is discontinuous, interrupted and fragmented' and 'its attempts at closure, at a unitary meaning, or a unified viewing subject, are constantly subjected to fracturing forces' (105). Individual texts are then subsumed within this whole, but equally on the level of specific popular realist texts, Fiske stresses how the 'generic' nature of such programmes makes them especially susceptible to the play of intertextuality and how the (segmented) forms of the series and serials means that narratives are continually interrupted.

Openness then seems always already to trump closure and television is defined as a site where 'the self-sufficiency of the single diegetic world of the traditional realist narrative can never be maintained' (145). Further, 'Television's foregrounding of its own discursive repertoire, its demystification of its own mode of representation, are central characteristics of its producerliness' (239). In sum, Fiske suggest that the very properties of the medium, it characteristic modes of meaning production on the level of individual texts and the ways in which it is consumed, function *fundamentally* as alienating or distancing devices.

While his emphasis on reception and his attention to particular representations implies that Fiske does not reduce the politics of a text to its form, he does seem to reduce the medium to a single aesthetic that corresponds to a particular model of subjectivity. Hence, Fiske states that both the text and the subjectivity of the

viewer 'are discursive constructs and both contain similar competing or contradictory discourses' (67). In some ways, this argument
represents a repetition of that offered by Baudrillard, in so far as the
aesthetics of television as a medium are, in effect, represented as a
new form of realism that both reflects and expresses the 'truth' of a
discursive, postmodern subject. However, whereas for Baudrillard
this (hyper) realism is inherently politically reactionary, for Fiske the
television text is a 'text of contestation' and the 'reading relations of
these texts are 'essentially democratic, not autocratic ones' because
'The discursive power to make meanings, to produce knowledges of
the world, is a power that both programme producers and
producerly viewers have access to' (239).

When Fiske *directly* addresses the postmodern on television, with
reference to *Miami Vice* (1984–9) and Madonna's MTV videos of
the late 1980s, he also argues that 'The postmodern language of
style is essentially democratic and empowering' (260), it 'crosses
genre boundaries as easily as those of gender and class' and it
'asserts ownership of all images' (254). Equally, the use of excess,
parody, pastiche and irony are assumed, in advance, to function self-
reflexively as alienation devices that prevent simple identifications,
transforming the apparent (Baudrillardian) celebration of surface
and style into a critique of commodification (248–54). The same
qualities, combined with the inherent producerliness of all television, also mean that the 'looking relations' set up by these texts,
which might have been read as voyeurism and objectification by
Mulvey, Bhabha et al., are transformed into a form of looking that
is 'participatory' and which 'destroys the difference between the
subject and the object of the gaze and produces empowering
pleasures for the subordinate' (254).

Exactly how this is achieved is unclear, but in Fiske's discussion
of Madonna it is notable that her gendered 'authorial voice' is
important to his reading of her work as empowering, subversive and
resistant. Yet overall, Fiske's argument could be taken to imply that
there is absolutely is no need for subordinate groups to struggle for
influence in the processes of production of television. The medium
itself is already inherently 'democratic', and 'democratising', and as
John Caughie put it, texts are addressed to 'naturally oppositional
readers who will get it right in the end' (Caughie, 1990: 55).

As part of a wider critique of 'banality' in cultural studies in the
1990s, Meaghan Morris describes Fiske's ideas as a redemptive,

'yes, *but* . . . discourse, that most often proceeds *from* admitting class, racial and sexual oppression *to* finding an inevitable saving grace' (Morris, 1990: 25, original italics). As such, she argues that this approach may be seen as a move to discredit certain voices such as 'those of grumpy feminists and cranky leftists', characterised in advance as positions 'from which anything said can be dismissed as already heard' (25). This 'discrediting' occurs partly because Fiske's approach in effect constitutes the postmodern as model of reading and partly because the slippage between television as a medium, specific television texts and modes of viewing means that *all* television production is more or less claimed for 'popular pleasures'. To criticise television production is then to criticise the (inherently democratic) pleasures of the 'people' and to position oneself as the elite and the undemocratic.

Susan Bordo argues that for Fiske there *are* no dominant meanings, or indeed no subject positions that are more socially and culturally dominant than others, since television viewers and producers are all represented as equally subordinate, equally empowered. As such, she asserts that his approach represents what she calls a 'characteristically postmodern appropriation of Foucault' that results in a 'flattening out of the terrain of power relations' (Bordo, 1995: 260–1). Rather than Hall's 'double movement' in popular culture, Fiske privileges subversion way over containment, and resistance way over power, in a fashion that seems to imply that the status quo is inherently progressive.

I would suggest that some of these problems with Fiske and other similar works arise because the ideas he borrows from Foucault, Derridian deconstruction and later work by Barthes represent methodologies and modes of analysis that may have political *implications* but do not in themselves constitute a political *position*. Hence, for example, feminist theorists have critiqued both Foucault's and Derrida's ideas as excluding any notion of political agency. Fiske's work *could* be seen as part of a discourse that attempts to redefine the political in the light of the historical failure of the Marxist-socialist experiment. However, the problem is that while he has apparently abandoned the concept of socialism, he continues to discuss *capitalism*, a term Marx originally defined in *opposition* to socialism and which as a concept it therefore repeats as well as differs from. A tendency to reject and repress rather than *interrogate* the legacies of socialism can easily make capitalism appear 'natural' and immutable in a manner that forecloses the thinking of possible alternative social and political structures. In *Spectres of Marx*, Derrida warns that the sort of postmodern discourse that repeatedly and triumphantly declares the death of Marxist-socialism may produce a reversal that slips from accepting the necessity of 'working within' to an outright celebration of capitalism (Derrida, 1994: 52). In fact, the inadmissibility of the concept of socialism within some postmodern theory is part of the rationale by which Baudrillard announces the death of politics, since he fails to recognise the type of politics represented by, for instance, feminism, anti-racism or queer. While Fiske borrows from feminism, for the most part, he refers in general terms to notions of 'social change' and to 'resisting' patriarchal capitalism from within, with little sense of the aims and objectives of this resistance, or the possible nature of this social change. In short, the failure to attempt to articulate a positive post-Marxist model of politics slides toward an acceptance of a triumph of capitalism that cannot be directly opposed and so instead is embraced and even celebrated, in so far as it is deemed more 'democratic' than its historical, socialist double.

Reconsidering realism and (post)modern television

If I seem to have been focusing heavily on Fiske, it is because *Television Culture* articulates a number of influential ideas which many other television theorists have had to refer back to, if only in order to differ from them. I also want to establish how despite its apparent focus on reception and on semiotics, this sort of position can still constitute a model of reading that emphasises the role of aesthetics in the signifying process, at the expense of the particularity of representations and also the social and material contexts of production. I am also concerned to demonstrate how within this model of reading something very like a postmodern aesthetic emerges as a new form of realism that is thought to express and reflect the 'truth' of a generalised postmodern subjectivity.

As Chris Barker points out, paraphrasing Gergen (1994), in fact 'a romantic view of identity based on the notion of a unified "deep interior" remains one of the central means in which people in everyday life justify themselves' (Barker, 1997: 146). By the same token, in his 1997 book *TV Drama in Transition*, Robin Nelson argues that in terms of specific texts, the dominant or habitual forms of popular television dramas are still realism and naturalism (Nelson, 1997: 118–19). Further, while he recognises the import- ance of the 'context of postmodernity', Nelson does not perceive this as a defining one in television (5 and 111) and he is critical of the way that Fiske's approach can place an 'over emphasis' on the 'active reader', which masks 'the endemic structural inequities of power and wealth in postmodernity's global village' (5).

Nelson describes his own approach as a Derridian 'both/and one'; amongst other things, this means he is concerned with aesthetics but also a wide range of other textual and contextual factors that affect the construction of meanings (8). He also refuses the collapse of realism into a monolithic, inherently conservative classic realism, and while he identifies certain trends in television drama that might suggest a 'transition' occurring between the modern and the post- modern, he understands *both* of these concepts in terms of resistance *and* containment. As part of this, he distinguishes between different sorts of realisms and naturalisms and between different sorts of post- modernisms circulating within contemporary television drama (4).

In terms of naturalism, he repeats Caughie's association between this form and the documentary look but points to how this can operate on a continuum between 'photographic' and 'critical natur- alism' (112). As such, he touches on but does not pursue the way that, in the last decades of the twentieth century, 'hybrid' fact/fiction forms like documentary drama have become increasingly common and popular. Earlier in the century these sorts of programmes were seen as problematic both within the institution of television and by successive governments, on the grounds that their convincing mimicry of a 'documentary style' might confuse the distinction between fact and fiction for audiences. Yet the most controversial works of this type were always those that explored important social and political issues from oppositional positions. In contrast, by the late 1990s the increased use of dramatic reconstruction in 'real crime' programmes such as the British series *Crimewatch* (1984–), and the rise of numerous reality TV formats from docusoap to pro- grammes based on CCTV footage, had caused debates about voyeurism but little serious discussion of form. At the same time, the use of a naturalistic or documentary look has increased across a wide range of television drama, starting most famously with North American crime shows such as *Hill Street Blues* (1981–7) but by the turn of the century spreading to many other genres. For instance, in television comedy the 'mockumentary' has developed into a genre in its own right and is exemplified in Britain by *The Office* (2001–2), reworked in 2005 for North American television. All of this might be seen, as Julian Petley claims, as evidence of the way in which 'under the influence of academic analysis, television has become acutely self reflexive and willing, even eager, to consider itself as constructed text' (Petley, 1996: 19). Alternatively, it could be argued that this style again simply represents a manner of delivering the 'external appearance of reality' but operating now as part of a postmodern aesthetic.

Nelson also picks out three main categories of realism, fantasy, formulaic and critical realism, while acknowledging that in practice the distinctions between these categories are often blurred and that the conventions for realism are unstable and open to change (112–21). While his defining of these categories starts with the concepts of 'mimetic' and 'referential' realism, as his argument unfolds it roughly embraces the various registers that Chris Barker notes in his ethnographic research carried out amongst British Asian teenage viewers of soap opera. Barker describes five different meanings in their usage of the term. These cover: 'mimetic realism' (providing the surface appearance of everyday reality); 'naturalism or literal realism' (relating to physical reality but also to 'plausibility of action and linear causality'); 'narrative or *soap world* realism' (relating to plausibility within terms of the diegetic world); 'emotional realism' (whereby 'the narrative while not necessarily conforming to the rules of naturalism or even narrative realism, does appeal to an array of personal problems to which we respond and identify emotionally) and 'mythic realism' (which again is not necessarily connected to naturalism but whereby texts are seen to embody 'deeper truths') (139–41). In short, in Bill Nichols's terms, these different registers of realism relate variously to 'disembodied (general, abstract, conceptual)' and 'embodied (local, concrete, experiential)' knowledges (Nichols, 1994: 133).

Nelson asserts that one of the reasons for the continuing dominance of realism on television is that it 'corresponds to human beings' strong inclination to make sense of the world, in the form of narratives' (1997: 118). From a poststructuralist position, identity is also understood as 'a narrativisation of the self' or a 'suturing into the story' (Hall, 1998a: 4). However, it is important not to assume that the sort of referential and mimetic realist and naturalistic narrative forms and structures that started to dominate mainstream cultural production in the nineteenth century and which still influence those used on television are the *only* ones than can and have provided models for 'sense making' and narrativisation of the self. Poetic, non-linear forms have often historically fulfilled such purposes and as such, on the level of reception, could be discussed in terms of the diegetic, emotional or mythic realisms that Barker considers.

Nevertheless, Nelson favours the modality of 'critical realism' for politically progressive television drama. With one exception, a common feature of the texts he places under this heading is that they are 'authored' rather than generic drama. Obviously, the collective processes of production within television have always rendered the ascribing of authorship problematic. However, as Nelson indicates, the postmodern turn to issues of reception, genre, intertextuality and the aesthetics of the medium as a whole means that like social-ism, discussion of authors apparently became inadmissible in tele-vision criticism (8). Yet as noted above, this concept *does* play a part in Fiske's discussion of Madonna, as it does in feminist essays on this performer such as the one by Anne E. Kaplan (1992). In fact, as I argue throughout this book, authorship is still clearly at stake within most contemporary political practice. In these terms it is worth noting that in 'What is an Author?' Foucault provides an exposition of the theories of intertextuality and iterability that undermines the concept of the author as the source of textual signi-fication. Yet rather than Barthes' death notice, this essay describes a move from a concern with authorial *intention* to the consideration of author *function* as contributing to determining and delimiting meanings (see Foucault, 1991 and Barthes, 1977).

Aside from authorship, Nelson's version of critical realism refers to drama which 'addresses a contemporary issue of ethical serious-ness, taking an unorthodox stance' (Nelson, 1997: 119). It uses ref-erential realism to 'construct convincing worlds to draw viewers in' (156), allowing for identification with characters, on the basis that 'sympathetic feeling as well as rational distance functions as an important part of cognition and by these means, realism at its best, can afford new understandings of human truths' (110). It 'shakes, if does not actually break, the frame of TV drama's realist model' (120) by 'small but significant devices of dislocation' (156). It takes a 'broad view embracing many perspectives', which allows human activity to be treated as 'situated practices' and 'connections to be made between human behaviour and the social, historical and political considerations of life which inform it' (120).

Nelson's prime example of critical realism is Peter Flannery's 1996 drama *Our Friends in the North*, which he admits is formally very much in the social realist tradition of Trevor Griffiths and Ken Loach. Dealing with the history of British socialism from the 1960s to the 1990s, it is also in that tradition in terms of content. However, Nelson also expounds his notion of critical realism with reference to such apparently aesthetically and thematically diverse works as adaptations of Jeanette Winterson's *Oranges are Not the Only Fruit* (1990), George Eliot's *Middlemarch* (1994) and *The X-Files* (1994–2000).

For Nelson one commonality between these dramas appears to be that their narrative structures can be defined in opposition to what he calls the 'flexi-narrative' structure. This 'denotes the fast cut, segmented, multi narrative structure which yields the ninety second sound and vision byte currently typical of popular TV' (24). According to Nelson, this structure 'has extended into virtually all popular series and serials' and has it roots in soap (24). Within flexi-narratives, 'new characters and narrative strands are introduced in each episode of a series' and while these narratives come to closure within the episode, a 'number of regular characters (smaller than in soaps) is involved in unresolved narratives, which give continuity across episodes' (34). By contrast, most of examples of critical realism he gives are mini-series. In direct contradiction to Fiske's celebration of the resistant potential of discontinuity and fragmentation within television, Nelson sees the *sustaining* of narrative or narratives, and space and time for development of relationships and of themes, as important markers for politically progressive efficacy (see 153). Nevertheless, he does not suggest that there is anything *inherently* progressive about sustained narratives, nor inherently conservative about flexi-narratives. He acknowledges that this latter can offer multiple perspectives on the action and may result in relatively 'open' texts. Yet he argues that, for a wide range of institutional reasons, flexi-narratives tend towards the repetitious and the formulaic, working against critical reflection (42–8). Again in direct contradiction to Fiske's position, for Nelson this is largely because they are designed to attract 'a *large* and *plural* audience' (48, my italics). Further, Nelson argues that 'The more open the text, the more the viewers seem to feel free to construct their own narratives, pleasures and meanings, providing that is, that the dislocations are not so great as to fundamentally disturb normative frames of reference' (68).

What delimits these dislocations is, according to Nelson, that the flexi-narrative tends to flourish as part of 'flexiad' drama, which 'echoes advertisements and pop video in deploying signifiers for their intrinsic "values and lifestyle" aesthetic appeal, rather than in any referential sense' (25). He sees this as part of the 'asetheticisation of the image' that increasingly 'distinguishes popular (post)modern TV drama output', with such dramas showing an increased tendency to visual spectacle and to extensive use of a musical soundtrack (24). For Nelson, this type of form at best 'corresponds to the postmodern market's need for diversity and flexibility' (213) and addresses the audience as individual consumers, in ways that commercially exploit difference (96). At worst it approaches Baudrillard's conception of the simulacrum, the hyperreal and pure relativism (87–8).

In general, then, Nelson does not reduce the politics of a text to its form. He also meticulously sets out an ethical position from which to evaluate television drama, drawing on structuralism and post-structuralism but insisting on attending to both the constitutive power of linguistic systems and the economic and material realities of everyday life, to signs and the things to which they refer, however conventionally and contingently (see Nelson, chapter 9). Further, one of his main concerns is to counter the tendency towards relativism that occurs in both celebratory and pessimistic accounts of postmodernism. On the level of the particular, however, his arguments favour a position that may embrace emotional identification, but he still privileges 'rationality' and shared 'human truths' in ways that appear to repeat the Marxist-socialist values traditionally associated with the type of critical realist aesthetic he praises. However, as with Fiske and other post-Marxist television critics, the concept of socialism does not appear as part of his discourse and he tends to define his political position mainly in negative terms, in *opposition* to the aesthetic practices and values he associates with capitalist postmodernity. Like Fiske, then, he does not clearly identify what might be the parameters of a *positive* (post-Marxist-socialist) political project, out of which a critique of postindustrial, postmodern capitalism might be concretely pursued. All of this raises the question as to what, or rather *whom*, he might mean exactly when he uses the term 'human'.

It could be argued that in chapter 9 of his book, Nelson is in fact refiguring the political through a Derridian reworking of ethics, as

Diane Elam does in *Feminism and Deconstruction*. However, as Elam's title suggests, she achieves this positively through the *politics* of feminism. She also acknowledges the problem of taking up 'oppositional' political positions such as feminism, which, based as it is on a sexed/gendered identification, remains within the system of binary hierarchical thought that has historically determined the limits of human subjectivity. However, like other postmodern feminists, anti-racist and queer theorists, she recognises the need *contingently* to make a self-conscious and positive political identification within this system, in order to be able to contest it and as a way, however flawed, of keeping open the possibility of thinking alternative models for politics in the future (Elam, 1994).

The problems arising from Nelson's hesitancy in either clearly owning a Marxist-socialist political position, or defining and taking up a post-Marxist one in positive terms, become clear in his discussion of a 'critical postmodernism'. Quoting Jim Collins, he suggests that such texts would be constructed to provoke 'a careful and purposeful consideration of representational alternatives' (see Nelson, 1997: 239). Nelson then examines this idea of a critical postmodernism in relation to David Lynch's series *Twin Peaks* (1989–91), which during the 1990s was the focal point of virtually every academic discussion of postmodern television drama. This is because *Twin Peaks* remains one of the few television dramas to (apparently) abandon linear narrative, naturalistic and diegetic plausibility and continuity. It also displays a self-conscious, self-reflexive intertextuality through an eclectic range of references to other fictions, cited in terms of irony, parody and pastiche. Most importantly, however, it *also* rejects psychologically motivated characters and performances. Further, it attracted a (demographically) significant enough audience to achieve the status of both a televisual and critical 'event'. As Nelson indicates, ironically, considering that in theory this text might be interpreted as foregrounding the decentring of the subject as author of meanings, this status was very much tied up with that of Lynch as a cinema 'auteur' (236).

This aside, in comparison to his enthusiasm for *Our Friends in the North*, Nelson is less persuaded by the critical potential of *Twin Peaks*, which he says:

> lies in its refusal to centre itself, to make discursive or narrative sense of its allusive, multi layered construct. But its critical efficacy is

realised only if it promotes through its multiple coding, a recognition
in the viewers of the constitutive nature of all discourse and of their
own subjectivity. (237)

This is a tall order, well beyond anything Nelson expects from his
critical realist texts, and even then he argues that there can be 'no
assurance that a resistant critical strategy, beyond psychological
empowerment, will result' (237). Actually, recognising the discursive
nature of subjectivity is not in and of itself 'psychologically empowering', but as Baudrillard's ideas suggest, can be experienced as a loss
of the self, truth and agency and/or can produce a relativism which
denies the individual and collective responsibility for the world we
inhabit. In sum, as with the Marxist-socialist position but going
beyond its understanding of the human, this recognition is only 'critical' when it operates to produce an understanding of the meaning
(both) of human subjectivity and of 'reality' as altering and alterable.
This must occur in a manner that leaves open the possibility of future
rearticulations of these concepts whilst operating within a framework of a positive and concrete commitment to the conceptualisation and production of more just social and political systems.

This is, of course, an even *taller* order for what is, after all, only
a television drama series. Not surprisingly, then, critics like Jim
Collins focus on the ways that within *Twin Peaks* 'tonal oscillation
and generic amalgamation' encourage viewers to 'activate ever shifting sets of expectations and decoding strategies', in which 'emotional involvement alternates with ironic detachment' (Collins,
1992: 347). For Collins, this oscillation between identification and
detachment is symptomatic of the 'suspended' nature of *all* television viewing, in which multiple 'viewing perspectives are no longer
mutually exclusive but in a sort of perpetual alternation' (348).
Collins relates this to 'the post-modern condition' within which we
'as individual subjects are constantly engaged in the process of negotiating the array of signs and subject positions that surround us'
(348). Collins asserts that, '*Twin Peaks* and other forms of hyperconscious popular culture address themselves *directly* to this condition, situating themselves in the arcs and gaps that result when these
positions don't coalesce' (348–9, my italics). For some it is through
the foregrounding of these arcs and gaps and the failure of the
subject positions that surround us to coalesce that such aesthetic
strategies potentially become political, providing a space for agency,

through the challenging of meaning and subjectivity as fixed and singular. For others these arcs and gaps are places where meanings multiply into pure meaninglessness. Yet while earlier in this essay Collins pays attention to the political dimensions of the 'post-modern condition', he concludes that these texts are 'responses to the contingent and conflicted set of circumstances that constitute cultural life at the end of the twentieth century' (349). In short, they could be understood as a new form of television realism that reflects and expresses a new dominant mode of subjectivity.

Personally, it has always seemed to me that on the level of specific *representation*, barely touched on by either Nelson or Collins, *Twin Peaks* repeats rather than subverts traditional discourses relating to gender, 'race' and sexuality, in ways that are *not* cancelled out by the 'polysemic, multi-accentual nature' of its form (Collins, 1992: 345). On similar grounds, I also find it difficult to agree with Nelson's enthusiasm for the progressive potential of *The X Files*, which he argues partly on the basis of it *not* using a flexi-narrative structure, even though it has many other qualities of flexiad drama. In fact, while the notion of flexiad drama is a very useful one, it can distract from what Nelson so clearly and usefully demonstrates throughout this book, which is how in terms of aesthetics much contemporary television drama can be seen to work on a continuum between realism, modernism and postmodernism, in ways that embrace the forms realism originally 'opposed', such as melodrama.

Within this continuum the boundaries between these different forms are already blurred; nonetheless, distinctions can and do emerge on the level of the located and the specific. Few dramas can be confidently placed at the extremes of this continuum, but very roughly and in terms of form only, British soaps like *Coronation Street* (1960–) and *Eastenders* (1985–) still mostly incline towards the realist end with an overlay of melodrama, while *Twin Peaks* remains more or less alone at the postmodern end with an overlay of high modernism. A few dramas, such as *Wild Palms* (1993) directed by Oliver Stone, or more recently Stephen King's *Kingdom Hospital* (2004), come close to *Twin Peaks* but are not in exactly the same place. In this continuum *The X Files* hovers somewhere around the middle, sometimes pulling one way, sometimes the other. Hence, in fact, Nelson refers to it as (post)modern. The over-whelming majority of television drama sometimes described as post-modern actually occupies this hovering 'middle', (post)modern terrain, and this includes North American dramas such as *Ally McBeal*, *Buffy the Vampire Slayer* (1997–2003), *The Sopranos* (1999–2005), *Six Feet Under* (2001–5). In Britain this category embraces the 'adult' soap *Night and Day* (2001–3) and comedy programmes *Spaced* (1999–2001), *The Green Wing* (2004) and indeed *The Office*. Like *The X Files* and the flexiad dramas Nelson discusses, these programmes might score highly in terms of display-ing some of the qualities of a postmodern aesthetic, thought to promote 'ironic detachment'. Rather than alternating detachment with emotional involvement, however, these texts ultimately pro-mote and privilege the latter through encouraging an identification with, and significant investment in, psychologically motivated char-acters and performances – far beyond the identification and invest-ment allowed by *Twin Peaks*.

This does not *necessarily* reflect on the politics of these texts and I am not suggesting that, as a general principle, emotional identifi-cation is problematic. It cannot be denied that it actually constitutes one of the chief pleasures of a very large number of fictional forms, popular or otherwise. Also, as Nelson notes, it is widely recognised that 'sympathetic feeling as well as rational distance functions as an important part of cognition' (Nelson, 1997: 110). Further (emo-tional) identification is also crucial in thinking around radical con-cepts of intersubjectivity and the *politics* of the relationship between self and other(s). On this basis, if long before Brecht emotional identification had been perceived as 'inferior', it is because of the association of emotion with 'subaltern' groups (women, children, homosexuals and ethnic 'others') within traditional models of subjectivity.

A politically progressive, critical postmodernism might then try to embrace *both* abstract and embodied knowledges, the emotional and the rational, identification and distance. However, the problem is that as a form of 'double coding', Collins's *ironic* distance might actually be no distance at all. As such it can function simply to reaf-firm the status quo. As Kay Richardson and Ulrike Meinhof indi-cate, 'in the first instance, audience uptake of irony cannot be guaranteed. And in the second the logic that equates excess with irony and irony with critical function is flawed' (Richardson and Meinhof, 1999: 130–1). The same applies to other so-called post-modern characteristics thought to promote critical distance, such as self-reflexivity, parody, pastiche, intertextuality, eclecticism, etc. All of these devices have been in circulation in western cultural production long before the modern era and can and have been used for the purposes of both reaction and resistance.

Conclusion

None of this is to deny the possibility of a politically progressive, critical postmodernism or (post)modernism, or a critical realism, or any other sort of critical 'ism', on television or elsewhere. Rather, my argument (and Nelson's) is that abstract and general formal strategies, however they are named and claimed, cannot in and of themselves be regarded as inherently reactionary or progressive, or as inherently encouraging distance or identification, passivity or activity in the audience. In this book then I am *not* attempting to define or privilege a particular form as being more or less politically progressive. Yet none of this is to suggest that form does not play a role in the signifying process, and an important one, especially in a relatively conservative medium such as television. Even so, as Nelson indicates (but overlooks with *Twin Peaks*), a range of other factors must also come into play in evaluating a text's progressiveness, because politics, like subjectivity and identity, is a matter of embodied, situated practices, as well as abstract theoretical generalisations.

In the following chapters, I do often focus on form in terms of both my more general discussions of feminism, anti-racism and the queer, and also my more specific discussions of television texts. As will be clear, my own political identification(s) with these positions also means that I *do* sometimes incline towards certain types of aesthetic judgements – a point I will return to in the conclusion. However, as part of my project of questioning (postmodern) narratives of progress/progressiveness, I also interrogate the assumptions about aesthetics and the politics of subjectivity and identity circulating within these positions. Yet because this is achieved from 'within' these positions, this provides a political context which acknowledges the theories and the television practice as 'situated practices' as well as abstractions. As a result, I consider a range of factors 'other' than form, as relevant to the particular topics and texts under discussion. Above all, in terms of the latter, explorations of form are always moderated through a focus on the specificity of representations.

2

The end(s) of feminism(s)?
From *Madonna* to *Ally McBeal*

Defining terms: the feminine, feminist, postmodern feminism and postfeminism

In an overview of the field since the 1970s, the editors of *Feminist Television Criticism* state that 'feminist television criticism has not adequately conceptualised its own meanings for feminism, but instead has mirrored the "common sense" meanings of feminism that circulate in both popular and academic cultures'. As they indicate, this 'sense' was not actually 'common' but rather reflected 'the place and concerns of white, middle class, heterosexual, western women'. They conclude that new directions for feminist criticism 'will involve a further critique of what is and has been meant by terms such as women and feminist' (Brunsdon, D'Acci and Spigel, 1997: 13).

Although some of the essays in *Feminist Television Criticism* date back to 1979, this collection was published in 1997. In June 1998, the cover of *Time* magazine carried a photograph of celebrated North American feminists, Susan B. Anthony, Betty Friedan and Gloria Steinam, alongside one of Calista Flockhart, the star of *Ally McBeal*, with a headline posing the question 'Is Feminism Dead?' If the answer is affirmative, any further critique of terms would seem pointless. Except, as Susan Faludi notes in *Backlash*, the very same headline featured in the print media in the early 1970s and again in the early 1980s and in fact, similar 'postfeminist' sentiments were expressed by journalists in the 1920s, just after women first got the vote in North America and Britain (Faludi, 1992: 70 and 101–5).

In the first part of this chapter I want to take the *Time* cover question as an opening to pick up on some of Robin Nelson's concerns in his article cited in the introduction (Nelson, 2000). However, rather than investigating 'gendering' in recent television drama,

I want to consider the progress/progressiveness of the representation and construction of *feminism* within this medium, and to examine the discourses that have informed and shaped feminist television criticism. In order to achieve this, I start by reflecting back on some of the various ways that the terms 'feminine', 'feminism', 'postfeminism' and 'postmodern feminism' have been defined and interpreted in the academic and public spheres, with reference to both politics and aesthetics. My emphasis is on how and why a confusion of these terms might have emerged and allowed for an appropriation, depoliticisation and trivialisation of the feminist debate. I also consider the ways that these issues can be seen to be played out in and around television works from the 1980s and 1990s and look briefly at Maureen Chadwick's *Two Golden Balls* (1994) and Fay Weldon's *Big Women* (1998) before focusing in detail on *Ally McBeal* (1997–2002).

The academic context: the poststructuralist 'feminine' aesthetic and postmodern feminism

In a later chapter in *Feminist Television Criticism* on 'Identity in Feminist Criticism', Brunsdon offered a typology of 'discernible historical paradigm shifts' in thinking about 'the relationship between feminism and women within feminist writing on the media' (Brunsdon, D'Acci and Spigel, 1997: 116). She argues that in the 1960s and 1970s feminist criticism posited a 'transparent', essentialist, relationship between feminism and women, in which the use of the pronoun 'we' represented a confident belief in the possibility of speaking about, to and even for *all* women as a group, 'who are subject to global patriarchal subordination and who thus have gender specific experiences in common' (117). The next phase, which she defines as 'hegemonic' or 'recruitist', entails 'the differentiation of the feminist from her other, the ordinary woman, the housewife, the woman she might have become', accompanied by 'the impulse to turn the feminine identifications of [these] women into feminist ones' (118). As Brunsdon notes, this was often a profoundly contradictory position, 'involving the repudiation and defence of traditional femininity' (118). Her final category is 'fragmented' and 'founded on the possibility that there is no necessary relationship' between 'feminism' and 'women'. In this instance, the term woman becomes 'a profoundly problematic category', and arguably, 'feminist becomes rather more stable' (120). She quotes Ang's and Hermes's call to 'jettison the figure of woman' and their argument that 'any feminist standpoint will necessarily have to present itself as partial, based upon the knowledge that while some women share some common interests and face some common enemies, such commonalities are by no means universal' (Ang and Hermes quoted in Brunsdon, 1997: 120). There has always been 'fragmentation' within feminism but the type indicated by Brunsdon was largely produced by the critiques and interventions of black feminist thinkers such as Audre Lorde, Hazel Carby and bell hooks. Such commentators pointed out that most types of feminism worked within essentialist and exclusive definitions of 'women', which failed to take into account differences of race, class and sexuality between women (see Chapter 3).

Within a 'high theory' context, these challenges to 'common sense' feminism are often subsumed in a narrative of the decentring of the stable and unitary enlightenment subject, within poststructuralist and postmodern theory. In these terms Brunsdon's second paradigm shift might be viewed in relation to 'French Feminism' of the 1970s and 1980s. This usually signifies the work of Hélène Cixous, Julie Kristeva and Luce Irigarary, although there are important differences between these three thinkers. Nevertheless, in general terms, they all use poststructuralist linguistic and psychoanalytical theory, mostly drawn from Jacques Derrida and Jacques Lacan, to perform a first- and (arguably) second-stage deconstruction of the western, patriarchal 'phallologocentric' symbolic system, that constructs woman and/or the feminine as the inferior other to man and/or the masculine. In practice, this is often pursued through the critical analysis of various canonical texts and the celebration of works of avant-garde, literary culture, thought to exemplify a 'feminine' aesthetic, defined in opposition to a dominant 'masculine' one. This latter is understood to claim a privileged relation to the 'real' and is based on concepts of linearity, rationality, singularity and the closure of meanings – qualities all associated with realism and naturalism. By contrast, the 'feminine' aesthetic embraces the emotional, the irrational, artifice and mimicry, is plural, shifting, polyvocal, fragmented and contiguous. It is also perceived as challenging and resisting the dominant patriarchal norms. The focus on the literary avant-garde means that these ideas have often been criticised as being elitist. They are also critiqued as being essentialist, because although these gendered positions and their corresponding 'aesthetics' are understood to be sociohistorical constructs, they also relate to presumed differences in the gendered experience of sexuality. This, plus the psychoanalytical framework in which they are articulated, tends to produce a privileging of biological sexual difference above all other differences.

This problematic was taken up by a *postmodern* feminism, which tends to draw on Michel Foucault alongside Derrida, rather than (or as well as) on Lacan. This position looks forward to a third stage of deconstruction, and the dissolution of all subjectivity and identity categories into a multiplicity of endlessly proliferating, differently marked positionalties. This vision was famously expressed in Donna Haraway's 1985 essay, 'A Manifesto for Cyborgs'. In this 'science fiction fantasy', Haraway posits a utopian, posthuman future, where all the binary oppositions that construct subjectivity and identity have been transcended and the world is inherited by 'cyborgs' who inhabit multiple, contradictory, fluid, nonoppositional identities (Haraway, 1990). However, some of those following in Haraway's wake overlooked her use of the future tense, to declare that under postmodernist theory, this utopian, third stage of deconstruction had already been achieved. Others, however, were extremely concerned by the way that in the *present*, the anti-essentialist drive of such theoretical approaches undermined the very concept of feminism as a political practice. One way or another, any concept of feminism is based on the existence of a relatively stable category 'women'. Yet postmodern feminism indicates that *any* citation or definition of the term 'women' will inevitably fail to encompass and represent all the possible differences between the multiple and contradictory subjects to which it traditionally refers. In effect, therefore, both 'women' and 'feminism' always privilege sexual difference over other differences and reinstate *some* hierarchical binary oppositions.

In short, despite Brunsdon's claim for the stability of the word feminism, in *theory*, postmodern feminism deconstructed itself out of existence, inspite of evidence that sexism and misogyny are still in play within the world's social and symbolic systems. For some thinking, though, this 'aporia' was a crucial part of the process of imagining other, more just ways of practising politics (see Elam, 1994). In the meantime, tactical solutions emerged, such as those offered by Ang and Hermes as cited by Brunsdon above, which, as

Judith Butler put it, involve a 'contingent essentialism' that recognises the necessity of 'provisional instating of an identity category' but attempts at the same time to open it up 'as a permanent site of contest' (see Butler, 1993: 222).

Butler's name is often taken to be synonymous with 'postmodern feminism' (also see Chapter 5). In fact her work in *Gender Trouble* (1990) and *Bodies that Matter* (1993) functions as corrective to the more 'utopian' versions of this thinking, in so far as she points out that at present, taking up one of the sexed positions remains 'one of the conditions that qualifies a body for life within the domain of cultural intelligibility' (Butler, 1993: 2). Yet Butler goes on to argue that while 'sex' appears to have a material basis, there is no access to the materiality of sex, except *through* gender as a discursive social construct, so that in practical terms, the difference between sex and gender is 'no difference at all' (5). Consequently, she argues that the sexed subject positions can be considered as discursive, 'regulatory fictions', which in Foucaultian terms produce and also enable the possibility of resistance. As part of this argument, Butler identifies the normative sexed/gendered positions as 'performative', a type of citation or repetition that 'enacts and produces' that of which it speaks, not through reference to any external reality but to *previous citations* (12–14). Hence, gender can be defined as a series of stylised acts, in which reference to any reality is 'suspended' and the process of repetition allows for and indeed makes *inevitable* 'unfaithful' repetitions. This opens up the possibility of the subversion and denaturalisation of the sexed/gendered positions, by self-consciously repeating them in ways that foreground their imitative and artificial nature. Butler then points to various strategies of 'subversive repetition' occurring within literary texts but also within drag performance and crossdressing. In the case of the former, this subversion appears to depend on formal devices that bear some resemblance to those of the 'feminine aesthetic' cited above, and in the latter, to those found within a generalised postmodern aesthetic (see Chapter 1).

Responding to *Gender Trouble*, Susan Bordo accused Butler and other postmodern feminists of treating the body as an 'abstract linguistic structure' and of being so 'intoxicated with interpretative and creative possibilities of cultural analysis' that they neglect 'to ask themselves what is actually going on in the culture around them' (Bordo, 1995: 292 and 295). In fact, *Bodies that Matter* is partly concerned with examining the way in which even if the historical 'norms' of the sex/gender system are 'regulatory fictions', they nonetheless continue to have concrete and embodied effects (Butler, 1993: 10). Yet Butler does focus largely on the textual, and it should be noted that while she *does* attend to differences of race and class, she tends to do so *through* the categories of sex and sexuality (see Chapter 5). Equally, while she discusses the gendered positions as plural, in fact she focuses exclusively on subversive repetitions of *femininity*, as a means of undermining the 'naturalness' of both, showing them simply to be a set of behaviours or attributes that could be inhabited and performed by either sex. Perhaps partly due to these factors, when taken up by others, Butler's ideas can come to function, in Sara Ahmed's terms, as the postmodern as a 'model of reading'. That is, the strategies of self-reflexivity, mimicry, irony, parody and pastiche she favours in drag performance, are presumed in advance to be always successful in producing subversion, understood as an 'overcoming' of a monolithic realism/masculinity (Ahmed, 1998: 149, see Chapter 1). As with Haraway's manifesto, Butler's ideas have also been taken to imply that the sex/gender system has *already* been (performatively) transcended so that there is no longer any *need* for feminism.

In *Feminism Without Women*, Tania Modleski notes that about the time feminists were beginning to jettison the notion of 'woman', the notion of the 'feminine' as a linguistic or textual subject position was being taken up by male scholars as a 'deconstructive figure'. This was carried out in ways that either 'efface female subjectivity by occupying the site of femininity' or affirm existing gender stereotypes by confusing 'feminism with *feminisation*' (Modleski, 1991: 3–8, her italics). Both Bordo and Modleski suggest that this might be seen as part of a process of appropriation and inoculation of feminism within the patriarchal institution of the academy. For some, it might also mark the beginning of the end of feminism, in terms of an (apparently) growing gulf between the popular and academic spheres. As Ruth Frankenberg and Lata Mani indicate, 'The integrity of the Subject may have been exposed as a ruse of bourgeois ideology by philosophers and cultural critics but law, to take one powerful institution, still operates as if this were not the case' (Frankenberg and Mani, 2001: 483). Equally, as Natalie Fenton asserts, 'in the present day political [. . .] it may be as Calhoun suggests that, "essentialist identities continue to be evoked and often deeply felt" ' (Fenton, 2000: 734).

The media context: from 'old' feminism to 'feminisation'

This evocation of deeply felt 'essentialist identities' is evident in journalist Natasha Walter's *The New Feminism* (1999), where it is clear that while she considers *feminism* to be a problematic category, the term *women* is inclusive and self-explanatory. Walter argues that feminism as a political movement is not dead, but it does require a new set of concrete, pragmatic and achievable social and political goals (Walter, 1999: 8). Walter dismisses academic feminism at the point when it 'began to theorise the very structure of language as oppressively patriarchal, or saw the very techniques of cinema as evidence of an oppressive male gaze' (6). Yet for Walter, this does not account for the estrangement of many 'ordinary' women from feminism. Rather, she suggests this was the product of feminism's 'attempt to direct women's private lives' in terms of dress, language and behaviour but *also* of a media discourse which represented the 'typical' feminist as man hating, puritanical, humourless, politically correct and unattractive (Walter, 1999: 4–5 and 36–9). In short, as Janet Lee puts it, 'A brown-rice-eating, dungaree clad lesbian, who is harshly judgemental of other women' (Lee, 1988: 172). Despite her rejection of the critique of form within the academy, aesthetics *are* important in Walter's own analysis; similarly, while she defines her own approach as 'materialist' – a concept derived from Marxist-socialism – she includes 'socialist' in her list of feminist negatives. Overall, while she admits this media image of feminism is a stereo-type, she affirms it, at least in part, as an accurate reflection of the 'rigid ideology of old feminism' that 'alienates and divides women' (Walter, 1999: 4–5). Disseminated in the public realm, even by figures represented *as* feminist spokespersons, this stereotype pro-duced negative connotations for the term 'feminist', even as femi-nism appeared to be having significant impact on culture and society. However, some of this impact was again a matter of *femi-nisation* rather than feminism.

As Lisa Adkins indicates, there were significant changes in the economic and cultural spheres during the 1980s. These embraced an increase in the number of women entering the workforce, the decline in traditionally male-dominated forms of industrial employment in favour of service industries, and a shift in emphasis in culture from production to consumption (Adkins, 2001: 670–1). Adkins lists the characteristics of this consumer culture in Baudrillardian terms as an *aestheticisation* of the public sphere. This is based on the sovereignty of the sign, appearance, image and style, the predominance of surface, simulation and masquerade and a de-differentiation of the social, the political and the domestic, that extended the private 'world of home and feelings' into the public domain (645 and 674–5). She points out that all these characteristics are *traditionally* understood 'to concern the very fabric of the feminine' – hence, alongside changes in work patterns, the perception of a 'feminisation' of all aspects of public life (675). For Baudrillard, the media and especially television are key factors in producing and disseminating this 'feminisation'. Significantly, in a 1988 article for *Screen* discussing 'new traditionalism and postfeminism', in relation to a rash of 'women centred' dramas on North American television, Elspeth Probyn quoted a *Newsweek* article stating that, 'The feminisation of television has surprisingly little to do with feminism' (Probyn, 1997: 130). Probyn goes on to assert that while feminism may be the implicit *'other'* to versions of women and home offered by these dramas, 'Of course, the word "feminism" is never mentioned in any of these shows; it's not even there as what Judith Mayne calls an "echo effect". Rather, feminism and feminist ideas are totally submerged – it is the word that cannot be said' (128).

Feminism on TV

In fact, feminism has *always* been a word seldom said in television drama. In the 1980s this was notable even in programmes like Lynda La Plante's *Widows* and *Prime Suspect* in Britain (see Chapter 3) and *Cagney and Lacey* (1982–88) in North America, in which, as Mayne puts it, 'feminist questions have been raised', or which feminists found 'progressive and satisfying' (Mayne, 1997: 84). For example, according to Lorraine Gamman, while *Cagney and Lacey* was originally created by 'feminist script writers' (Barbara Avedon and Barbara Corday), at the height of its popularity the show's production team and its British fan club were unwilling to either discuss or 'own' the feminist content of the episodes, and Sharon Gless, who played Cagney, publicly rejected the description of the show as feminist, as 'too limiting' (Gamman, 1988: 25). Such refusals mean that what feminism is or might be remains uninterrogated. As Judith Mayne argues with reference to *LA Law* (1986–94), this allows for the 'stereotypically feminine, if not necessarily to undermine, then at least to complicate female challenges to male power' and this becomes even more acute when feminism is confused with feminisation (Mayne, 1997: 94). This holds for *LA Law*, which as I note in my discussion of *Ally McBeal* might itself be seen as a feminisation of the law drama series, but also for the vast majority of 'women-centred' television drama of the 1990s and indeed the early 2000s.

All of this has meant that unless feminist television criticism wished to function only in a humourless, divisive, politically correct mode, for the most part it *had*, as Brunsdon puts it, to turn 'feminine' identifications into 'feminist ones' (Brunsdon, D'Acci and Spigel, 1997: 118). As such, in the 1970s and 1980s many theorists focused on soap opera, following a strategy established in film studies of revaluing genres *aimed at* and apparently enjoyed *by* women, in ways that did not necessarily claim them as feminist but did allow them to be perceived as transgressive, empowering or subversive. However, after the widespread critique of the essentialism within influential ideas such as those of Laura Mulvey (1975) on gendered spectatorship, many sought to make a distinction between 'the female spectator', as interpellated by the dominant discourse of the text, and the 'female social audience'.[1]

Hence, in advance of Fiske, Brunsdon argued that while texts may construct preferred spectator positions, historical 'socially situated subjects' may or may not take up these positions (see Brunsdon, 1982 and 1994). However, the reason given for the appeal of such programmes to female subjects in the first case, was that such programmes 'call on traditionally feminine cultural competencies', which while not *natural* attributes of one gender or the other, are 'under present cultural and political arrangements' more *likely* to be possessed by female viewers (Brunsdon, 1982: 36). While not defining soap as politically 'progressive', then, Brunsdon affirmed the value of previously overlooked, despised feminine skills and competencies said to be required and mobilised by these texts (37). As Brunsdon herself acknowledged later, one of the dangers with this approach was that 'Instead of being a difficult and contradictory psychic, historical and cultural formation, towards which feminists have been ambivalent, femininity becomes an explanatory category'

(Brunsdon, 1994: 345). Women are then represented as 'lik[ing] these texts because they (both the texts and the women) have feminine concerns' (345). In fact, as Elspeth Probyn pointed out, due to a combination of such revaluings and poststructuralist articulations of a 'feminine aesthetic', by the late 1980s femininity or rather 'the feminine' came to be perceived by some as *automatically* and *inherently* a site of disruption, subversion and resistance (Probyn, 1997: 133).

Probyn points towards this in John Fiske's discussion of soap opera as a 'feminine' genre (Probyn, 1997: 133–4). Fiske cites Tania Modleski as having suggested that soap has the 'characteristics of a *feminine* aesthetic', which he reads as corresponding to a model of feminine sexuality/subjectivity (Fiske, 1991: 197, my italics). Following this, while he does consider that soap may be 'working to naturalise patriarchy in the feminine subjects who suffer from it', he concludes that it is subversive and resistant, 'whittl[ing] away at patriarchy's power to subject women' by legitimating 'feminine values', and that this 'produces self-esteem for the women who live by them' (197). In actual fact, Modleski argued that potentially soap operas 'are not altogether at odds with a possible *feminist* aesthetic', yet to be developed (Modleski, 1997: 47, my italics). Despite efforts to distinguish between them, then, Fiske blurs the distinction between a feminine aesthetic, femininity, female and feminist, in the ways noted by Brunsdon above. As Probyn, quoting Meaghan Morris, points out, this allows 'the feminine' to become a 'means to redemption' of soap, which 'discredits' in advance certain voices such as 'those of grumpy feminists and cranky leftists' (Probyn, 1997: 133 and Morris, 1990: 25). Yet as Shelagh Young asserts, this blurring may equally demonstrate that, in fact, there are no 'solid boundaries' between these terms (Young, 1988: 188). However, the failure to distinguish between them allows for a *re*naturalisation of the relationship between sex and gender, and for the 'feminine' as a singular category to substitute both for 'women' as a plural and differentiated category and for 'feminist' as a self-conscious, political identification.

Probyn argues that Fiske's notion of the feminine was already dated in academic circles by the mid-1980s, and other commentators have pointed out that soap is 'a woman's form no more' (see Geraghty, 1991). Nevertheless, I would argue that the idea of certain formal strategies, traditionally seen as concerning 'the very fabric of the feminine', as being *inherently* subversive and resistant is evident

in debates around Madonna as a postfeminism icon in the late
1980s and early 1990s.

Postfeminism

As is clear from both Shelagh Young's and Sherry Grant's essays in
The Female Gaze (1994), to be critical of Madonna is to be dis-
credited as an 'old-style' puritanical feminist and to risk appearing
'elitist' in a postmodern period, when, as Young puts it, 'the dominant intellectual project sometimes seems to be to prove the *popular*
is also *political*' (Young, 1988: 17). The aesthetic qualities of
Madonna's video performances were variously used to exemplify a
democratised, postmodern 'resistant' popular culture; a postmodern notion of subjectivity as fluid and discursive; and a Butlerian
strategy of subversive repetition which 'denaturalises femininity'
and challenges *both* genders because it reveals 'gender as a sign
system that does not necessarily co-inside with identity' (Kaplan,
1992: 272). Finally Madonna's performances were also claimed for
postfeminism, which is sometimes assumed to be identical with
postmodern feminism.

According to Faludi, Lee and Young, 'postfeminism' was primarily
a media construct of the mid-1980s and has at least two distinct, if
often overlapping strands. In the positive version, postfeminism
accepts that old-style feminism, despite its flaws, succeeded in its goals
and is therefore no longer relevant to 'today's young women'.
Interestingly, if Lee, Young, Walter and others are correct, *today's
young women*, have remained consistent in this position since the
1980s. If this version of postfeminism has connections with a *postmodern* feminism, it is with the utopian version which assumes that
the sex/gender system has been deconstructed everywhere and for
everyone. As a result, women are now free to 'perform or mimic femininity' and celebrate their sexuality free of any (old feminist) fear of
being objectified and defined in an inferior relation to men. This postfeminism includes a certain fluidity in terms of sexuality, notable in
Madonna's flirtations with bisexuality and in the image of the 'lipstick' lesbian of the 1990s. Yet the negative tone of media speculation
on the sexuality of another 1990s postfeminist icon, Spice Girl
Melanie Chisholm, when she gained weight, suggests that the power
of girls to transgress the heterosexual imperative remains the privilege
of those who conform to dominant norms for feminine attractiveness.

The second strand of postfeminism is more ambivalent to the legacy of feminism and reasserts traditional paradigms of sex and gender. In this instance, as Faludi points out, the tropes are of 'man shortage', 'ticking biological clocks' and women's discovery, usually at the age of 30, that they cannot 'have it all' (unless they actually *are* Madonna) (Faludi, 1992: 101). These women 'miss out' on relationships and children because they are too focused on their careers and/or are too 'choosy' and/or because feminism has produced a 'crisis' in masculinity whereby 'men have been "usurped", neutralised, marginalised, emasculated' (14). Those who do attempt to 'have it all' are torn between conflicting demands, usually at the expense of their children's well being. It is notable that this view seldom incorporates the notion that some types of women have always *had* to work and that one of the goals of feminism was to change the social structure in order to support them. Rather, as Isobel Armstrong notes, in this discourse *feminism* is held responsible for a wide range of social problems and is portrayed as a source of oppression for women, men and children (see Armstrong, 2000: 198).

In the mid-1980s, Susan Faludi argued that both modes of post-feminism were part of a right-wing, anti-feminist patriarchal backlash (Faludi, 1992). For Modleski, texts that 'proclaim or assume' the advent of postfeminism are 'in effect delivering us back into a pre-feminist world' (Modleski, 1991: 3). In 1988, writing about the 'yuppie' television series *Thirtysomething* (1987–91), Probyn defined the postfeminist discourse represented by this series as useful 'in provid[ing] a public language to talk about me and other similar women' but as ultimately a 'liberal feminism shorn of its political programme' (Probyn, 1997: 194). More recently, Armstrong asserted that much postfeminism 'fuel[s] female misogyny' and that this discourse functions on a 'rhetorical level that prevents careful analyses of the "predicaments", which it identifies' (Armstrong, 2000: 203).

During the 1980s, however, Shelagh Young questioned the right of white, middle-class, intellectual feminists to 'say what is, and what is not a feminist representation, or who is and who is not a feminist' (Young, 1988: 174 and 181). Drawing on Foucaultian theory, she went on to assert that what she defines as 'popular' post-feminism was indicative of, 'not a rejection and a negation of feminism' but of its *success*, a recognition that 'feminism is at last a force to be reckoned with, a system of power being actively resisted' (184). However, as Susan Bordo, also a Foucaultian, points out, 'even the work of white, upper class, heterosexual women is not located at the *center* [*sic*] of cultural power' (Bordo, 1995: 224, original italics). It is also striking that although Young *refers* to the multiple differences of race, ethnicity, class and nationality within the category 'women', her *examples* of popular, postfeminist resistance are Madonna and two white, British, Conservative politicians of the time, Edwina Currie and Margaret Thatcher. She asserts that '*Arguably*, these successful popular figures are speaking to all women' (Young, 1994: 180, my italics). bell hooks for one *did* argue that owing to the particular construction of black female subjectivity in relation to sexuality, Madonna's performance could only be interpreted as 'liberating' from a white perspective' (hooks, 1992: 159–60).

As Ien Ang points out, 'spotting the difference' between repetition and subversion in Madonna's performance may be a matter of perspective(s) and of what contexts are taken into account in terms of both production and consumption (Ang, 2001: 399). As such, Kaplan, Lee and Young all agree that from some perspectives if Madonna is a postfeminist icon, the difference between this and some earlier forms of feminism may be that this is an individualistic, 'free-market', postindustrial, capitalist feminism. Hence Young's apt comparison between Madonna, Currie and especially Thatcher, who as Prime Minister of Britain between 1979 and 1996 was a champion of exactly these values. Significantly, Young also argues that one of the reasons why many (old) feminists found it difficult to 'love Madonna' is because they believed that feminist politics 'must necessarily be linked to the socialist tradition' (Young, 1988: 180). For Young, as for Walter, this alliance with socialism was a major factor in (old) feminism's divisiveness. Yet Young herself clearly indicates a debt to Marxist-socialism when she talks of 'class', just as Walter does when she talks of 'materialism'. As noted in Chapter 1, a tendency within post-Marxist, postmodern thought to reject rather than *interrogate* the legacies of socialism can slip from accepting the necessity of deconstructively 'working within' capitalism to a celebration of the status quo.

As Sara Ahmed points out and as evinced in Young's essay, within some postmodern feminist theory, categories such as 'race' and 'class' are cited as 'figures for difference' rather than as a 'constitutive and positive term of analysis' (Ahmed, 2000: 41). Ahmed argues that as a result, a philosophy of difference can actually involve universalism, allowing, for example, a speaking from the place of the privileged white subject who 'reincorporates difference as a sign of its own fractured and multiple coming into being' (42). In short, a postmodern postfeminism may represent a reversal and a substitution of the old 'dominant norms' that reaffirm the 'superiority' of the white, bourgeois subject by other means, whilst retaining an aura of progressiveness through its association with (old) feminism.

This is the argument made by Lisa Adkins in her analysis of Linda McDowell's study of service-sector professionals, in which McDowell draws on Butler's discourse of gender performativity. McDowell argues that the premium increasingly being placed on traditionally 'feminine' skills and attributes, such as 'flexibility', interpersonal skills and appearance, suggests that 'the performance of femininity – for all workers – constitutes workplace resources' (Adkins, 2001: 669). McDowell describes these 'performances' as 'strategic', claiming that in the workplace men and women are beginning to 'do' gender, so as to denaturalise it, opening up 'complex and generative subject positions for both sexes' (McDowell in Adkins, 2001: 684). Yet this might simply indicate a 'feminisation' as part of the production of a model of subjectivity suited to the demands of patriarchal, postindustrial capitalism. Indeed, Adkins asserts that there is evidence in McDowell's study to suggest that while *male* workers might be able to 'take on the aesthetics of femininity' and perform 'new gender hybrids', in contrast 'performances of *masculine* aesthetics have negative workplace consequences' for *women* workers, who are simultaneously understood to have 'natural' advantages in the feminised workplace, which therefore do not merit recognition or reward (695). In short, as Adkins notes quoting Judith Habelstram, 'women's mobility is *within* the genre of femininity, suggesting that 'gender it seems, is reversible *only in one direction*' (Habelstram in Adkins, 2001: 685, my italics). This might be seen as a consequence of poststructuralist and postmodern strategies of subversive repetition, which focus on demonstrating the constructedness of femininity, which has *always* been understood in terms of mimicry and artifice, and which assume that this *also* denaturalises masculinity. It must also be noted that some men, in some contexts, have *always* been 'feminised' by dint of their subaltern position in terms of class, ethnicity or sexuality. Significantly, Adkins also cites Mantia Diawara's analysis of the emergence of 'mobile subject positions' in relation to race on film, in which Diawara examines how certain white male characters are 'strategically' able to take on the 'aesthetics of blackness' in terms of language and bodily style, whilst black characters tend *only* to perform this aesthetic (Adkins, 2001: 687–8, my italics). 'Feminisation', then, may be matter of privileged access to 'cultural resources' whereby white middle-class masculinity is refigured as the position of fluidity and mobility, in opposition to 'naturally' fixed and limited 'others', in ways that may reverse but do not suspend or displace the 'old' norms of enlightenment subjectivity.

Judith Butler is at pains to point out in *Bodies that Matter* that not all ironic or parodic repetitions of the sex/gender positions are necessarily subversive. Neither is there anything 'inherently' subversive about irony, self-reflexivity or parody; nor, indeed, as Charles Jenks (1986) indicates, is there anything inherently *postmodern* about these devices. Nothing, furthermore, 'naturally' or 'essentially' links qualities of mimicry and artifice to the category 'women', or those of realism to the category 'men'. As such, 'spotting the difference' between subversion and containment in any given performance of gender cannot be reduced to a matter of form or style alone but depends on what contexts are taken into consideration and on the particularity of representations.

Case studies in feminism, postfeminism and pre-feminism: *Two Golden Balls* and *Big Women*

Before turning to *Ally McBeal* I want to refer briefly to two pieces of British television drama from the 1990s. These shows are notable because both are scripted by women and both make rare direct representations of old-style feminism. Like *Ally McBeal*, both are comedies and both also draw intertextually on genres often associated with the 'feminine'. I would also argue that ultimately they both utilise the feminine to undermine the feminist. However, the differences and similarities between these shows and the later far more markedly postmodern *Ally McBeal* are indicative of some of the different ways in which this is achieved.

Two Golden Balls (1994) was written by Maureen Chadwick and directed by Anya Camilleri. A self-contained two-hour comedy drama, it follows the story of Linda (Claire Skinner) and her journey from naïve, muddle-headed, muddle-haired, dungaree-wearing old-style feminist, to a glamorous, 'feminine' and sexually fulfilled woman. This is achieved when her political activities land her in prison and she shares a cell with a porn star, Sidnie, played by Kim Cattrall, who later played Samantha in *Sex and the City* (1998–2004). Sidnie convinces Linda to throw off her feminist shackles and join her and her colleague Mariella (Rowena King) in seizing the means of production from an exploitative male pornographer, to create their own commercially successful, female-centred porn. This allows Linda to discover and celebrate her sexuality and also leads to the sexual liberation of her 'emasculated', pro-feminist husband Dexter (Angus Macfayden), with whom she then disappears into a self-consciously theatrical sunset. This happy ending 'playfully' repeats that of classic romance and there are also marked fantasy or 'fairytale' elements within the style and structure of the piece. These genres have been claimed as 'feminine' forms within literary criticism and there are overtones of a popularised version of 'French Feminism' in some of the dialogue which emphasises the 'revolutionary' potential of female sexuality. All these aspects of the drama are played out in the registers of irony, parody and pastiche. Nevertheless, while far from naturalistic, characterisation and performances remain within the conventions of psychological realism and the narrative structure, camera work and editing all favour an emotional identification with Linda, and to some extent, Sidnie and Mariella. These female protagonists are all young, conventionally attractive and markedly heterosexual. Female characters who do not fit this profile, in terms of age, such as Linda's mother, or appearance, such as a 'butch' prison warder to whom Sidnie refers as a 'dyke', are like the group of feminists to which Linda originally belongs, represented as humourless and oppressive to other women. They are also the subject of misogynistic jokes within the overall diegetic frame.

The portrayal of male characters makes an interesting contrast. Whereas Linda's sexual awakening is strictly heterosexual, there is an implication that Dexter's occurs through a close encounter with an attractive gay/bisexual man, whose representation is in stark contrast with that of the 'butch' female prison warder. Unlike Linda's mother, the older *male* figure, Viscount Osgood (Lesley Philips), who 'worships' women for their erotic power, is represented in wholly positive terms. This also points to a class dynamic in *Two Golden Balls*, in so far as sexism and the sexual exploitation of women is remarked as the territory of its white, working-class villain Randall (Nicholas Boulton), rather than of the aristocrat or the middle-class male. As noted in Chapter 3, racism is often represented as a 'problem' primarily of the working class. In terms of a discourse of 'race', it is notable that King, who plays Mariella, is the only black performer in the cast and the representation of this character abounds with intertextual references to Cleopatra and to ancient sex goddesses. This might be seen as affirming the traditional construction of black female subjectivity as exotic and hypersexual (see Chapter 3). In short, this is postfeminism in celebratory and recuperative mode. Old-style feminism is portrayed as repressive and oppressive for both men and women, and empowerment is achieved by a feminisation of pornography, as a commercial enterprise that is actually underwritten by the wealthy Osgood. Any 'mobility' allowed to the female characters is strictly *within* the parameters of normative femininity, and arguably this is *confirmed* rather than opened up by the self-conscious intertextual references to 'feminine' fairytale and romance genres.

Adapted by Fay Weldon from her novel of the same name, *Big Women* (1998) also represents a journey from feminism to post-feminism but in less positive terms. Weldon emerged as a successful female novelist in the 1970s, when, as *Big Women* indicates, these were a rarity. As a result, she has frequently been called on by the media to act as a spokesperson for both women and feminism, although some of her public statements have been described as 'anti-feminist'.[2] *Big Women* was produced by Tariq Ali, known for his radical political activism in Britain in the 1960s, and directed by Renny Rye, who also directed many of Dennis Potter's celebrated television dramas. This four-part mini-series takes place between the early 1970s and the mid-1990s and portrays the rise and fall of 'Medusa', a British feminist publishing house which is clearly modelled on the (real) Virago Press.

Structurally, this drama is reminiscent of Peter Flannery's 1996 series *Our Friends in the North*, which Nelson uses to exemplify progressive critical realism in television drama (see Chapter 1). Both dramas follow a small group of protagonists over several decades, interweaving the historical, the personal and the political, with *Our Friends* focusing on socialism and *Big Women* representing key moments and debates in the recent history of feminism. However, whereas *Our Friends* was critical of British socialism but supportive of its ideals, *Big Women* is highly ambivalent in its attitude towards feminism. While male characters and patriarchal structures are represented as unequivocally misogynist, feminism is portrayed as the refuge of discontented or dysfunctional white middle-class women, who lack any genuine sense of solidarity with other women. Strikingly, the scenes dealing with the famous women's anti-nuclear peace protest at Greenham Common in the early 1980s almost exactly reproduce the pejorative manner in which these (actual) events were portrayed in the media of the time. Protesters are mostly portrayed as humourless, dungaree-wearing extremists who are aggressive to both men and to other more 'feminine' women. As Layla (Daniela Nardini), one of the drama's central characters, says, 'they are unable to decide who they hate more – men, the bomb or each other'. Layla also critiques the protesters for stirring up fear of nuclear war in children, as if it were possible to protest against weapons of mass destruction *without* referring to their effects. While Layla is, like most others in this drama, an ambivalent character, these statements remain uncontested within the diegesis. At other times, the criticism of old-style feminism(s) is more balanced. Yet this drama itself repeats some of feminism's errors; so, for instance, feminism's failure to take account of differences of ethnicity, gender and sexuality is addressed by one of only two black characters in the drama, both of whom make strictly 'token' appearances.

It might be argued that this is a matter of naturalism or mimetic realism in relation to its social milieu, but *Big Women* is *not* realism. Rather it offers highly stylised dialogue and exaggerated performances. It also draws heavily on the structures and images of classical mythology and on the 'feminine' genres of melodrama, fairytale and gothic romance. Although this is achieved intertextually and in the register of parody and pastiche, as with the earlier adaptation of Weldon's *The Life and Loves of a She Devil* (1986),[3] this drama very much *repeats* classical notions of the irrational, 'monstrous', supernatural feminine. As such character is rendered in terms of *archetype*s that owe much to Jungian psychoanalysis and are defined in terms of one or two attributes (Layla's hedonism, Stephanie's excessive political idealism, Zoe by her 'victim' status, Bull by being a bully, etc.). These characteristics are portrayed as at once (human) saving graces and 'fatal flaws' in the Aristotelian sense.

Each episode attempts to locate and historicise its action through film footage of current events of the period, accompanied by appropriate popular music. However, this is counterbalanced by the numerous references to classical mythology, combined with a structure in which flashbacks to early scenes of the founding moments of Medusa/feminism are used to 'explain' later events. This mainly occurs as the drama moves into the 1990s and features the grown-up children of the protagonists, including various emasculated and feminised young men and the distinctly 'postfeminist' Saffron. Saffron's first appearance as an adult is preceded by footage of Margaret Thatcher and is accompanied by the Spice Girls' famous 'girl power' song *Wannabe* (1997). She also 'flaunts' her femininity, as the camera focuses lovingly on her long legs in short skirts, her blonde hair and beautifully made-up face. However, these attributes are represented as tools that she uses in her ruthless, equal opportunities manipulation and exploitation of others in her climb up the ladder within the world of commercial publishing, which culminates in the literal 'selling out' of the Medusa Press.

Saffron is frequently described by older characters as a 'chicken come home to roost', a sort of 'nemesis' – the implication being that if she is a monster, she is one created *by* feminism. Despite the historicisation and contextualisation of events, then, there is a sense of 'evolutionary determinism' in this drama. While the self-conscious stylisation might potentially create a postmodern 'ironic distance', the classical references allow for these devices to produce an identification *of* rather than *with* the characters, as embodying essential and universal human qualities. In fact, within *Big Women*, both feminism and postfeminism are recuperated to a discourse of an eternal 'war of the sexes'. In this context, the unaltering and unalterable flaws of woman/the feminine mean that all feminism, and perhaps all politics, is 'fated' to end in selfish individualism and there is no possibility of social and political change, only of the reversal and substitution of existing power relations. In short, *Big Women* clearly belongs to a tradition of classical satire that pre-dates the modern and has always used irony, parody and pastiche to expose the folly of 'universal human nature'.

Significantly, the earlier adaptation of Weldon's *She-Devil* provoked a fair measure of feminist debate in the British media (see Brandt, 1993). However, the potentially more provocative *Big Women* barely produced a ripple of interest, even though it appeared in the same year that *Ally McBeal* was causing controversy on both sides of the Atlantic. This may be because, as the combination of Weldon, Ali and Rye indicates, *Big Women* was a type of British-authored 'quality' mini-series that might be understood as appealing primarily to a white, middle-class, middle-aged audience. In contrast, *Ally McBeal* was a long-running 'popular quality' series, clearly aimed at a younger demographic. Yet the difference in response to these dramas might equally be taken to signal a widespread inoculation and depoliticisation of feminism, through a very postmodern confusion of the distinction between politics and aesthetics, feminism and feminisation, postmodern feminism and postfeminism.

Ally McBeal: the terms of the debate

Ally McBeal was created by writer/producer David E. Kelly, who worked on *LA Law* before developing his own series, including *Chicago Hope* (1994–), *Ally McBeal* (1997–2002) and the 'serious' law drama *The Practice* (1997–). In North America the debate around *Ally McBeal* was initiated by the 1998 *Time* cover cited above, and the accompanying article, 'Feminism: It's All About Me!' by Ginia Bellafante. Bellafante defined old-style feminism as the product of 'an upper middle-class intellectual elite', and asserted that if feminism has come to seem 'divorced from matters of public purpose', this was partly due to shifts in the academy, focusing more on 'symbols of the body and less on social action and change' (Bellafante, 1998: 3). However, for the most part, she mounted an attack on postfeminism, using the character of *Ally McBeal* as an example of what she termed the 'Camille Paglia syndrome', whereby claims for the power of female sexuality have produced an obsessive focus on the sexual, 'wed to a culture of celebrity and self-obsession' (3–4). Along with novelist Helen Fielding's creation Bridget Jones, she used Ally to indicate how much feminism has 'devolved into the silly', with 'powerful support' from popular culture 'offering images of grown single women as frazzled, self-absorbed girls' (3). These comments appeared as part of a wider argument that cited a number of other actual and fictional figures and actual North American social and political events and statistics. However, the explosion of commentaries that appeared in this article's wake often concentrated wholly on *Ally McBeal*, debating whether or not this character was an accurate reflection of the state of postfeminism, and whether, for good or ill, she functioned as a 'role model' for 'today's young women'.

Some of the show's defenders argued that many young, single women *did* positively identify with this character's dilemmas, whilst others warned against confusing television characters with real people. There was often a strong 'hyperreal' dimension to this debate, initiated perhaps by both the *Time* cover and Bellafante placing together *actual* feminist activists and *fictional* female characters, as if to imply an equivalence. Press coverage of Calista Flockhart also often blurred the distinction between performer and character, to the point where Flockhart was provoked to comment:

> People are saying I'm the spokeswoman for postmodern feminism, and I never thought I would be that, I mean I consider myself – Calista Flockhart – a feminist. The sole purpose of *Ally McBeal* is entertainment, and people need to take it in the spirit it's given. I'm just an actress trying to play a part.

Yet she then went on: 'There's no denying that people are thinking of Ally as a role model [. . .] To me the interesting question is why? What's lacking?' (quoted in Rosenthal, 1988: 2).

Character and plot

Ally McBeal does seem an unlikely role model. In 'One Hundred Tears Away' in season 1, Ally, an attractive, white lawyer faces a bar association hearing on her emotional competence to practise law. A female judge defends her on the basis that when men get passionate about something they are seen as 'strong and impassioned' but when women do so they are seen as 'weak and emotional'. This 'feminist' argument is somewhat undercut by the fact that Ally *is* consistently portrayed as emotionally 'out of control' in both her personal and professional life and this is reflected in Flockhart's twitching, pouting, finger-sucking and hair-twirling performance of the character. Even Ally's therapist Tracey describes her as a 'little weakling' ('The Playing Field') and in season 1, other characters frequently comment on her neurosis and her self-absorption (see 'The Blame Game' and 'Happy Birthday Baby'). Yet at other times, as Ruth Shalit points out, Ally's stereotypically feminine 'romantic idealism, her emotionalism, her intuitiveness, her girlish indifference to such manly concerns as law and logic and reason' are represented as positive qualities and even an 'asset' or professional resource (Shalit, 1998: 7).

In fact, there is also no denying that the first season of *Ally McBeal* did locate itself in relation to popular *postfeminist* discourse. In the pilot episode, Ally, who is approaching 30, offers an account of her single status, in which she describes herself as being a 'victim of my own choices' and 'choosing myself out of happiness'. Later, when Ally has hallucinations featuring a 'dancing baby', her flatmate Renee suggests that they are a manifestation of Ally's 'ticking biological clock' ('Cro-Magnon'). The legacy of feminism is taken as a 'given', with Ally saying 'I know women can change the world', but she continues 'I just want to get married first' ('The Blame Game'). In season 2, Ally did also sometimes seem to be offered up as a postfeminist role model, when the makers appeared to respond to the media debate about the show from *within the show*. For instance, 'It's My Party' delivers an unequivocal postfeminist rebuke to repressive old-style feminists, who objected that Ally's wearing of micro mini-skirts in court was symptomatic not just of the character's lack of professionalism but of a trivialisation of female lawyers in general (see 'The Plain Dealer', 1998). This episode represents a conservative Christian man as less 'prejudiced' and less likely to judge on appearances than such feminists.

However, for the most part the show's attitudes to the character of Ally and to the female, the feminine, feminism and postfeminism were all marked by ambivalence and contradiction. To follow through one example, in 'The Playing Field', Richard Fish (Greg Germann), senior partner at Ally's firm Cage and Fish, tries to win a highly questionable sexual harassment case by claiming in court that the existence of the sexual discrimination laws proves women's inability to cope in the workplace, and argues that all women should qualify under the Federal Disabilities Act. Challenged by his colleague Georgia (Courtney Thorne Smith), he borrows her high-heeled shoe and asks, 'Why would a grown person walk around in something like this?' To which he answers 'because men like it – don't talk to me about equality, and don't tell me you're not disabled'. As a character, one of Richard's functions is to be chronically and comically 'politically incorrect', but neither an outraged Georgia nor Ally seems able to refute his arguments. It is Ally's therapist, Tracey, in a scene in the bar, who offers the postfeminist counter-argument, urging them to realise that 'sex is power and it's ours, you assume its men's and it's ours', pointing to Renee as an example of a woman 'in charge of her own sexuality' ('The Playing Field'). These assertions are also confirmed in a conversation between Richard and John Cage (Peter MacNicol). Putting aside an established running joke when Ally constantly 'falls off' her high heels but continues to wear them ('Theme of Life', 'The Inmates'), Tracey's argument is undermined in the next episode. Renee, whose hobby is kick boxing, is shown unambiguously 'leading a date on' and then using excessive violence to defend herself, when this expression of her 'sexual power' is misread as consent to sexual intercourse ('The Inmates'). The man is seriously hurt and in the next episode Renee is on trial on a charge for assault. Although Renee wins the case, the structure and narrative of these episodes do not entirely favour her perspective. She eventually admits her responsibility in this incident to Ally, revealing that her apparent sexual confidence hides anger and aggression towards men, developed through experiences in her early teens ('Being There'). In this sequence of events, discourses of the female, the feminine, the feminist and the postfeminist are all deployed in turn to undercut each other, producing a shifting of perspectives that is so contradictory it is impossible to determine a 'dominant' discourse.

In short, *Ally McBeal* often demonstrates an openness to interpretation that *could* potentially be claimed as characteristically postmodern. This very much relates to its form, something that is lost by a tendency of the show's detractors to focus more or less entirely on plot and character. In contrast, many of the show's defenders frequently point to its 'cartoonish' special effects and its narrative and stylistic strategies of exaggeration, transgression, contradiction and comic undercutting. Actually, I would argue that *both* of these responses are prompted by the show itself, in ways that account for its controversial nature. On one hand, *Ally McBeal* employs a postmodern aesthetic that self-reflexively remarks its own textuality, producing ironic distance from characters as fictional constructs. On the other, it asserts and affirms a particular version of reality, portrays its characters in terms of traditional psychological motivation and privileges emotional identification with them, as representations of universal 'human truths'.

Genre, form and intertextuality

Many commentators describe *Ally McBeal* as belonging to a sub-genre of women's sitcom that goes back to *The Mary Tyler Moore Show* (1970–77). Hence, most episodes take place in the same limited number of locations (the office, the bar, the court, Ally's apartment), Ally's work colleagues function as a surrogate family and the action always relates in some way to the 'situation', defined as Ally's idealistic desire for heterosexual, romantic fulfilment. Yet this series actually uses a version of Nelson's flexi-narrative structure, with each episode offering a self-contained story that involves new characters but with some storylines continuing across more than one episode and/or season. This creates space for the sort of narrative progression and character development typical of soap, enabling the show to enter the preserve of 'drama'.

This is not just a matter of the way that all episodes contain switches of emotional register from comedy to a more serious consideration of themes raised by the narrative. While rarer in British sitcom, this is common in North America. However, for example, it is virtually unknown for *any* sitcom to include the death of a member of the core cast. Yet in season 3, Ally (character and series) carried on with barely a pause after the death of Billy (Gil Bellows). As such, the show has often been referred to as comedy drama or 'dramedy'. In fact it draws intertextually on a number of different genres including law-firm drama series like *LA Law* and *The Practice*, which also use (post)modern flexi-narrative structures and have taken on elements of soap. Yet *Ally McBeal* draws on these genres in a manner that recalls Susan Harris's groundbreaking series *Soap* (1977–81). This North American sitcom parodied soap-opera conventions, satirising the emotional and narrative excesses of the genre, whilst depending on those excesses at its more serious moments, so that at some level it also parodied itself.

To a large extent, then, *Ally McBeal* is a sitcom that parodies law-firm drama, in ways that could be said to take to comic excess the (post)modern aestheticisation or 'feminisation' of this genre as evinced in *LA Law*. For example, *Ally McBeal* can be seen to take to an extreme the way that in such shows, law suits always overlap with events in the characters' private lives, or offer parallels to their emotional concerns. In doing this *Ally McBeal* also potentially comments on its own construction in ways that devolve into self-parody.

This becomes evident when, in the first season, characters from Kelly's 'straight' law drama *The Practice* were brought in to assist Cage and Fish on a murder case ('The Inmates'). The contrast with the more sombre and serious *The Practice* self-reflexively underlines Cage and Fish's status as a 'joke' law firm full of hyper-emotional, cartoon characters, working in a feminised office furnished in light pastel colours and staffed by beautiful women in expensive and revealing designer outfits. Of course, this conjunction also potentially points up the fictional status of *The Practice*, not least when despite the bizarre behaviour of the Cage and Fish lawyers and the ludicrous nature of the case, the character of Bobby Donnell is 'won round' by Ally's reminder that 'there's more to life than being a lawyer'. Later in the season, when he returns to ask for their help on another case, he is attracted to Ally but claims he does not mix the personal and the professional, but then admits (as regular viewers of *The Practice* would know) that *all* his relationship have done exactly that.

Yet in its more 'serious' moments, such as those which occur in the Renee narrative in 'Being There' cited above, *Ally McBeal* simply repeats the conventions of these law-firm drama series, including, for instance, the power of the 'big speech' to effect justice. Similarly, it also uses elements originating in soap but now also common to many drama series, such as the convention whereby the 'camera lingers on the telling expression to allow the viewer not just to experience the emotion of that character but to imagine what constitutes the emotion' (Fiske, 1991: 183). The feelings between Ally and her ex-lover Billy in the first three seasons are usually represented through just such 'lingering on telling expression', underlined by the use of soft focus and key lights in the eyes. Yet this convention is also sometimes taken to parodic excess, comically foregrounding its melodramatic nature. For example, in 'Fools' Night Out' in a lift sequence Billy and Ally execute a whole 'conversation' consisting entirely of exaggeratedly 'speaking' looks.

The same play between (North American) soap realism, parody and self-parody is in evidence around the character of Ally herself. This is most clear in the contrast between the recurring scenes of Ally on her own that end most episodes and the use of special effects to show what Ally is thinking/fantasising. The former are nearly always set at night and she is often shown walking through dark streets accompanied by expressive musical soundtrack. The latter include, for example, the feeling of lust being signified by a huge tongue hanging out of her mouth, or emotional pain by her body being shot full of arrows. These two different styles of shot indicate the changes of register in the show from comic to serious but they also offer two contradictory perspectives on the character. The stylistic conventions used in the alone/walking sequences conventionally signify depth or 'interiority', an 'inner life' behind Ally's neurotic, comic posturing, which the viewer is invited to imagine, identify with and experience through an act of empathy. In literally 'showing' us what Ally is thinking, the highly coloured, comic fantasy shots constitute an ironic comment on, rather than expression of character, creating distance by portraying her as a transparent two-dimensional figure. In short, these two devices indicate an alternation between emotional identification and ironic distance, something like what Jim Collins ascribes to '*Twin Peaks* and other forms of hyperconscious popular culture' (Collins, 1992: 348, see Chapter 1).

It is noticeable, however, that as the seasons progressed the visual special-effects sequences became less frequent, with their function being taken up by musical effects. In the first episodes, music, usually popular ballads or soul, was a key part of the show's 'serious' emotional register. As such it tended to move between an extradiegetic soundtrack, which the characters 'can't hear', and intradiegetic music performed by Vonda Shepard in the bar, which they can. A song might start playing extradiegetically under a scene but the scene would then cut to the bar where it was being sung intradiegetically by Shepard. Again these are well-established conventions, but the centrality of music in both registers in *Ally McBeal* was always highly unusual for a sitcom, soap or law series, with some episodes verging on becoming music videos.

These conventions were also complicated by the gradual establishing that Ally and also John could also 'hear' or 'play' music in their heads, audible to the audience, although not usually to other characters (see, amongst others, 'Cro-Magnon', 'The Playing Field', 'Once in a Lifetime'). From this point, music might initially appear to be extradiegetic but then be revealed as 'really' playing in Ally or John's head. This is often signified by the sudden intrusion of 'stop' and 'rewind' or 'winding down' sound effects, or as in 'The Playing Field' by a song abruptly stopping and starting at a different speed. This is complicated to the point that in 'I Will Survive' in season

3, apparently extradiegetic music is first revealed as coming intradiegetically from the radio but continues in Ally's head when she switches it off and finally is shown to come (intra and/or extradiegetically?) from a hallucination of (the real) Gloria Gaynor, singing in Ally's shower.

It could be argued that some of these devices reinforce a sense of the character's 'interiority', giving the viewer the *experience* of Ally's tendency to confuse the 'real' and the 'imagined' within the diegetic world. However, they also play on audience expectations in relation to such conventions, drawing attention to their conventional nature. Alongside and as part of this play on and with music, as seasons progressed numerous regular and guest characters started singing intradiegetically in the bar, which also featured artists of the status of Tina Turner and Barry White as themselves, and songs were also performed elsewhere, so that the show virtually became a musical. This self-reflexivity was acknowledged by an increasing number of episode titles that were quotes from songs, and finally in season 3 by means of an episode entitled 'The Musical, Almost', which like the whole series at this point is a musical, almost.

In short, the show foregrounds the formulaic and constructed status of devices that at other times it still employs straightforwardly, especially in the alone/walking scenes which were part of the show's *own* formula. This drama then moderates between simple reiteration of these conventions, commenting on them and self-reflexively commenting on its own use of them. Similarly, it quotes from other genres, comments on them and then comments on its own quoting. In doing so, it draws attention to its own status as a fiction that refers only to other fictions, in ways that in theory should allow its characters to appear as constructs, and which might potentially reveal the performativity of gender in the context of television as an institution. However, while the musical is considered one of the most 'feminine' and artificial of dramatic genres, paradoxically the actual *musical* element, as opposed to narrative, character and mise en scène, like *all* music is nevertheless often perceived in terms of emotional and mythic realism. I would argue that, with its dependence on music, *Ally McBeal* operates in a very similar paradoxical fashion and that its contradictions are recuperated because episodes always *end* with the walking/alone or very similar sequences, articulated visually and musically in the show's 'serious' register. These scenes could be said to signify sitcom closure – a return to the status quo after comic and parodic disruption. They also privilege interiority and a 'depth model' of subjectivity, so that Ally's and other characters' emotional concerns are universalised into representations of human (a)loneliness in the absence of romantic (heterosexual) love and marriage.

Subjectivity and identity

The model of subjectivity constructed within *Ally McBeal* becomes evident in the way characters' behaviour, both 'cartoon' and 'serious', is so frequently explained through a popular Freudian discourse, whereby childhood experiences and traumas are shown as determining their identities. Again, the show parodies this Freudian discourse through its array of eccentric therapists, its obsession with toilet jokes and the acknowledgement of Ally's neurosis. However, it also privileges this discourse in moments of revelation in the show's serious register, in ways that resolve any apparent contradictions or inconsistencies in the characters' behaviour and encourages the viewer to perceive the human 'truths' behind the cartoon facades. For example, Ally is represented as incapable of forming an adult relationship because she seeks to recreate the innocence of her childhood romance with Billy (pilot episode, 'The Playing Field', 'The Real World'). In season 3 this is also linked to her overtly Oedipal relationship with her father and the classically Freudian trauma she experienced at 3 years old, of seeing her mother having sex with another man ('Troubled Water'). Similarly, Renee's sexual aggression is the result of the unwanted attention she attracted when she developed breasts early, John Cage's eccentricities are linked to his experience of being a bullied outsider as a child, Elaine's exhibitionism is related to childhood economic deprivation, Richard's fear of commitment is produced by his parents' bitter relationship, and so on. Despite all the postmodern formal devices that remark the fictional nature of these characters, the viewer is therefore invited to identify with them as fixed, stable and psychologically motivated subjects, available to be explained in terms of linear cause and effect.

This also means that their identities are established through reference to a paradigm within which white, western, middle-class, heterosexual norms of 'femininity' and 'masculinity' may be thought as social behaviours, but are nonetheless affirmed as stable and universal. The series may comment on these 'norms' and even at times

parody them but ultimately this parody only reinstates the difference *between* men and women, represented as undifferentiated
groups. Further, while male central characters sometimes exhibit or
take on 'feminine' attributes, and 'guest characters' include a male
to female transgender character, Barry Humphries in his drag
persona Edna Everage and various famous 'out' lesbians, the main
female characters remain firmly within the genre of femininity. If
they do transgress feminine norms, like the 'cold', unemotional and
ambitious Nelle, they are portrayed as unsympathetic.

In a popular mode, Freudian discourse can amount to a denial of
responsibility for one's behaviour as an adult. Interestingly, in *Ally
McBeal* childhood is simultaneously figured as a site of defining and
determining trauma *and* as a site of innocence, freedom and imagination. In 'Over the Rainbow', Richard states a wish to create this
'childhood world' at the firm, and this is also the diegetic world of
the show, a fantasy world in which unicorns can exist, dreams can
come true and someone as child*ish* as Ally McBeal can be a successful lawyer. In short, it is a world that at is at once feminised and
child*like* (see 'Making Spirits Bright', 'The Playing Field', 'The
Inmates', 'The Real World').

In these terms, this show might be said to be reiterating traditional,
patriarchal discourse that equates the feminine and the feminised
with the *infantile*. Significantly, although the self-reflexivity in the
series may remark the world of Cage and Fish as a fantasy, it is also
frequently compared to its 'other' – 'the real world' – in ways that
suggest a conservative dominant discourse. For example, this 'real
world' is frequently invoked in cases where Cage and Fish are called
on to represent otherwise exemplary employees who have been fired
on the basis of being unattractive or 'different', usually in terms of
physical appearance. These cases are nearly always lost to arguments
that, like it or not, in the 'real world' people *are* judged on their
appearance, as much as or even more than their abilities (see, for
example, 'Odd Ball Parade', 'Mr Bo'). While these episodes initially
appear to put this 'law' of 'normative' physical appearance in question, its inescapable, unalterable 'reality' is confirmed, just as it is
(self-reflexively) in the offices of Cage and Fish. Not only do all female
personnel fulfil certain conventions for attractiveness but 'fatness' in
women is a constant source of Richard's transgressive humour.
However, the diegesis assumes these conventions as a norm and this
is evinced in a 'running gag' in the third season, when under the

influence of a hallucination induced by a brain tumour, Billy 'comically' expresses sexual desire for a large, older woman. Despite a continuing theme in the show that asserts the power of the childlike imagination to *transform* reality, the show raises such questions only to further consolidate a strictly defined and normative status quo.

When complaints were made about the show's failure to acknowledge or explore issues of ethnicity around Ally's relationship to African American Dr Greg Butters (Jesse L. Martin) or her flatmate Renee, Kelly claimed that this was a deliberate 'colour blindness' that reflected the *fanciful, whimsical* world of the show, proposing a 'naive dream' devoid of racial tension in which 'All people are one under the sun' (quoted in Braxton, 1999). Heidi Safia Mirza describes such colour blindness as 'the polite language of race', a 'well meaning false optimism' that does not challenge racism but 'maintains the status quo, it validates inequalities' (Mirza, 2000: 296). In *Ally McBeal* this colour blindness does appear questionable when considered in relation to gender, sexuality and class. John Cage often 'strategically' mimics black masculinity in the form of Barry White, to give himself 'sexual confidence'. Even more striking is the way that Asian American Ling (Lucy Lui) and African American Renee and the white but 'blue-collar' secretary Elaine (Jane Krakowski) are all far more overtly sexualised than the white, upper-middle-class Ally, Nelle and Georgia. These representations then seem to exhibit the classic traits of 'fetishistic disavowal' as outlined in Chapter 3, in relation to gender and 'race' and also class, whereby a questionable fascination or desire is simultaneously indulged and denied.

Conclusion

It is always possible to find moments of contradiction and subversion in such a long-running series, especially one where jokes and comic function are more important than consistency. However, overall the fantasy world of *Ally McBeal* does seem to reiterate conservative dominant norms for perceiving and defining 'reality'. Yet so do many other television series, and I would suggest that the particular controversy surrounding *Ally McBeal* may relate to the way its shifting of perspectives, its self-reflexivity and its strategies of parody and self-parody could be seen to function to 'discredit in advance' certain voices such as 'those of grumpy feminists' (Morris,

1990: 25). The show appears to represent a fantasy cartoon world, where all reference to reality is suspended, so that its repetition of discourses of irrational and infantile femininity, of misogyny and homophobia, can be claimed as operating as self-conscious transgression and subversion. Yet at the same time, it continues to strongly encourage emotional identification with psychologically motivated characters and to make 'common sense' truth claims about reality that are gendered, sexed, raced and classed. While there may be an alternation between ironic distance and emotional identification, the latter is privileged in ways that close down meanings at the end of each episode, with a return to the status quo, in terms both of the show's 'situation' and of traditional models for subjectivity and identity.

I am not suggesting that any of this is a matter of conscious intention. Rather, *Ally McBeal* is part of a larger, deeply ambivalent media discourse around the female, the feminine, the feminist and the postfeminist. This ambivalence is complicated but not resolved by the employment of elements of a postmodern aesthetic, which gives the show an aura of formal progressiveness but which, rather than guaranteeing subversive repetition, represents a relativism that reaffirms the status quo by other means through an equation of *feminism* with *feminisation*. None of this is to say that *Ally McBeal* is not often clever, funny and even provocative – and indeed it fulfils one criterion for political drama, in so far as it has caused public debate. However, perhaps it is not so much the show itself but the debates around it and other postfeminist dramas such as *Sex and the City* that should be a matter of concern. It seems to me that many of the commentaries on these dramas (including, perhaps, my own) implicitly *accept* and *confirm* the trivialisation and depoliticisation of feminism that has been characteristic of media representation since the 1970s.

As the seriously flawed but nonetheless 'serious' British mini-series *Sex Traffic* (2004), focused around the international trade in forced prostitution, might suggest, outside the privileged world of a minority of affluent, white, western women there are more crucial issues at stake for feminism than skirt lengths, neurosis and romantic aspirations. Part of the problem with *Sex Traffic* is, in fact, the nature of the realism it employs and especially its drive to closure in the form of a (relatively) happy ending, which privileges a white, masculine, bourgeois perspective. Nevertheless, in terms of *what* it represents, it is a reminder that as Judith Butler's *Bodies that Matter* signals, the point of the deconstruction of the subject was to challenge definitions of the human that allowed some categories of persons to be thought of as less than properly human, or even as *non*human, and therefore without 'rights' even to their own bodies. In short, and at the risk of seeming humourless, *Sex Traffic* might serve as a reminder that the violence, abuses and inequalities that feminism set out to address have not been overcome for all or even most women in the world and cannot simply be 'laughed away'. This can be lost in too great an emphasis on strategies of subversive repetition based on irony, parody and pastiche.

Notes

1 For critiques of Mulvey, see for example Jackie Stacey in Gamman and Marshment, 1988.
2 Weldon attracted strong criticism for her negative comments on feminism in articles for *The Guardian* ('Pity Poor Men', December 1977) and *The Times* ('Rape Isn't the Worst Thing that Can Happen to a Woman', 1998).
3 Weldon was passed over for creating the adaptation of *She-Devil* in favour of writer Ted Whitehead. The novel was also made into a film in 1989, starring Roseanne Barr and Meryl Streep.

3

Divided duties: diasporic subjectivities and 'race relations' dramas (*Supply and Demand, The Bill, Second Generation*)

In a 1998 article for *Screen*, Charlotte Brunsdon discussed Lynda La Plante's *Prime Suspect* (1991) with reference to the way in which some 1990s British crime drama had become concerned with an 'equal opportunities discourse' (Brunsdon, 1998). Brunsdon mainly concentrated on issues of gender but touched on 'race', implicitly raising the question of whether, in these terms, British crime drama had become any more (or less) progressive, since earlier in the decade Jim Pines asked whether it could be defined as 'inherently racist' (Pines, 1995). Pines pursues this question in relation to form but also to genre, authorship and representation. In the first part of this chapter I want to contextualise Pines' concerns in relation to thinking within anti-racist and postcolonial theory, with particular reference to the rejection of realism in favour of a 'diaspora aesthetic'. Returning to Pines' argument and the crime genre, all these themes and issues are then opened up specifically in relation to the pilot episode of La Plante's series *Supply and Demand* (1997) and an episode of *The Bill* (1984–) broadcast in November 2000. The chapter then concludes with a brief consideration of the workings of a 'diaspora aesthetic' in some more recent 'authored' drama.

Defining terms: problematising the discourses of 'race' and 'ethnicity'

It could be taken as a sign of progress(iveness) that within an academic context, as Mary Maynard indicates:

it is virtually impossible to embark on any discussion of 'race' without first drawing attention to the problematic nature of the term, along with others associated with it [. . .]. It has long been recognised that races do not exist in any scientifically meaningful sense. (Maynard, 2001: 122)

She continues, 'None the less, in many societies people have often acted, and continue to act, as if "race" is a fixed objective category' (122).

Within the academy, as with gender, the concept of 'race' has been subject to a process of deconstruction for over thirty years. As such, it is understood to be the product of a social and historical discursive formation, usually traced back to enlightenment thought, allied to capitalism, colonialism and the emergence of the nation state, and supported by ideas drawn from the fields of biology and anthropology. Within this discourse, western culture was constructed as the product of particular type of 'naturally' (biologically) advanced or evolved rational white subject, and assumed to be the model for all human progress. This subject was defined through a binary relation of superiority to 'primitive', irrational others, conceived of as not just 'essentially' inferior but perhaps not even 'properly' human. In the process whiteness was naturalised as the 'norm' and as such did not signify *as* a racial identity – so that 'race' came to be seen as a determining quality of these 'others'.

In principle, then, to continue to employ the word 'race' and terms such as 'black' and 'white' is to risk reaffirming the truth claims of this discursive formation. Yet as Maynard remarks, deconstruction 'is not the same thing as destroying or transcending the categories themselves, which clearly continue to play a significant role in how the social world is organised on a global scale' (Maynard, 2001: 129). Or as Atvar Brah asserts more strongly, 'However many times the concept is exposed as vacuous, race continues to operate as an irreducible mark of social difference' (Brah, 1996: 95). In fact exactly because 'race' *is* a discursive fiction, *racism* can easily be reconstituted by other means, so that as Maynard notes, 'Common sense understandings of "race" have concentrated on such variables as skin colour, country of origin, religion, nationality and language' (Maynard, 2001: 122). As Lola Young affirms, then, 'Racism is not attributable to a single factor' but is rather 'in a continual state of flux and subject to the political, social and economic imperatives of a particular moment' (Young, 1996: 40). Since *racism* persists, paradoxically, anti-essentialist attempts to displace the signifier 'race' can, as Paul Gilroy has argued, function to distract from and even conceal 'the lingering power of specifically racialised forms of power and subordination' (Gilroy, 1993: 31). For this reason, many black theorists have been reluctant to embrace alternative terms such as 'ethnicity'. In its contemporary articulation, ethnicity is presumed to signify culture and an affiliation to a tradition or way of life, thereby potentially breaking down the categories of black and white into multiple, nonbiological positionalities. As with utopian postmodern feminism, this rather assumes that a 'third stage' of deconstruction of 'race' has been achieved across the social and political spheres.

However, suspicion of the term ethnicity arises because of its association with 'official', liberal discourses of multiculturalism at the level of government. As Sara Ahmed amongst others has argued, while such multiculturalism supposedly embraces and celebrates a plurality of cultural identities and communities within a nation, it can often work on a superficial level of surface and style that ultimately operates to 'exclude any differences that challenge the supposedly universal values on which the culture is predicated' (Ahmed, 2000: 106 and 110). She goes on to quote John Frow and Meaghan Morris, who state that the category of culture within which multiculturalism operates 'tends to reproduce imaginary identities at the level of the ethnic "community"' and thereby to screen out differentiations and contradictions within that community (quoted in Ahmed, 2000: 105). Further, in common usage in Britain and North America, the term 'ethnic' mostly functions as a prefix to the term 'minorities', in ways that allow for the ethnicity of the 'majority' (white) population to remain the unspoken norm. As a result, 'culture' can harden back into 'nature' to produce cultural or 'differentialist' racism, based not on biological hereditary but on the 'insurmountability of cultural differences' (Balibar quoted in Brah, 1996: 186). Terms such as ethnicity can then be deployed as replacements for, rather than actual displacements of, the concept of 'race'. As such, many theorists still use the term 'race', understood as referring to a discursive fiction, which nevertheless continues to have very real material effects.

'Black' as a political category

Use of the term 'black' dates back to the American Civil Rights movement of the 1950s and the 'Black Power' movements of the

1960s and 1970s, which also functioned as models for 'black consciousnesses' movements elsewhere. It has therefore always signalled a *political* identification based on 'the common experience of racism and marginalisation and the gulf this creates between white people and those they oppress, both on an institutional and a personal basis' (Maynard, 2001: 123). In the 1980s, in both Britain and North America, this often allowed it to operate as a signifier for resistance 'amongst groups and communities with, in fact, very different histories, traditions and ethnic identities' (Hall, 1992: 254). However, the North American black consciousness movement *also* produced a desire to reclaim a positive, independent black identity, other to that imposed and determined by white culture and society. As signalled by Alex Haley's celebrated 1970s television series *Roots*, this was effected by looking to Africa as the epicentre of black culture and the celebration of a 'pan-African identity' as a distinctive cultural heritage, counter to centuries of Eurocentricism (217). For some, this was again primarily a matter of a political identification but for others, such as Patricia Hill Collins, it was based on an understanding that 'in spite of varying histories, black societies reflect elements of a core African value system that existed prior to, and independently of, racial oppression' (Hill Collins, 2001: 188). As noted in Chapter 1, this identity was affirmed and celebrated through a range of aesthetic strategies associated with this cultural tradition and defined as both separate from and in opposition to a Eurocentric one. This, then, might be seen to constitute a 'first stage' of deconstruction, which performs a reversal that may reclaim the traditionally 'inferior' position in positive terms but remains in the system, potentially affirming the 'reality' of 'race' by other means.

While many black British subjects also connected to this 'pan-African identity' and the cultural forms associated with it, by the late 1980s, as Lola Young indicates, some black British theorists started to question the dominance of North American modes of 'consciousnesses', asking:

> to what extent is the North American experience of racial differentiation applicable elsewhere, and in particular to Britain? [. . .] Although there are many similarities, it is important to remember that British experiences were dissimilar in important respects, and colonialism and imperial conquest have operated quite differently in North America. (Young, 1996: 10)

Within this British context, theorist Stuart Hall might insist that the term 'black' indicated a 'politically and socially constructed category' with 'no guarantee in Nature', and as such, embraces a plurality of ethnicities (Hall, 1992: 252). However, as Maynard points out, in common usage this term is often exclusively associated with those of 'sub-Saharan descent' (Maynard, 2001: 123). As such, even when the focus was *specifically* on what it meant to be black in Britain, it could remain within a discourse of 'race' and function as a homogenising and essentialising term that conceals differences of ethnicity, class and gender. As Bakare-Yusef notes, in the public sphere and partly due to patterns of immigration in mid- to late twentieth-century Britain:

> It was the under class and working class Jamaican cultural practices which were called upon to speak for and represent the cultural taste of all Britain's blacks [. . .] This was the case in both black and white cultural practices, 'yoof' media discourse, and also in cultural studies. (Bakare-Yusef, 1997: 82)

This was evident in the portrayal of black British subjects in mainstream television drama, where black was often represented as synonymous with the aesthetics, if not the politics, of Rastafarianism. Moreover, as black feminists pointed out, in all these spheres it was black *masculinity* that tended to signify black identity (see Young, 1996: 149 and Mirza, 1997: 272). At the same time, according to Young, *racism* was often represented as an attribute of working-class white men, and sometimes of women (regardless of class), but seldom of white, middle-class men (Young, 1996: 109).

Both these tendencies point to the ways in which the discourse of 'race' is bound up with those of gender, sexuality and social class. In the political movements of the 1970s to the 1980s, these were often (and still are) represented as separate issues, or one is given priority over the other in a 'hierarchy of oppressions', resulting in a 'the lack of attention to the points at which these politically constructed categories intersect' (Young, 1996: 176). However, Young insists that, in the words of Atvar Brah, while racism may always be a 'gendered and classed phenomenon', 'race' is neither 'reducible to social class or gender nor wholly autonomous [. . .] all of these are best construed as historically contingent and context-specific relationships' (Brah, 1996: 156 and 110). Under the influence of poststructuralism and postcolonial theory, this thinking challenged the assumptions of both white-dominated feminism and the supposedly gender-neutral discourses of black politics, and was concerned to dislodge the essentialism implicit in both. Brah then posited a black British feminism, created through a coalition between the 'project of African-Asian unity, feminism and gay and lesbian politics', which 'asserts the specificity of black women's experiences' but at the same time understands this category as 'highly differentiated in terms of class, ethnicity and religion'. It also includes those 'who had migrated from Africa, the Asian subcontinent and the Caribbean, as well as those born in Britain' (Brah, 1996: 113). Brah concludes by articulating this position in terms of 'new formations of *diaspora* subjectivities and identities' (113, my italics).

Diaspora and the diaspora aesthetic

Referring to the condition of 'any people globally dispersed or scattered', as Imruh Bakare puts it, the concept of 'diaspora' has 'gained particular significance to the ethnic or national identities which have been globalised in the process of movement and migration, ostensibly linked to the expansion of capitalism' (Bakare, 2000: 232). Despite important contributions to thinking through diaspora by feminist scholars internationally, in Britain most discussions of this concept tend to refer back to ideas derived from Homi K. Bhabha via Stuart Hall and Paul Gilroy.

Some of Bhabha's work has been compared to Judith Butler's. Like Butler, Bhabha operates on a Foucaultian understanding that regulatory discursive regimes create and enable possibilities for subversion and resistance, and on the recognition that history and identity are constantly in a process of being negotiated through the play of repetition and difference. Like Butler's, Bhabha's work has been accused of being overly theoretical and elitist. Butler's conceptualisation of the performativity of gender also has much in common with Bhabha's of 'colonial mimicry' (see Bhabha, 1994: 111–21). In this argument, Bhabha develops a notion of 'subversive repetition', whereby the subaltern colonised subject's mimicry of the coloniser's identity can operate to foreground the constructed nature of the 'original' and its fundamental dependence on its 'poor copy' for its meaning. This suggests a relationship of mutual interdependence and exchange in the production of *both* identities, so that the Eurocentric must be understood as being defined through and as part of, rather than simply opposed to and separate from, the Afrocentric – and vice versa.

This deconstructive logic also informs Bhabha's formulation of the cultural hybridity of diasporic identities, which he describes as being formed on the boundaries 'in between', or in excess to, 'the sum of the parts of difference', including culture, locations, history and temporality but also class and gender (Bhabha, 1994: 2). For Bhabha, this hybridity refuses 'the binary representation of social antagonism' and can function to undermine the imaginary purity or homogeneity of national and/or cultural identities (Bhabha, 1998: 59). Bhabha is then concerned with the potential of this hybridity to challenge and rethink Eurocentric metanarratives of the past, and to undermine and destabilise dominant identity categories in the present and in the *future*, to produce 'something new and unrecognisable, a new area of meaning and representation' (Bhabha, 1990: 211). In short, he understands this hybridity as a potential means of (eventually) producing a third stage of the deconstruction.

Both Hall and Gilroy draw on Bhabha's ideas but are more concerned with exploring *specific* articulations of hybridity in relation to African and Caribbean diasporic identities in the present, as expressed through an identifiable, albeit shifting, aesthetic and understood as a potential site of political agency, out of which to destabilise the dominant identity. Hall points to the way a sense of identity based on a narrative of Africa as a lost site of imaginary unification has been produced *retrospectively* by the common experience of discontinuity and dislocation, created by the uprootings of slavery and transportation (Hall, 2000: 23). This produces a proliferation of different identities formed in between 'history, memory, fantasy narrative and myth', in between the past, present and future and in between the 'black triangle', or in Gilroy's terms, 'the Black Atlantic' that links Africa, Europe, North America and the Caribbean (Hall, 2000: 24 and Gilroy, 1993). As Hall indicates, then:

> The diaspora experience [. . .] is defined not by purity or essence but by the recognition of a necessary heterogeneity and diversity; by a concept of 'identity' which lives through, not despite difference; by hybridity. Diaspora identities are those which are constantly

producing and reproducing themselves anew, through transformation and difference. (Hall, 2000: 31)

The same principles hold for diaspora aesthetics, which Hall describes in terms of 'recombination, hybridisations, blends' or 'cut and mix' (31).

Despite Hall's insistence on difference, heterogeneity and diversity, as both Bakare and Young indicate, within black British film making as elsewhere, in the 1990s diaspora aesthetics came to be associated with a particular set of formal strategies. These were constructed as inherently progressive, in so far as they were defined in opposition to and understood as undermining the dominant form of realism (see Bakare, 2000: 273 and Young, 1996: 188). As noted in Chapter 1, this critique of realism intersected with similar debates within feminist and queer film criticism and represents an attempt to move beyond issues of positive or negative representations of black British subjects, to focus on how the controlling white colonial gaze has determined and objectified the subaltern colonised subject. However, as Young and Bakare indicate, the influence of these ideas led to a rejection, not only of the realist aesthetics of the white mainstream, but also of *black* realist film production, and the production of a 'canon' of highly praised and influential 'non realist experimental texts' (Young, 1996: 188). Young concedes that 'realist practices in film and television have been a major component in determining how the "problem" of blackness has been defined and perceived' (136). However, she *also* points out that while 'there may be constraints in certain realist forms of representation, it is by no means the case that all realisms are reactionary or that the rejection of such forms results in politically progressive, complex films' (159).

Bakare also notes that discussions of diasporic aesthetics of this period often focused on the work of African and Caribbean British film makers. This was often at the expense of acknowledging the specificity of *British Asian* productions, with their very different histories in relation to both cinema and Britishness, and also the *different* ways various modes of hybridity are enunciated in relation to gender, class and sexuality in these works (Bakare, 2000: 231). In short, any attempt to define or describe diaspora aesthetics and/or and cultural hyrbidity, *especially* if and when this is achieved in opposition to a 'monolithic' notion of realism, can constitute a reversal and a substitution that continue to privilege some differences over others.

To borrow from Judith Roof writing on queer, ideas of diasporic cultural hybridity can be seen as one of many 'different manifestations of the same complex cultural impetus' that are dubbed postmodern (Roof, 1997: 180). As such, it is significant that to Hall's list of characteristics of diaspora aesthetics (recombination, hybridisations, blends, cut and mix), Nicholas Mirzoeff adds that *all* diaspora aesthetics are 'necessarily intertextual' (Mirzoeff, 2000: 7). Moreover, Bhabha's concept of 'colonial mimicry' embraces strategies of irony, parody and pastiche. Described in terms of the general and the abstract, then, a diaspora aesthetic (singular) can begin to sound very like a (generalised and singular) postmodern one, which, of course, is also frequently defined in opposition to realism as singular and monolithic.

As a result, as Alan Sinfield argues, cultural hybridity sometimes appears as part of a relativist discourse that posits *any* sort of 'instability' of categories as *inherently* progressive, ignoring the fact for instance that according to Marx capitalism thrives on instability and depends on the production of the 'new' (Sinfield, 2000: 105). Hence, as I explore in Chapter 3, notions of cultural hybridity are sometimes appropriated to conceptualise a 'new' mode of subjectivity, eminently suited to the demands of western-dominated global capitalism. This is possible, partly because as Bakare asserts, ultimately *all* cultures, traditional, modern or postmodern, can be understood as 'hybrids forged through syncretism, regardless of the ways in which their identities may be imagined at a particular historical moment' (Bakare, 2000: 234). It is then a small step to relativism, whereby all cultures and identities are understood as hybrid *in much the same way*. As such, it is important to remember that as Naz Rassool asserts, if black British cultural hybridity can be perceived as a challenge to 'a society constructed around an ethnically homogenous norm', equally it can also refer

> to the reality that in an ongoing quest for rootedness within a society so fundamentally hostile to their presence that black people have to continually learn to adapt, adjust and change their cultures, their customs, behaviours and cultural consciousness, in order to belong socially, as well as to identify culturally and politically within the dominant culture. (Rassool, 1997: 189)

In short, as Shohat and Stam point out, it is crucial 'to discriminate between diverse modalities of hybridity: colonial imposition, obligatory assimilation, political co-optation, cultural mimicry, and so forth' (Shohat and Stam, 1994: 43).

In fact, neither Bhabha nor Hall suggests that cultural hybridity and/or diaspora aesthetics are 'essentially' subversive, not least since they are defined as repeating *as well as* differing from the identities and practices of the normative mainstream. In these terms Sinfield points to Kobena Mercer's example of the workings of a diaspora aesthetic in relation to hairstyles. Mercer demonstrates how the signifiers of cultural hybridity can variously indicate resistant subculture production *or* mainstream appropriation and commodification, and sometimes both at once. As such, Sinfield asserts that hybridity 'must be addressed not in the abstract, but as a social practice', one that works on a dialectic between imposition and dissidence, subversion and recuperation, difference and repetition (Sinfield, 2000: 106).

This 'dialectic' is also exemplified by the popularity of the aesthetics of Indian 'Bollywood' films within British film, theatre and television in the early 2000s. This may reflect a 'transformation' and subversion of mainstream British culture, produced by the impact on that culture of second- and third-generation Asian British subjects. Yet it may also reflect a process of commodification whereby, as bell hooks put it, 'ethnicity becomes spice, seasoning that can liven up the dull dish that is mainstream white culture' (hooks, 1992: 21). This is not least because these aesthetics frequently appear in the register of ironic, postmodern camp.

Working through these issues, Lola Young concludes, 'No textual practice is inherently reactionary or progressive. It is much more complex than that, bell hooks puts it thus "The issue really is one of standpoint. From what political perspective do we dream, look, create and take action"' (Young, 1996: 191). This suggests a 'contingent essentialism' in terms of a return to notions of authorship, or at least a Foucaultian 'author function', as one of the means by which political meanings are produced. Certainly in terms of television drama, the works that might most clearly be identified as using a 'diaspora aesthetic' are those that come under the category of 'authored' drama. This is perhaps because 'authored drama' has always been the primary space on television for formal and political experimentation. I will offer a brief consideration of some authored

works that display evidence of diaspora aesthetics at the end of the
chapter. First, however, I want to consider the representation of
'race' and ethnicity in some generic drama.

Direct and inferential racism, realism and the postmodern in British crime drama and sitcom

In terms of representation, Ellis Cashmore picks out two consistent
stereotypes for black characters on television: either 'as hopeless
figures of fun with limited intellects; or as victims crawling despair-
ingly towards drug addiction, crime or prison, usually all three'
(Cashmore, 1994: 101). Stereotypes for Asian characters vary somewhat but nonetheless it is significant that in the mid to late twentieth century, when represented at all, most 'minority' ethnic groups
were more likely to appear within sitcoms or crime fiction than
other sorts of television drama (Hall, 1981: 32). It is not surprising,
then, that in the early 1990s Jim Pines posed the question as to
whether or not 'the generic codes and conventions which circum-
scribe black related themes and images in crime fiction' could be
considered to be 'inherently racist' (Pines, 1995: 68).

Pines did discover some signs of progress in the representation of
marginalised ethnic groups within North American series such as
Hill Street Blues (1981–87) and *NYPD Blue* (1993–2005) and in the
British series *The Bill* (1984–). As Pines acknowledges, the tendency
to more ethnically integrated casting in such shows may have been
related to the emergence of a significant black middle class, which
provided a new marketing opportunity for television producers. The
notable increase in the representation of Asian British subjects on
television may be the result of a similar development.

However, Robin Nelson also uses *Hill Street Blues* and *NYPD
Blue* as early examples of the 'flexi-narrative structure'. On this
basis, at the time, they were deemed formally progressive, and Pines
also sees them as extending the boundaries of (racial) characterisation beyond the binary oppositions of 'positive and negative
imagery' (Pines, 1995: 74 and 76). Yet Pines tends to agree with
Nelson's view of flexiad drama as commercially exploiting difference (Nelson, 1997: 97). For instance, he is critical of *NYPD Blue*
for the way in which racial tension is sublimated through 'male
bonding' and argues that, 'The celebrated open narrative structure
that characterises *Hill Street Blues* enables the drama cleverly to

elide moral issues and to play down racial conflict (which is always present just beneath the surface) and other important social issues' (Pines, 1995: 74). He also argues that within the 'postmodern style' of series such as *Miami Vice* (1984–89) or the earlier British series *Gangsters* (1975–78) 'the "otherness" of the black subject and its socially marginalised location, have been thoroughly exoticised and pushed to the extremes both visually and narratively' in ways that reinforce existing racist imagery, 'only now in a seductive and stylish fashion' (75–6).

Nevertheless, Pines concludes that the crime genre is not *necessarily* 'inherently racist' but becomes so because most white writers 'seem unable (or unwilling) to approach black subjects imaginatively', and 'have rarely attempted to incorporate black imagery *within* the conventions of the genre' (76). As a result, he suggests that crime drama tends to draw on the 'reality effects', or as he puts it more strongly, 'the effluence of tabloid realism', constructed on the 'basis of popular racist imagery connected with the reporting of "black crime"' (69). Instead, Pines calls for crime drama that engages 'experimentally with the possibilities of the genre conventions', rather than simply grafting black characters onto existing forms (74). His main concern is that this grafting on produces 'race relations dramas', with 'race' occupying a 'privileged space in the narrative' (68–9).

Stuart Hall drew similar conclusions in 1981, discussing sitcoms such as *Til Death Us Do Part* (1965–75), *Mind Your Language* (1977–86), *Love Thy Neighbour* (1972–76) and *It Ain't Half Hot Mum* (1971–81). Hall noted that these programmes were defended on 'good anti-racist grounds' on the basis that 'the appearance of black characters alongside white ones would help normalise and naturalise their presence in British society' (Hall, 1981: 42). He attributes this defence to 'the liberal consensus', which he describes as 'the linchpin of what I call inferential racism', which 'keeps active and organised racism in place' (48). For Hall, the 'inferential' nature of racism within television was evident in the way these sitcoms did not just *include* black characters but were *about* 'race', and so repeated 'the same old categories of racially differentiated characters and qualities [. . .] these relations of superior and inferior, provide the pivots on which jokes turn, the tension points which move and motivate the situations in situation comedies'. At the same time, the 'comic register' in which they are articulated 'protects and defends viewers from acknowledging their incipient racism. It creates disavowal' (43).

Both Hall and Pines, then, critique the way that the tendency to mainly represent black and Asian characters within 'race relations' narratives on television can make racism seem an issue *of* and *for* these groups, rather than the white population. In both instances, while form may be at issue, a range of other factors, generic, discursive, authorial and institutional, are also in play.

Lynda La Plante's 'dual address'

As part of his discussion of the use of 'tabloid realism' in British crime drama, Pines cites Lynda La Plante's first series *Widows* (1983). Describing the series as 'in most other respects [. . .] a relatively sophisticated crime series, featuring (working class) women in the principal roles, the presence of the black member in the group of women was marked pejoratively, by the use of such parochial devices as racial badgering' (Pines, 1995: 72). Pines suggests that this was meant to signal 'white working class racial prejudice', but argues that it has 'no *ethical* value within the drama, its only dramatic purpose was to provide "light relief", in a racist manner which traces back to the British sitcom tradition' (73).

La Plante's crime drama presents an interesting and complex case, in so far as it might be considered as *both* generic and authored. Further, from *Widows* onwards, La Plante has been recognised as achieving for gender something very similar to what Pines calls for in terms of ethnicity. In the first instance, as with the later La Plante series such as *Prime Suspect* (1991–2003) and *The Governor* (1995–96), the characterisation of the female protagonists in *Widows* was more varied than in most television drama of the time, and went beyond the binary oppositions of positive and negative images of women. In the second, as both Gillian Skirrow (1985) and Charlotte Brunsdon (1987) indicate, *Widows* simultaneously 'troubled' *both* genre and gender conventions. Skirrow argued that it subversively repeated generic conventions, 'questioning them at the same time; a constant process of negotiation with the expectations of both the audience and the institution of television' (Skirrow, 1985: 174). While for Brundson any subversion of gender and 'race' in *Widows* was eventually recuperated by the demands of realism, in a later article, she implies a more successful negotiation of genre in relation to gender in *Prime Suspect 1*. In this instance, she argues that this drama offers a 'dual address' to both a 'liberal feminist audience' and a more 'masculinist (smoking and drinking) tabloid constituency', 'a balancing act' which she says 'leads to real ambivalences' (Brunsdon, 1998: 232). Potentially there is a class dynamic implicit in both Brunsdon's and Pines' use of the term 'tabloid'. This could be taken as part of a discourse, noted by Young above, whereby sexism and racism are portrayed primarily as attributes of white, *working-class* men and women. It is important to note, then, that I take this term to refer to the 'reality effects' produced by the more reactionary sectors of the 'tabloid' media, rather than to any of the social groups that might constitute their audience.

Nevertheless, it does seem to me that some sort of contradictory dual address or interpellation is a feature in the structuring of *all* La Plante signature drama. This is most obvious in the *Trial and Retribution* series (1997–), where split-screen techniques are used to show either different versions of events, separate, simultaneously occurring incidents, or varying perspectives on the same scene. However, even less formally experimental series such as *Prime Suspect* and *The Governor* show many of the characteristics of the type of critical realism discussed by Nelson, which 'shakes, if not actually breaks, the realist frame' (Nelson, 1997: 120). They also tend to be structured around parallels, contradictions and reversals, employing dialectical narrative structures and modes of characterisation to expose contradictions between the personal, the professional and the political, in ways that are never entirely resolved by the closure of the narrative. All of this potentially complicates the process of identification, so that the main protagonists are seldom entirely sympathetic in terms of either 'liberal feminist' or 'tabloid' positions. The ambivalences this produces may provoke a questioning of the assumptions and prejudices implicit in *both* these positions.

However, as Mike Wayne has noted, 'flawed' and 'contradictory' heroes are common within the context of crime drama and these ambivalences are always open to recuperation by a realist focus on individuals, rather than social forces (Wayne, 1998: 31). Nonetheless, I would argue that this duality of address opens up a relatively complex understanding of power relations, in terms of gender and class and of the police as an institution. As such, figures such as Dolly in *Widows*, Jane Tennison in *Prime Suspect* and the working-class Mike Walker in the *Trial and Retribution* series are portrayed as oppressed by but also *reproducing* the unequal power relations that circulate within both their professional and personal spheres.

From *Widows* onwards, La Plante signature dramas have also been notable for engaging with issues of ethnicity and sexuality, in ways that often negotiate with audience expectations of the genre and of television as an institution. At the very least, these dramas provide complex roles for black performers on British television, at times when these are sparse, and later works such as *Trial and Retribution* (1997–), *Mind Games* (2000) and *Prime Suspect* 6 and 7 (2002–3) have featured integrated casting, where 'race' is not at issue. However, Bella in *Widows* aside, black characters have seldom been main protagonists, *except* in race-relations dramas such as *Prime Suspect 2* (1993), which brings me to *Supply and Demand* (1997).

Supply and Demand as a race-relations drama

The two-hour pilot episode for the series *Supply and Demand* was produced and written by La Plante with Steve Griffiths and directed by Peter MacDonald. The plot focuses on a joint undercover investigation by the Metropolitan Police and the North West Division, into a Manchester-based drug dealer, Lance Anthony Izzard (Freddie Starr) and Somers (Anthony Higgens), his upper-class, cocaine-addicted backer. However, the narrative pivots mostly around the relationship between two black police officers. DS Jake Brown (Eamon Walker) is an experienced, 'deep undercover' drugs specialist, with martial arts and boxing skills, who infiltrates Izzard's operation as a bodyguard and driver. DI Carl Harrington (Ade Sapara) is a public-school-educated Cambridge graduate, on a fast-track career trajectory within the Metropolitan Police Force, who has no previous experience of undercover work or drug-related crime. In the course of the operation Jake is coerced by Harrington into tutoring him to imitate a Rastafarian 'Willy-boy', who is killed in an accident when driving a drugs shipment for Izzard but whom Izzard has never met. To convince Izzard of his authenticity, Harrington takes drugs with increasing willingness and, when the real Willy-boy's death is discovered, is force-fed crack cocaine at the Somers' house. Ordered by Izzard to kill Harrington, Jake takes him to a safe house to help conceal his burgeoning addiction, and (apparently) to save Harrington's career, Jake also seduces his female superior officer, DI Chomsky. The penultimate sequence is concerned with a darkly comic triple cross, which leaves the police with a large quantity of sugar, Somers in custody and Izzard dead. The final scenes show the creation of a special undercover drugs force, which will be the focus of the ensuing series.

Professionalism, class and cultural identity

Despite the unlikeliness of the plot, to some extent *Supply and Demand* appears to answer Pines' call for crime fiction with 'complexly drawn, black central characters' and even 'flawed black cop heroes', although Jake is more satisfactory in this respect than Harrington (Pines, 1995: 74). This is mainly due to the subtlety of Eamon Walker's performance, which encourages emotional identification, but is also because, initially at least, Harrington is defined primarily in contrast with Jake. Yet through Harrington *Supply and Demand* also appears to subvert genre conventions and audience expectations in terms of race-relations crime drama. In an introductory sequence, the camera passes across ranks of white male and female police officers, within which a single black face is only just visible, while over a loud musical soundtrack an upper-class voice is giving a speech. Becoming increasingly audible, the voice states 'there must be no discrimination in the Metropolitan Police Force, no sexual or racial discrimination, what is important is professionalism, that is what makes us the finest police force in the world'. The end of this speech coincides with a reverse shot of Harrington. The initial withholding of the identity of the speaker, the cut from a wide shot to a big close-up and the speed of the edit, appear to be designed to create surprise and play on assumptions that the voice will belong to a white senior officer.

This is followed by a briefing scene in which the spatial dynamics, camera work and performances suggest a distance between Harrington and his white senior officers, despite the fact that they comment favourably on his record of achievements and his 'excellent leadership skills'. All of this suggests a scenario in which Harrington is positioned as an 'outsider' in the police force, similar to the model of Jane Tennison in *Prime Suspect* but with 'race' rather than gender as the point of tension. When Harrington expresses a desire to work on drug-related crime, because he states 'black culture seems inextricably linked to this issue', it seems probable that the narrative will unfold in the manner Jim Pines suggests is common to many race-relations crime dramas. Harrington will be the exceptional noble black cop hero, 'whose mission is to clean up the criminalised black neighbourhoods' (Pines, 1995: 74). Yet Harrington's status as hero is undercut by his dialogue, which is full of military jargon and pompous expressions. Together with Sapara's performance, these establish Harrington as naive and self-important. This is further emphasised when he explains his desire to work on drugs in terms of needing 'street credibility'. At this point the action cuts from a close-up of Harrington to a close-up of Jake, who in a parallel but more informal briefing scene is established as an expert on drug-related crime, and as having abundant street credibility. Subsequently, the first half of the drama continues to set up an opposition between Jake's flexibility, professionalism and competence, and Harrington's arrogance and inexperience. While Harrington is distanced from both the police and the black community, Jake is portrayed as at home in any situation and as having the ability to switch seamlessly between a range of different bodily styles and modes of speech. These range from 'Estuary' English to pure Jamaican patois via stages in between. Harrington's colleagues also include Frankie Li (Benedict Wong), DC Irwin (played by Ramon Tikaram, who has played both Asian and South American roles), blond and blue-eyed Teller (Jonathan Phillips) and DI Chomsky (Juliet Aubrey), whose name suggests a history of immigration. In this ethnically diverse context the implication is that, if looks and derogatory remarks are exchanged behind Harrington's back, this is *not* a matter of racism. Instead, it is because Harrington uses his *class* position to pull both rank and strings and takes personal credit for the team's successes, demonstrating inappropriate, childish displays of triumph, all of which rather contradicts the earlier assertion of his leadership skills. Nevertheless, the implication is that what is at stake in this narrative is *not* racial discrimination in the police but, as stated in Harrington's first speech, the issue of professionalism and of the preferral of Harrington in the force, by dint of his class identity and education at the expense of the hard-won, hands-on experience of working-class figures like Jake.

Interestingly, while the undercover team are portrayed as ethnically diverse, the main criminals are not only white but their whiteness is exaggerated through costume, make-up and lighting.

Somers is fair and pale, and both Izzard and Julia Somers (Fiona Ramsey) have aggressively bleached blonde hair, with her pallor being accentuated by blood-red lipstick and brightly coloured power suits. Their international supplier is tall with long blonde hair and blue eyes and is first introduced backlit in darkness, descending from a light aircraft and wearing a long black coat and flying boots.

Form and narrative structure

Within *Supply and Demand*, then, there is evidence of a liberal, multicultural discourse in the diversity of the police team. In the portrayal of differences between Jake and Harrington there is also some acknowledgement of the heterogeneity of diasporic British subjects, and in that of the 'villians' even perhaps a remarking of whiteness *as* ethnicity. In Jake's characterisation there is also a suggestion of cultural hybridity. The dialectical structuring of scenes and the play of oppositions between Jake and Harrington and between Jake and Chomsky recall structures characteristic of Nelson's critical realism, and the piece contains some 'still' black and white photo shots that might be seen as 'shaking' the realist frame.

However, *Supply and Demand* also has elements of '(post)-modern', flexiad drama, and the realism it draws on is borrowed from North American crime drama and Hollywood comedy action films, like the *Lethal Weapon* series (1989–98) starring Danny Glover and Mel Gibson. As such, *Supply and Demand* favours the visual and the spectacular, and naturalism and referential realism are subsidiary to opportunities for action sequences involving guns and chases in cars, jeeps, light aircraft and a helicopter. A strong musical score with a repeating whistle motif is employed to underline and comment on character and action to comic or ironic effect, in a manner that verges on the self-reflexive. Similarly, the exaggeration of the whiteness of the main villains verges on excess, parody and pastiche, something that is reinforced by the casting of popular comedian Freddie Starr as Izzard. In line with his celebrity persona, Starr portrays this character as aggressive and hysterical but nevertheless comically bungling and hence a 'lovable' working-class rogue, just as Somers is the epitome of snivelling and effete upper-class decadence, his wife a Lady Macbeth figure and the international supplier is represented through codes associated with film 'Nazis'.

However, if these postmodern tendencies could be understood as drawing attention to the constructedness of this drama, as Pines argues, they do not necessarily preclude the repetition of existing racist imagery 'only now in a stylish and seductive manner' (Pines, 1995: 76). The racial badgering that Pines critiques in *Widows* has not entirely disappeared (72–3). At one point Izzard calls Jake 'black boy', provoking Jake to announce firmly, 'The name is Jake, Mr Izzard, *Sir*'. This scene may add something to Jake's characterisation but again serves no clear *ethical* purpose in the drama, other than to demonstrate white, working-class racism. These attitudes are absent in the upper-class Somers and in the representation of higher-ranking white police officers.

More importantly, the tendency towards ironic self-reflexivity in this drama does not counteract the fact that although the humour is supposedly at Harrington's expense due to his *class* background, the scene in which Jake teaches an inept Harrington to impersonate Willy-boy comes uncomfortably near 'eliciting an exaggerated racial effect as comic relief' (Pines, 1995: 72). While this scene *could* be interpreted as a subversive repetition through Bhabha's notion of colonial mimicry, its effect has to be read as part of a whole in which *Supply and Demand* is still actually very much a race-relations drama, on the model described by Pines.

In fact, the ethnic inclusivity of the undercover team in contrast to the ranks of white, uniformed officers shown in the introductory sequence *confirms* Harrington's assertion in the briefing scene that black (and other ethnic minority) culture is 'inextricably linked' to drugs. This is not balanced out by the drama's 'social message', articulated towards the end by Jake, that the 'real' problem is not with users (with the exception of Somers, all represented as black) but with dealers, suppliers and financiers (represented as exclusively white). It is not just that the victimisation of the black community is rendered pathetic by the representation of the villains in cartoonish and melodramatic terms. It is also that in the second half of the drama Harrington discovers an 'authentic' black identity, based on the experience of drug culture.

I would argue, then, that *Supply and Demand* can be discussed in terms of both generic realism and an ironic (post)modern or 'flexiad' register, which correspond to a dual address to liberal (feminist) and tabloid constituencies. In this instance, however, the 'ambivalences' created can be seen to function as part of a strategy of disavowal, signalled by the initial proposition that this drama is 'about' professionalism, which serves to distract from the fact that in *both* instances the address is also, implicitly, white.

Disavowal and the doubleness of the white gaze

Discussing disavowal in relation to racial fetishism, Homi Bhabha describes this as a process whereby a fascination or desire is both indulged and denied:

> A non repressive form of knowledge that allows for the possibility of simultaneously embracing two contradictory beliefs, one official and one secret, one archaic and one progressive, one that articulates the myth of origins, the other that articulates difference and division. (Bhabha, 1986: 168)

In fact, not only are the differences between Jake and Harrington constantly being foreclosed from the very start of the drama, but the *manner* of portraying their differences might illustrate assertions by Franz Fanon, Hall and Bhabha, amongst others, as to the way, historically, the ambivalence or 'doubleness' of the white gaze has constructed the black man as at once childish and hypersexual. It may be possible to perceive Jake as a resistant 'reverse stereotype', with his street credibility, marshal arts, boxing skills and seduction of Chomsky. However, when he is placed together with the naive, excitable Harrington they appear as the two sides of this older coin. A shared, racially marked identity is also suggested in the opening credit sequence, which intercuts almost identical shots of both Jake and Harrington with and without dreadlocks. Achieved by hair extensions as part of his impersonation of Willy-boy, this hairstyle is later remarked as a signifier of Harrington's newly discovered 'black identity', yet within the diegesis Jake appears with dreads only briefly in his very first scene. In some scenes together, they are also shown in two shot, rather than through reaction shots, so that the camera looks *at* them as a pair, as opposed to *with* them as individuals. However, a tendency towards voyeurism and objectification is most noticeable in the way in which their bodies are overtly displayed. Harrington is shown either topless or completely, if discreetly, naked on four different occasions. Jake appears in a boxing strip, sparring with another black character and watched by an excited Izzard, whose tongue protrudes suggestively between his teeth. After the seduction scene with Chomsky he is shown in a tight cut-away vest, while she is fully dressed.

Both visually and in narrative terms, these scenes could be said to repeat the way that in a white-dominated culture, 'the exotic character of the black body takes on an absolutely powerful charge and becomes a particular and ambivalent subject of desire' (Hall, 1998: 41). This particular mode of ambivalence works on a dialectic, whereby on one hand, as Franz Fanon argued, the 'white gaze' generally reduces the black man 'to the biological and specifically to a penis' (Fanon, 1986: 170), while on the other, it performs a 'form of symbolic castration that denies both [their] masculinity and agency, in an attempt to render the black male body, once again controllable by white supremist patriarchy' (Carrington, 2000: 142). In conversation with Chomsky, a senior officer describes Jake as 'cocky' – a remark she takes up in inescapably pointed fashion. In planning his seduction of Chomsky, Jake jokes to Harrington, 'You know what they say about the black man'. Both of these comments are signalled as 'ironic' but their status as such is rendered questionable by a 'castrating' impulse that occurs around Jake and Harrington, whereby their scenes of undress always occur within sequences in which they are subject to comic or serious humiliation and loss of agency, and in Harrington's case, to attack and brutalisation.

This dynamic climaxes in a scene in the safe house when a drug-crazed and semi-nude Harrington attacks Jake, who overpowers him and holds him in a tight embrace as a means of restraint. When Jake lets him go, Harrington collapses to the ground and this is followed by an unconventional shot from Harrington's point of view, with Jake towering over him in a way that emphasises Jake's hyper-masculinity and Harrington's childlike loss of agency. Jake says, 'I warned you about undercover' and Harrington replies that he has 'been living it [undercover] all his life'. He talks of the survival tactics necessary to 'the only black kid at public school – laughing at racist jokes in order to "blend in" ' until 'you begin to forget who you are', and concludes 'fucked up as I am now I truly believe that this is the first time I've ever known who I really am'. It *may* be possible to interpret this scene in terms of Harrington abandoning a mask that has been imposed by white culture in favour of a politicised black identity, grounded in the common experience of racism – except this identity is itself 'mimicry', achieved through a superficial imitation of a Rastafarian, and by taking drugs, consorting with a white prostitute and being brutally beaten up by both black and white men. All of this confirms the 'tabloid' representation of black British subjects at the time. Significantly, Jake appears to share this identity. When teaching Harrington how to impersonate Willy-boy, Harrington naively asks how long it took *him* 'to get it', and a furious Jake replies 'I *am* it'. The 'it' in question is clearly not an identification with Willy-boy as an *actual* Rastafarian, since one plot point hinges on the fact that no *actual* Rastafarian would work for the police. Clearly, in this instance, a generic Rastafarian 'aesthetic' is being used to signify *all* 'black' subjectivity. Further, Jake later reveals that his bond with Harrington is the basis of his own experience of nearly being addicted to drugs. Despite the initial differences between them, these characters are revealed to be fundamentally 'the same', in a manner that could be said to draw on tabloid reality effects. From this perspective at its most extreme, Harrington's discovery of 'who he really is' might be read as affirming expectations of an 'authentic' black subject, at best as a victim and at worst as naturally belonging to a criminalised underclass. In these terms, the symbolic emasculation of Harrington that leads up to this scene might be construed as a punishment for his usurpation of the privileges of white, upper-class masculinity, and it is significant that his collapse is brought on by Somers (the real thing) force-feeding him crack cocaine.

This sequence ends with Jake helping Harrington up and a close-up of their clasped hands, symbolically affirming an identification that transcends the differences between them. This bond produces ambivalences in relation to the theme of professionalism in the police, since as Chomsky points out later, it is achieved at the expense of both of them behaving in a wholly unprofessional manner. In *Supply and Demand*'s diegetic world, where there appears to be no (overt) racial discrimination in the police as an institution, this might easily confirm a discourse whereby 'racism' is a matter of and for ethnic 'minorities'.

'Race', gender and sexuality

This hand clasp is followed by Jake announcing his plan to seduce Chomsky to keep her quiet for Harrington's sake. This appears as a classic homosocial gesture, in which women function as the 'glue' between men and which is in turn sometimes interpreted as a disavowal of homosexuality. In fact, the relationship between Jake and Harrington, especially as realised visually in this sequence, is exactly the sort that often provokes queer reading (see Chapter 5). Yet what may be subversive in terms of the construction of whiteness, gender and sexuality is far more complex when 'race' and class enter the equation. As Ben Carrington indicates in his discussion of black sportsmen, a 'white male homoerotic fascination with the black male [sporting] body' is an aspect of racial fetishism (Carrington, 2000: 136). Carrington describes this fascination in terms of the subjugation and controlling of black masculinity, directed to the maintenance of a discourse that posits the inherent superiority of *white* masculinity. This is not necessarily undermined by the confusions of gender and sexuality produced by this homoeroticism, or even by the intervention of 'actual' homosexual desire (142). Carrington also argues that in the tabloid press the sexualisation and objectification of black athletes often finds expression 'disguised as features for a female audience' (136). Significantly, if in *Supply and Demand* Harrington is 'punished' for his usurpation of white privilege in terms of class, Jake is punished for his personal and professional 'cockiness' by Chomsky.

A level of sexism in Jake's attitude to Chomsky is indicated from the start, in a series of incidents around the making of coffee, and in his casual assurance that he can seduce her into concealing Harrington's drug problem. When he first kisses her and she responds, he comments, 'So you do fancy me – I was beginning to wonder if you were a dyke or a bike'. Chomsky's answer is 'Try superior officer', underlining the fact that his professionalism has never included acknowledgement of her status. After they have sex, however, there is something of a reversal, with him making her coffee and running after her as she leaves to ask for a 'proper date'. As they speak on the stairs, they are passed by a female prostitute showing out a client. An implied parallel becomes clear in later scenes, when Chomsky's evasions around this date suggest that rather than him using her sexually, she has used and discarded him. If the focus is solely on the gender dynamic, this role reversal may be considered as moderately subversive from a white, liberal, feminist perspective. However, in relation to the discourse of 'race' this scenario is dangerously close to repeating the historical representational/social practice whereby a black man who expresses desire for a white woman must be 'put in his place' through actual or symbolic emasculation.

However, Walker's portrayal of Jake is nuanced enough to allow for a reading of his initial sexist arrogance as bravado that hides his 'real feelings'. Equally, like so many of La Plante's female protagonists, Chomsky is not a particularly sympathetic character, mainly because she is 'masculinised' and on two occasions she is shown to exactly repeat the insensitive behaviour of a male superior, which she has already criticised herself. As a result, when she does report Harrington, her style of professionalism appears ruthless and ambitious in contrast to Jake's more appealing codes of personal loyalty. Yet Chomsky has the last word. In the final scene when her name is not included in the list of those chosen for a newly formed, special undercover force, Jake and Harrington are triumphant because, as Jake puts it, 'we are in and she is out'. However, in a final twist, it is revealed that her name was not on the list because she will head the team. Initially, the visual and narrative structure of the scene encourages the viewer to share in the male characters' triumph, but the whistle motif on the soundtrack underlines the reversal of expectation and remarks the implicit sexism of their assumptions. As the camera focuses in on Chomsky, these (black) men are, once again, put 'back in their place'.

There is a sense then in which the relationships between Chomsky, Harrington and Jake seems to be designed to signify a multi-axial understanding of power relations, 'highlighting the way in which one group constituted as a "minority" along one dimension of differentiation, may be constituted as a "majority" along another' (Brah, 1996: 189). Yet, this sort of approach is always open to falling into relativism. In this instance, gender, 'race' and class are played off against each other, as if they were 'independent variables', as opposed to 'mutually constitutive', in ways that oversimplify their intersection (109). This might be a matter of a popular realist text attempting to appeal to too many different audiences at once, which in Nelson's terms, ends up by exploiting difference for commercial reasons (Nelson, 1997: 96). In any case, in this instance, a dialectical narrative strategy that brings into operation both liberal (feminist) and tabloid interpellations does not necessarily expose contradictions in terms of 'race'. Rather it can confirm the historical ambivalences around this discourse, remaining caught up within 'the complex dialects of power and subordination' through which 'black male identities have been historically and culturally constructed' (Mercer and Julien, cited in Hall, 1997: 272).

Discussing *Supply and Demand* with a group of students, I was once asked if maybe I was 'reading too much in'. Unquestionably, I have subjected *Supply and Demand* to a level of scrutiny in relation to the discourse of 'race', under which very few such television programmes would stand up. As such, I want to stress that it is not my intention to critique this *particular* drama, which ironically, I chose because in many ways it is far more progressive than the majority of others of its time and genre. Rather, the problem is with the way racist discourse has been naturalised within and through genre conventions and by means of the (white) gaze of the camera. The issues I have identified are then partly a matter of genre conventions and of form but not purely a matter of realism, not least since *Supply and Demand* shows certain hybrid and postmodern influences. Rather, they are the product of a deeply embedded inferential racism that still circulates within television as an institution, across genres and forms.

The Bill: race-relations drama in the twenty-first century

It is interesting to offer a progress check by comparing *Supply and Demand* with an episode of *The Bill* broadcast in November 2000. This was after the publication of the Macpherson inquiry, with its conclusions concerning institutional racism within the police force (see Chapter 1 and Conclusion). Obviously, there are limitations in comparing a high-budget, self-contained pilot with a biweekly police series, which can be more 'topical' but is constrained by format and by an early evening family viewing slot. *Supply and Demand* is more 'filmic' in terms of its visual style, scope and ambition and offered a sustained and self-contained narrative, whereas *The Bill* is closer to soap and has a flexi-narrative structure as described by Nelson (see Chapter 1).

'Carnival' was scheduled early in a series advertised as a 'new-style' *The Bill*. This was partly a matter of significant changes in cast and narrative circumstances occasioned by the ending of the previous series, but also an updating of its visual style. These formal innovations were based around increased use of the sort of naturalistic style of camera work pioneered in *Hill Street Blues*, and at this point similar innovations were evident in other British popular drama series, such as the teen soap *Hollyoaks* (1995–). Yet often as in *The Bill* these devices tend to be 'grafted on' to a baseline of the realist conventions of British soap. As a result, *The Bill* makes greater claim to referential realism than *Supply and Demand*, but occasionally in 'Carnival' the camera performs sudden shifts into disorientating angles and odd visual perspectives. This may also owe something to the innovative, politically radical British series *The Cops* (1998), where it functions as something of an alienation effect. In 'Carnival' the motivation of these shots is not clear, although they tend to suggest suspicion or paranoia.

Unlike *Supply and Demand*, there is no disavowal that 'Carnival' is a race-relations drama, not least in that it is set against a background of the Notting Hill Carnival, the most publicised celebration of Caribbean and West Indian diasporic cultural identities in Britain. In this and the next but one episode, 'The Gathering Storm', officers are also shown attempting to apply the lessons of the Macpherson report concerning institutional racism in the police.

Character: professionalism, class and cultural identity

However, there are some striking parallels between the narratives and central characters in the two dramas, because 'Carnival' focuses primarily on two black British officers, Detective Constable Danny Glaze (Karl Collins), who is working undercover on a drugs case and a university educated police constable, Gary McCann (Clive Wedderburn), who is on normal duties. Like Jake and Harrington, after initial hostility these two achieve some sort of bond with each other. In this case, however, it is Gary who is characterised as the more professional and as part of the team, while Danny is the outsider. In scenes between them, it is Gary's perspective which tends to be privileged, and the majority of the 'disorientating' shots noted above occur around Danny, for instance, in a scene where he is shown eavesdropping on a conversation between senior officers. These render him a not entirely trustworthy figure. However, Wedderburn's performance tends to portray Gary as defensive and self-righteous, while in scenes outside the station Collins lends Danny a sense of vulnerability. Neither figure, then, is either 'simply' a positive or negative representation.

In fact, Gary points out that Danny's 'street credibility' is largely a self-delusion. This is signified by his 'Afro' hairstyle, which according to Gary makes him an object of derision in the local black community. Associated in 1960s and 1970s with the Black Power movement, at the time of this episode this hairstyle mainly appeared in a high-fashion, ironic, retro context and is often taken as an inter-textual reference to 'blaxploitation' films like *Shaft* (1971). In fact, Collins appears with the same hairstyle in the drama series *Meterosexuality*, playing a gay DJ, where the Afro signals post-modern, diasporic camp (see Chapter 5). However, in *The Bill*, Danny's hairstyle is remarked as an anachronism by several black characters. As such, his or rather the programme maker's choice of 'undercover' hairstyle does indeed seem odd and it supports Gary's implication that Danny is attempting to imitate a black cultural identity that is not his own. The 'fake' nature of Danny's streetwise persona is also underlined in scenes in which his cover fails to con-vince the Jamaican criminals he encounters and this, alongside his failure to function as a team player with other (white) officers, creates a situation where he is nearly killed in a shoot out.

Gary also objects to Danny speaking to him in patois and assum-ing a cultural affinity between them in front of white colleagues. Yet, rather than insisting on the heterogeneity of black British identity, Gary seems to imply that Danny is attempting to exploit the sensi-tivity concerning racial discrimination produced by Macpherson to the advantage of his career. This perspective is also voiced in polit-ically questionable terms by a white officer, PC Smith, who claims that 'he is only saying what everybody else is thinking'.

Yet despite an excellent record, Gary's own career has stalled because he has previously failed his sergeants' exam on 'presenta-tion' – which is a matter of the (white) examiner's judgement. Gary hesitates to take the exam again, because he fears, not that he might have failed previously due to racial prejudice, but that next time he may succeed by means of *positive* discrimination. His professional-ism, then, relates to the desire to be recognised for his merits and abilities rather than the 'colour of his skin', and he is portrayed as resenting the way that, post-Macpherson, he is being defined as a 'black officer' rather than simply an officer. Yet in a contradictory fashion, he also refers to the experiences of an older generation of black officers, to admit that in the past 'colour blindness' in the force has been a matter of black officers having to conform to a white cul-tural identity in order to survive, let alone gain promotion. Significantly, we see Gary distancing himself from the local black community as well as Danny. Yet at the climax of the drama, it is

Gary's understanding of Jamaican patios (even though his family are from Grenada) that allows him to save Danny's life. This gives Gary the confidence to retake his sergeants' exam, and although not clearly enunciated, might be interpreted to indicate a recognition that his 'cultural hybridity' can be an asset in his professional work. By contrast, the last shot of Danny shows him demoted back to uniform and shaving off his Afro.

Like *Supply and Demand*, then, 'Carnival' explores questions of professionalism and cultural identity in relation to two black police officers. Like *Supply and Demand*, the plot of 'Carnival' also revolves around drugs, in this instance with a Jamaican 'posse' as suppliers being double crossed by a brutal black British gang. This repeats the tendency of the genre to criminalise black subjects, but nevertheless the narrative features a range of male *and* female black characters with heterogeneous national, class and gender identities and varying modes of cultural hybridity. While there may be issues of 'authenticity' around Danny's 'black' persona, Gary and Danny start to bond at the point when they jokily acknowledge that their animosity may arise in part from differences in Danny's Jamaican and Gary's Grenadian family backgrounds. There is also no evidence of the objectification and sexualisation that occurs around Jake and Harrington in *Supply and Demand*.

'Carnival' and Macpherson

On the other hand, the carnival context of the drama potentially widens the implications of the episode to symbolically embrace much of the black British community, not just in terms of drug culture and violence but its position on Macpherson. Earlier in 2000, allegations were made that police officers had been encouraged to turn a 'blind eye' to criminal activities during the Notting Hill Carnival, for fear of accusations of racism post-Macpherson. In December 2000, William Hague, the then Conservative Party leader, argued that the effect of the Macpherson report was to put *ethnic minorities* at risk, because the police now felt constrained in dealing with street robberies committed by young black men (see Travis, 2000).

Against the context of such public debates, 'Carnival' could be seen as part of a discourse which sought to deny or deflect attention from the conclusions of Macpherson. At best, it presents the report as primarily a problem for *black* officers, potentially affirming racism in the police force as 'something to do with the presence of black people' (Brah, 1996: 105). At worst, in a (white) liberal relativist mode, it chooses to explore the dangers of *reverse* discrimination, so that it is not the institution but *Danny's* professionalism that is put into question, through his insistence on cultural difference. In 'The Gathering Storm', similar questions of professionalism arise around PC Smith cited above, who fails to save Gary from a savage beating at the hands of an extremist racist group. However, the focus on this extremist group again avoids the issue of racism in the police and leaves open the question of how far within this drama professionalism is implicitly coded in terms of conformity to a white cultural identity.

It is not possible to draw conclusions concerning the operation of the discourse of 'race' within mainstream crime drama, let alone British television as a whole, from these two examples. However, while the differences between them do perhaps indicate certain changes in the representation of black British identities within television drama, the similarities are telling.

Post-Macpherson: authored drama and diaspora aesthetics

In the aftermath of Macpherson, the BBC and other terrestrial providers also admitted to the overwhelming 'whiteness' of their organisations.[1] Channel 4 has a history of (some) specialist programming for ethnic minorities and gave significant support to black cinema in the 1980s and 1990s. However, if there has been only a limited representation of diasporic subjects, let alone diasporic aesthetics, within mainstream British television drama, it is partly because there have been so few diasporic subjects in positions of authority within television as an institution. In 2003, Fiona McKinson pointed to signs of progress in *front* of the camera, especially in the rise in the number of ethnic 'minority' characters in soaps and medical dramas, and these numbers have continued to rise across a number of genres. However, McKinson also quotes Lord Herman Ouseley, pointing to the way a lack of multicultural knowledge on the part of television decision makers and executives in the BBC means that 'racist decisions are probably made every day' (McKinson, 2003: 2). Similarly, at a seminar at the British Academy of Film and Television Arts in 2004, Shobna Gulati, a performer in the British soap *Coronation Street*, asserted that 'the people commissioning storylines and creating characters for black and Asian actors are out of touch with the real world', and called for representations that are not 'parodies of ourselves as human beings' and which represent 'the particulars of our lives and cultures' (quoted in Gillespie, 2004). It is certainly noticeable that, as remarked above, 'diaspora aesthetics' tend to be far more in evidence when a work is to some extent 'authored' by a diaspora subject, although this is not necessarily a guarantee of progressiveness.

BabyFather

For McKinson at least, *Babyfather* (2001 and 2002), a popular drama series based on the novel of the same name by Patrick Augustus, was 'groundbreaking'. Like *Supply and Demand* and 'Carnival', *Babyfather* also focuses primarily on black masculinity, although it does contain substantial roles for black women. McKinson praises it for moving away from 'simple positive representation' of black British subjects and exploring 'fatherhood and friendship as issues both in cultural terms as well as a more universal context' (McKinson, 2003: 2). Yet, she also notes the advertising image for the series of the four male protagonists naked in a shower, asking 'was this feeding into the myth of the sexual prowess of the black Male or are we reading too deeply into things?' (2). Moreover, during the second series, Augustus accused the BBC of reducing his characters to 'racist stereotypes' by adding material relating to domestic violence and drug use. Defending the BBC, Hilary Salmon denied that these things featured significantly in the series, which she pointed out had been written by three well-respected black writers and had won two awards from the Commission for Racial Equality (see BBC News 2002).

Babyfather does clearly remark the heterogeneity of second-generation black British subjectivities and the complexity of their relationship to the dominant culture. However, as with *Supply and Demand* and 'Carnival', evidence of diaspora aesthetics occurs only on the level of representation of the attitudes and lifestyles of psychologically motivated characters. Otherwise *Babyfather* has many of the stylistic features of Nelson's popular 'flexiad' drama.

White Teeth and Second Generation

There is evidence of a diaspora aesthetic on the level of *form* as well as representation in *White Teeth* (2002) and *Second Generation* (2003). Again both were based on novels, but in contrast to *Babyfather* both were mini-series and both show more evidence of the sort of 'literary' influences found in traditional 'quality, authored' television.[2]

Adapted by Simon Burke from Zadie Smith's prize-winning novel and directed by Julian Jarrold, the four-part *White Teeth* focuses on a wide range of different diaspora subjectivities, in ways that touch on questions of ethnicity, gender, sexuality and class. Overall, its pace is far slower and its narrative both more fragmented and expansive in social and historical scope than most realist popular drama. It also uses a far broader vocabulary of shots and unusual visual strategies. Its characters and performances work outside the norms of psychological realism, tending to the fragmentary, the 'excessive' and the contradictory. Overall the style could be defined as a mix of magical realism and ironic postmodernism that recalls a diasporic literary tradition which embraces novelists such as Salman Rushdie and Hanif Kureishi. Kureishi's own novel, *The Buddha of Suburbia* (1990), was adapted for television in 1993 and has been analysed in terms of both a commodified postmodernism and a diaspora aesthetic by Bruce Carson (Carson and Llewellyn-Jones, 2000). There is less evidence of 'commodification' within *White Teeth*, but inevitably the representation of some of the female and the younger male characters sometimes repeats, as much as it subverts, a mode of objectification that the drama itself clearly wishes to 'comment on'.

Traces of a similar formal mix are evident in the two-part *Second Generation*, written by Neil Biswas and directed by Jon Sen. It also features an extensive soundtrack by composer Nitin Sawhney, whose work is notable for crossing boundaries between cultures and between the popular and the 'high'. However, in contrast to *White Teeth*, while still involving a wide vocabulary of unusual shots, the visual style of *Second Generation* leans far more to MTV. Its pace is faster, its narrative is more condensed and its characters and performances are closer to the norms of psychological realism. While overall less 'literary' than *White Teeth*, *Second Generation* draws on the narrative of Shakespeare's *King Lear*, focusing on an ailing patriarch and his three daughters, who are closely modelled on Regan, Goneril and Cordelia in terms of both characterisation and dramatic function. Like some nineteenth-century reworkings of this play, it offers a happy ending, with the Lear figure (played by Om Puri) reunited with Cordelia/Heere (Parminder Nagra) and her partner Sam Khan/Edgar (Christopher Simpson). These two had been lovers but in the past were pushed apart by parental disapproval arising from religious difference. As with *King Lear*, *Second Generation* concentrates on two families where the mothers are dead, so there are no older-generation Asian women amongst the main protagonists. This forecloses the possibility of exploring tensions that relate to gender and between generations of women of the sort that featured in British Asian productions such as *Bhaji on the Beach* (1993) or in comic register in the television sketch show *Goodness Gracious Me* (1998–2000). Indeed, while *Second Generation* appears to propose female figures as central characters, as with *King Lear*, the focus is actually on the male figures. Hence, as with Cordelia, Heere's narrative arc focuses on her 'divided duty' towards her father and her two lovers (one white, one Asian), and the character has little existence outside these relationships. It is then the male experience which symbolises the cultural, generational and religious themes of the drama. This may be a matter of the *gendered* positionality of the writer and the director, but it is strongly reinforced by the drama's intertextual dependence on *King Lear*. Significantly, the director, Jon Sen, states that 'This is not a cynical attempt to cash in on the "fashionability" of British Asians. It's just a brilliant love story that everyone can hook onto' (*Asians in Media*, 2003: 2). This opens the question of the 'commodification' of Asian ethnicity but also of how far it is possible for cultural hybridity to 'transform' this canonical western text, without either repeating its particular structuring of gender and/or reaffirming the colonialist myth of Shakespeare's work as 'universal'.

Conclusion

In fact, Sen's comment, like McKinson's on *Babyfather*, exemplifies the dialectic between imposition and dissidence, subversion and recuperation, difference and repetition, homogenisation and heterogeneity, inevitably in play within hybrid diaspora subjectivities and aesthetics – not least in the context of white-dominated commercial television. Similarly, 'real world' events at the start of the twenty-first century clearly indicate the way in which the discourse of 'race' can be constantly reconstituted by other means, a point I shall return to in the next chapter.

Notes

1 See, for example, archived articles for 2001 at BBCNews.com.
2 *White Teeth*, *Second Generation* and *The Buddha of Suburbia* all featured many of the same performers, already familiar from similar roles in both film and television. Crosschecks across a range of dramas suggest a fairly limited pool of black and Asian British performers in work at any one time, another point that might signify a continuing institutional racism in television and related institutions.

4

The world of enterprise: myths of the global and global myths (*Star Trek*)

Globalisation as a performative metanarrative

In 1999, Doreen Massey stated that 'Globalisation is currently one of the most frequently used and most powerful words in our geographical and social imaginations' (Massey, 1999: 33). Massey's stress on the imagination echoes that of other theorists, some of whom describe it as a 'fantasy, a set of practices and a context' (Franklin, Lurie and Stacey, 2000: 5). In fact, the concept of globalisation functions as a mode of 'emplotment', or a metanarrative, providing a framework for 'identifying, defining and analysing a set of processes that are said to be transforming the world at an unprecedented speed' (Franklin et al., 2000: 1). Like science fiction, these accounts are frequently *speculative* as much as descriptive, slipping between tenses and extrapolating from the past and present to predict the future. Added to the sheer weight of repetition of references to globalisation in both popular and academic realms, this can give the impression that, if globalisation is not already a singular and coherent condition that embraces the whole world, its achievement is inevitable. Citing a particular 'neo liberal version', Massey asserts that 'it is not so much a description of how the world is, as an image in which the world is being made' (Massey, 1999: 36). The discourses of globalisation, then, have significant constitutive or performative power simultaneously describing, producing and naturalising certain processes and effects. From the 1950s onwards, television has been understood as central to imagining and producing the global, and while it would still be inaccurate to suggest that every person on the planet now has access to television, it factors in the lives of a high percentage of the world population.

In the first part of this chapter I want to interrogate some accounts of globalisation as narratives of progress/progressiveness or decline, with specific reference to thinking around the role of television in constructing new forms of global identity. I then move on to draw some comparisons between these accounts and what Daniel Bernardi refers to as the *Star Trek* 'mega-text', as both a global commodity and as a fantasy of a globalised world, with specific reference to the first season of *Enterprise* (2001) (Bernardi, 1998: 7).

Time–space compression

Most accounts relate globalisation back to the historical development of the economic, political and military institutions of western modernity, culminating in those of postmodernity. Virtually all of them understand the development of new technologies in the nineteenth and twentieth centuries as having produced 'time–space compression', or rather 'a *perception* of a shrinking of the world through new technologies and mobilities, and a speeding up of processes no longer inhibited by national boundaries or by geographical locations' (Franklin et al., 2000: 1–2, my italics). These mobilities embrace flows of people across borders but also the flows of 'mediascapes, ideoscapes, ethnoscapes, financescapes and technoscapes' (Appaduria cited in Franklin et al., 2000: 2).

It is mostly taken as a given that these mobilities are inextricably linked to the free flow of capital. Hence, Massey comments on 'the spectacle of world economic leaders gathering to flaunt and reinforce their powerfulness, a powerfulness which consists in insisting that they (we) are powerless in the face of globalising market forces, there is absolutely nothing that can be done. Except, of course, to push the process further' (Massey, 1999: 36). As a result, anti-capitalism protests around institutions such as the World Trade Organisation and the International Monetary Fund have frequently been characterised as anti-globalisation. Actually, many protesters advocate planetary consciousness and global interconnectedness based on concerns for human rights, ecology and a more equal division of world resources. There is little argument that transnational corporations now account for about a third of world economic output and two thirds of world trade (Spronk, 2002: 2). However, to accept the inevitably of some form of globalisation is still not *necessarily* to accept the inevitability of a model based on western capitalist structures of social organisation.[1] In most other areas there are competing interpretations, not so much over the forms globalisation has taken or is taking, but concerning its meaning and impact. These interpretations range everywhere between the utopian and the apocalyptic, with the latter tending to dominate in the wake of the events of 11 September 2001 in North America.

Utopian and apocalyptic narratives in the 1990s

In early 1990s, many western cultural theorists favoured positive accounts of globalisation that owed much to Marshall McLuhan's 1969 vision of the world as a single media system, or as Barbara Spronk put it 'the glitzy, networked global village' inhabited by cosmopolitan, global subjects (Spronk, 2002: 1). This is what Massey calls 'the extreme (and though extreme none the less highly popular) version of globalisation, which offers visions of unfettered mobility, of free unbounded space' (Massey, 1999: 33). In this version, global flows are represented as democratising, reconfiguring previous 'core' and 'periphery' distinctions, undermining the old nation state system which is understood as a source of conflict and division, and producing new 'hybrid' global forms of identity. As Aijaz Ahmad points out, 'the underlying logic of this celebratory mode is that of the limitless freedom of a globalised market place' (Ahmad, 1995: 116). Sara Ahmed argues that within such discourses, cultural or other differences are redefined in terms of commodity or as surface lifestyle, to be tried and discarded by 'sophisticated, free wheeling global consumers' (Ahmed, 2000: 116–17). As she also indicates, these ideas draw on postmodern and postcolonial theory in ways that assume a narrative of progress/progressiveness, within which the historical legacies both of colonialism and of the western enlightenment subject are figured as having been 'overcome' and transcended (10). As such, the emphasis on mobility in such accounts can amount to a denial of 'the complex and contingent social relations of antagonism, which grant some subjects the ability to move at the expense of others' (83). They also tend to overlook the ways in which not all such movement is voluntary and how the 'global free market' has produced 'new' forms of slavery, both literally in terms of, for example, the international trade in forced prostitution, and virtual, in terms of the economic exploitation of migrant workers or workers in indigenous sweatshops.

In her celebrated 'A Manifesto for Cyborgs', Donna Haraway points out that most of the technologies speeding globalisation were produced by the western, industrial military complexes during the second world and cold wars, and can operate as an 'informatics of domination' (Haraway, 1990: 203). As Jackie Stacey notes, global consciousness and interconnectedness is also sometimes figured as 'apocalyptic', relating to a shared sense of planetary vulnerability in the face of the dangers posed by the impact of these technological processes on the environment and/or by weapons of mass destruction (Franklin, Lurie and Stacey, 2000: 28). Paradoxically, these dangers can be used by the very nations who developed these technologies in the first place, to justify militaristic or political interventions into other states, which have acquired them subsequently.

Global television and cultural imperialism: production

Ultimately, Haraway, who is a postmodern, materialist feminist, argues that these technologies have the potential to be *both* instruments of global domination *and* oppression and of positive social and political change. Similarly, when discussing television, most post-Marxist media and cultural theorists have tended to negotiate a middle ground between utopian and apocalyptic accounts of globalisation. Few dispute the significance of the role television plays in the production of time–space compression, or that cable, digital and satellite technologies have increased the permeability of national borders. However, there is significant debate concerning how far television produces a 'globalised sense of reality' which constitutes 'cultural imperialism' – that is, the 'process of disseminating western and often specifically North American commodities, values, priorities or ways of life, and by extension models of subjectivity and identity, to the rest of the world' (Robins, 1991: 25).

If McLuhan's famous assertion that 'the medium is the message' is correct, then regardless of content, the basic experience of watching television as an invention of western technological societies might in and of itself function as a mode of cultural imperialism. McLuhan's ideas clearly influenced postmodern thinker Jean Baudrillard. However, McLuhan saw television's 'message' in terms of benign unification, while Baudrillard perceives it as creating a sense of globalised *hyper*reality, in which viewers are interpellated as passive consumers of signs and can no longer tell, or care to tell, the difference between one place and another, fact and fiction, the news, an advert or a soap opera.

Most recent criticism tends to reject both McLuhan's and Baudrillard's focus on television as a *medium*, to concentrate on specific issues of production and reception. Commentators like Chris Barker acknowledge that digital, cable and satellite technologies have prompted the creation of giant transnational media conglomerates, such as Viacom and the Murdoch News Corporation, which 'at one point potentially had a global reach of some two thirds of the planet' (Barker, 1997: 60). Like Farell Corcoran, Barker also allows that North American programming accounts globally for 75% of all television programme exports (Corcoran, 2002: 3). Nevertheless, Barker asserts that it is unwise to generalise about such figures, which can obscure where these programmes are exported to, differences between types of programmes exported and levels of consumption (Barker, 1997: 49). Corcoran, like many others, also cautions against 'conflating economic power with cultural effects and the economist notion that culture is just another by-product of the capitalist world economy' (Corcoran, 2002: 4). Instead, both Corcoran and Barker emphasise the complex and contradictory nature of the relationship between the local and the global.

Summing up a range of arguments on this theme, Barker cites a number of theorists, including Appaduria (1993), Robertson (1995) and Giddens (1994), who draw on the logic of deconstruction to assert the relationship between the local and the global as one of interdependence and ongoing, mutual constitution. As such, they insist that global flows are not only 'one way' – not least because in a global market place, 'diversity sells' (Barker, 1997: 200–6). Therefore, Barker argues that while 'an element of cultural homogenisation seems undeniable, mechanisms of fragmentation, heterogenisation and hybridity are also at work', and citing Robertson, he concludes 'it is not a question of either homogenisation or heterogenisation but both at once' (Barker, 1997: 205).

This sort of argument is often supported with reference to the way that new technologies have facilitated the development not only of giant transnational media corporations, but also of national, local and community television around the globe (see Dowmunt, 1993). This includes, for example, companies such as the British-based Kurdish-language MED-TV. This describes itself as 'using satellite technology to speak to a transnational, multi-cultural audience and to give a voice to a suppressed and marginalised people – enabling them to learn about their heritage and about each other' (MED-TV, 1999: 1). Organisations like MED-TV support Joseph Straubhuar's argument that rather than a single global market for television, there are several 'geo-cultural markets, primarily characterised by language and cultural tradition, which tend to be seen as regional but spread by colonisation, slavery and migration, can also be trans-national' (Straubhaur, 1997: 291).

Yet Ulrike Meinhof and Kay Richardson also argue for the continuing importance of the *national* voice in television, stating that 'Viewers prefer, so the evidence suggests, to watch programmes made for them, where they are' (Richardson and Meinhof, 1999: 5). In these terms, Corcoran notes that the global flow of television programmes is inhibited by 'cultural discount'. This is defined as 'diminished appeal that is based on viewers' difficulty in identifying with aspects of its form and content', and this he says occurs 'even in same language television markets' (Corcoran, 2002: 3). According to Corcoran, recognition of these factors has led 'localisation to become another mantra in the international trade press', and has produced a range of 'adaptive manoeuvres' (3–4). These are often pursued through co-production between global giants and local partners, a pattern employed, for instance, by MTV. These strategies vary from simple dubbing to providing programme frameworks of pre-recorded material designed to be customised locally, or the franchising of programme formats.

However, this sort of localisation is still based on formats developed in western cultural contexts. This might therefore be understood to lead to greater global homogenisation, in terms of establishing certain aesthetic strategies as an international norm. Significantly, Barker claims that one of the ways that television can be said to be 'global' is in evidence of 'similar narrative forms being produced around the world, including soap opera and particular ways of structuring news, sports, quiz shows and music videos' (Barker, 1999: 54). Focusing on soap, he remarks that 'the emergence of an international prime time, soap opera style, may be partly attributed to the universal appeal of particular open ended narrative forms, the centrality of personal and kinship relations, and the possibility it offers for examining local issues in real settings' (54). Yet, neither open-ended forms nor personal and kinship relations are perceived and function in *exactly* the same way worldwide, and as Barker also acknowledges, the spread of this form may equally be due to 'the emergence of an international style embedded in the traditions of Hollywood' (54). Earlier in the 1990s and in stronger terms, Ellis Cashmore argues that 'America has defined the form television should take and the American formulas have become converted into universal conventions to be copied by all' (Cashmore, 1994: 195). Similarly, Peter Dahlgren points to an increasing standardisation of news programmes under the influence of Euro-American, transnational news agencies like CNN (Dahlgren, 1995). For some, such as Tom Perlmutter, this effect is 'two way' in that the need to please a widely varying foreign market means that 'American programming is being squeezed to conform to a homogeneous, globalised standard' (Perlmutter, 1993: 20).

Reception: global resistant readers

Some governments and theorists, notably those *not* operating from a Euro-American cultural perspective, take the threat of cultural imperialism through television very seriously. For instance, Kalyani Chadha and Ananndan Kavoor quote sources from Singapore, India and China all expressing fears of the influence of western media on indigenous traditions and values, in the strongest possible terms (Chadha and Kavoor, 2002). As a result, these and other countries, including some within the European Union and Canada, have put in place what Daniel Bilteryst calls 'national gatekeeping policies', in favour of domestically produced programmes (Bilteryst and Meers, 2002: 412).

However, many argue against an over-emphasis on the dangers of cultural imperialism. This is often achieved by focusing on reception, in a manner reminiscent of John Fiske's approach as discussed in Chapter 1. Dowmunt points out that there is 'no single homogenous global audience' (Dowmunt, 1993: 1) and Street observes that there is no 'global process of cultural interpretation' (Street, 1997: 81), with both making the case for television as a site of 'resistant reading'. As with Fiske's ideas, however, at the point at which they start to generalise from the particular, such approaches can easily slip into asserting the democratic and democratising potential of television, in ways that 'flatten [. . .] out of the terrain of [global] power relations' (Bordo, 1995: 260–1). They can also move from an apparent critique to a celebration of the dominant, western model of capitalism. For instance, writing on MTV in 1993, Corinna Strummer concedes that 'it typifies and exists to serve, the interests of advanced consumer capitalism' (Strummer, 1993: 60). However, she also suggests that it might be seen as 'opening avenues of opposition for Europe's youth, resisting either oppressive national identities, or the values and life styles of an older generation' (51). On this point, Dowmunt adds that this role might have been especially important in the late 1980s in communist Eastern Europe and Russia, 'where western culture has had a symbolic value as resistance to totalitarianism. Demonstrating once again that what for one community may be media imperialism, may for another be a liberating force' (Dowmunt, 1993: 14). The problem is that, historically, western culture has often justified imperialism through concepts of liberation and modernisation, so that looking to MTV in such ways may be *already* symptomatic of cultural imperialism. Speaking as diasporic subjects from within North America, Alexander and Mohanty refer to this nation's self-perception as 'the democratic nation par excellence' and its deployment of a rhetoric within which words like 'freedom, equality and human rights are defined in terms of economic access, choice, private property and ownership, so that capitalist values infuse ideas about citizenship and liberal democracy' (Alexander and Mohanty, 2001: 508). These values are taken as given within the large majority of North American television programmes, and in many countries instead of, or as well as, symbolising resistance or liberation, might equally function to foreclose thinking around possible 'alternative' models of political and social organisation.

Transnational hybrid identities?

However, in an extension of the 'resistant reading' thesis, Chris Barker argues that *all* identities, including national ones, can be understood as 'imaginary'. He also asks 'at what level is the national culture under threat located, the government or the dominant ethnic group? Cultural identities, it is argued, are always already far more diverse and hybridised than allowed for by national ones' (Barker, 1997: 194 and 197). He goes on to assert that globalisation is producing:

Post-traditional and translocal identity formations [which] involve the production of multiple identities or identifications, many of which have little bearing on the question of national identity, but focus on issues of sexuality, relationships, age, work etc. Television is one resource, albeit a significant one, in that process. (Barker, 1997: 206)

How far television is understood as part *of*, or simply responding *to* the development of such post-traditional identities is unclear. However, drawing on similar theoretical sources to Barker, Timothy Havens seems to suggest that, for some at least, the latter is the case, since it is argued that 'homogenous national identities are increasingly ineffective for drawing audiences [. . .]. Instead audiences coalesce around various transnational identities, such as gender, ethnicity and "race" or age' (Havens, 2000: 372). This raises the question as to why many *British* television programmes are remade for the North American market? *Queer as Folk*, for example, would seem (as discussed in the next chapter) to offer plenty of scope for a transnational identification on the basis of sexuality but was remade to take account of North American national and cultural differences.

In fact, studying the North American *Cosby* (1996–2000) in relation to the notion of 'race' as a 'transnational identity', Havens identifies a wide variety of responses to the show by viewers in the numerous countries where it has been syndicated. While he found evidence of identifications on the basis of 'race' in South Africa, the Caribbean and the Middle East, in the same locations and ethnic groups, he *also* found disidentifications on the basis of class, economics and culture. Yet, these aspects of the show sometimes provided grounds for identifications *across* racial lines, for instance, among white South Africans (Havens, 2000: 386). Summing up, Havens suggests that these responses offer further evidence 'that viewers understand international television though the twin discourses of racial and regional identity. Political or historical relations between nations and communities worldwide, determine which of these identities operate for which viewers' (385).

Yet in Havens's study, some Caribbean viewers disidentified with *Cosby* on the basis of the particular style of *masculinity* represented by the main character (385). This suggests, as Barker notes above, that rather than just the twin discourses of 'race' and regional identity, multiple identities and identifications may come into play in such readings. However, there are several potential problems with this thesis of television and transnational identities, not least that the examples available focus on global responses to *North American* products, and there seems little evidence of a two-way process. As importantly, it *starts* from a (secular, western) post-modern, post-traditional model of identity, taken as an assumed global 'norm'. This is not the model of identity which dominates most television production – unless Baudrillard's contention and John Fiske's implication that it dominates the *medium* are taken as accurate. Nor is it actually one subscribed to by a significant pro-portion of socially situated, global subjects. Moreover, within this model, it is actually the historical, shifting and contradictory rela-tionship between *all* categories of difference, including national and cultural differences, that allow all or any of them to be revealed as constructed and imaginary. Identifications based on 'race', gender or sexuality may put national or cultural identities into question, whilst simultaneously reinscribing these former categories as 'fixed and universal'.

Havens acknowledges that the concept of 'race' as a 'trans-national identity that can bind together audiences across national lines' owes much to Paul Gilroy's 1993 book *The Black Atlantic* (Havens, 2000: 372). Gilroy, Stuart Hall and Homi Bhabha also clearly influence ideas of television and hybrid, transnational identities, as articulated by Barker. However, as noted in the previ-ous chapter, both Gilroy and Hall discuss a very particular mode of diasporic identities, formed in *exchanges* between Africa, the Caribbean Islands, Europe and the Americas. Gilroy also developed his argument largely through reference to music and other fields, where the conditions of production and dissemination have, for centuries, allowed for multiple-way flows of global influence, far more than is currently the case with television. Moreover, Bhabha posits his notion of cultural hybridity as part of an analysis that looks *forward* to a 'third stage' of deconstruction, which will produce something as 'new' and as yet unthinkable (Bhabha, 1990: 211). As already noted in Chapter 3, in the present, especially when taken as a generalised, postmodern model for identity, the notion of cultural hybridity can fall into relativism. The understanding that, historically, as Imruh Bakare notes, 'all cultures, traditional, modern, or post-modern, are hybrids', can as Ruth Frankenberg and Lata Mani put it, lead to the notion that we can all be defined as 'decentred, multiple, minor or metiza, in exactly comparable ways' (Bakare, 2000: 234 and Frankenberg and Mani, 2001: 487).

In short, deep-rooted historical and context-specific differences can be figured as superficial, a matter purely of aesthetics or surface lifestyle, and it is surely only on this basis that most television is a 'resource' for identity construction.

Cultural hybridity, then, can be appropriated to a new 'global', postmodern norm of identity, which is implicitly advanced as progressive in so far as it opposes the *old* (western) traditional norm. Yet, what might actually be at stake in defining translocal, transnational subjectivities is 'a certain kind of western subject, the subject of and in [postmodern] theory' (see Ahmed, 2000: 83). This simply reinscribes a hierarchy in which those who do not participate in this theoretical model are implicitly figured as more 'primitive' and less advanced 'others'. A distinction therefore continues to be made between those who '*know* the difference' and can exploit mobility of identity as a 'resource' and those who *are* the difference, who remain 'still' (see Ahmed, 2000: 116–17). In short, this version of postmodern subjectivity can come full circle, to represent, once again, a failure to engage with otherness and difference, except in terms of either pure relativism or more primitive versions of the assumed postmodern 'norm'.

Globalisation as complex and paradoxical

The above version of cultural hybridity may be most clearly in evidence in the more utopian versions of globalisation but its traces can appear in more 'balanced' accounts, such as that offered by Barker. Barker is well aware of the dangers of leaving behind 'what is core to the cultural imperialism theses, namely ideas of power and inequality' (Barker, 1997: 200). Having said this, Barker then goes on to quote Pieterse:

> Relations of power and hegemony are inscribed and reproduced within hybridity [. . .] Hence, hybridity raises the question of the *terms* of the mixture, the conditions of mixing and melange. At the same time it's important to note the ways in which hegemony is not merely reproduced by but refigured in the process of hybridisation. (Pieterse, 1995 in Barker, 1997: 201)

The fact is that, once again, this comment moves from stressing the historical and the context specific to a generalisation, and in the process '*from* identifying dominance and oppression to always finding a means of redemption' (Morris, 1990: 25, original italics; see Chapter 1). In a sense, this signals one of the key weaknesses of *all* accounts of globalisation, in so far as they tend to function as metanarratives, which generalise from the specific. As is clear from the range of arguments cited above, when the field is broad as the whole world, on the level of the local and specific it is possible to find examples to support any number of conflicting and contradictory general arguments.

To be fair, if this seems to occur with Barker, it is because he is attempting to summarise a wide range of such accounts (as am I), and ultimately he is keen to assert the paradoxical, contradictory nature of globalisation, albeit as a set of processes, rather than as a metanarrative. In the 1999 version of his book on television and globalisation, he asserts that globalisation is best understood as a:

> series of overlapping, over determined, complex and chaotic conditions which, at best, can be seen to cluster around key nodal points. This has led, not to the creation of an ordered global village, but to multiplication of points of conflict, antagonism and contradiction [. . .], arising from unpredictable over determinations of which television forms a part. (Barker, 1999: 41)

There is plenty of evidence as to the paradoxical nature of globalisation in the way that global anti-capitalism protests have depended on the same technologies and mobilities that enable global capitalism. Equally, the terrorist attacks of 11 September 2001 in North America can be read as being both produced and enabled by the very 'flows' of globalisation which they sought to assail. In their aftermath, these events simultaneously produced signs of transnational identifications *and* an upsurge of nationalism and racism at the same time, in the same countries. In the longer term, they became the impetus for political and military interventions into other nation states on the basis of global security. A large part of the global impact of these attacks was also unquestionably due to the rapid and continuous dissemination of horrific live television pictures across the world by satellite. Yet I am not sure that describing these events as part of the overdetermined, complex and chaotic nature of globalisation is especially useful in understanding the specific historical and political contexts of which they are part. Above all, it seems to me that this sort of 'complexity theory' narrative can allow for a forgetting of history and an avoidance of political responsibility. It can also induce a sense of powerlessness, in which globalisation takes on the status of a force of 'nature'.

Before 9/11 and from their particular diasporic, feminist materialist position, Jacqui Alexander and Chandra Talpade Mohanty understand globalisation as a continuation of colonialism, or rather argue that 'global realignments and fluidity of capital have simply led to a consolidation and exacerbation of capitalist relations of dominance and exploitation – in what we refer to as process of re-colonisation' (Alexander and Mohanty, 2001: 496). In this process, the 'hierarchical relationships amongst racial groups and geographies have not disappeared' (499). In 2002 feminist economist Barbara Spronk also points out that *some* analysts of globalisation 'see the rise of nationalist and fundamentalist movements round the world – movements that are of course political as well as cultural – as a direct response to this threat [of culture imperialism]'. These are then 'struggles to retain or recreate individual and collective sense of self defined by place, language and belief' (Spronk, 2002: 8).

These identities may, from a western, postmodern perspective, be 'imaginary' but they are nonetheless deeply felt and produce material effects. There may be numerous factors that offset the threat of cultural imperialism via television. However, not to fully acknowledge that for many in the world this threat is experienced as very real is a failure of empathetic identification, not least in the light of evidence of continuing investment in ideas of an 'essential' national culture and identity within the countries that actually pose the threat. A *politicised* postmodern notion of global (inter)subjectivity, rather than a relativist one, understands 'others' as *both* different and *also* as part of the same. It recognises and interrogates its own postionality in the globe and its implication in unequal economic and cultural power relations, in ways that cannot be subject to metanarratives but must approached 'as historically contingent and context-specific relationships' (Brah, 1996: 109).

Case study: *Star Trek* as myth of the global and global myth

It may seem bathetic to move from these 'real' and serious issues to discussing *Star Trek*. Nevertheless, since the 1960s this science-fiction fantasy has predicted, engaged with and/or reflected most of the key tropes of both utopian and apocalyptic accounts of globalisation. It has even sometimes rehearsed the arguments of those situated somewhere between these poles. Mostly, however, the *Star Trek* universe privileges a version of the global articulated through a discourse of technological determinism, as part of a narrative of progress/progressiveness. In the *Star Trek* universe, the development of technologies which allow for mobility through space (and time) is remarked as a major, if not the *primary* marker of the 'advanced cultures' that make up a 'Federation' of planets, which functions very much like the (actual) United Nations. Yet access to the same technologies by *culturally* less 'advanced' species constantly produces the threat of global, and sometimes universal, apocalypse. This is always narrowly avoided by the intervention of the Federation's 'Star Fleet', the headquarters of which are to be found in San Francisco, California, Earth. On this Earth, technological 'progress' has produced a democratic, unified (supposedly) multicultural, global, social and political system, without war, disease or poverty and 'beyond' modes of social inequality relating to gender, 'race' or class.

While clearly not 'referential realism', I would argue that, in certain senses, this science-fiction fantasy is no more or less 'imaginary' than some of the other accounts of globalisation above, and it is on this basis that I want to set up a comparison. As a brand, *Star Trek* is also a 'global product' and therefore may be considered as a potential purveyor of cultural imperialism. However, in 1992 Mel Harris, then president of the Paramount group which produces *Star Trek*, was convinced that it offered a view from everywhere and nowhere, suggesting that it could function as a model for a 'universal language of television that can travel across language and cultural barriers', going on to ask 'What country is *Star Trek* from? It's not from any country [. . .] It has no base. It doesn't reflect any point of view' (quoted in Perlmutter, 1993: 21). A similar belief in the 'universality' of *Star Trek* informs journalists Jeff Greenwald's series of online articles entitled Planet *Star Trek* (Greenwald, 1997a and b). Greenwald's main premise is that *Star Trek* is not just a 'myth of the global' but also has the status of a 'global myth', and he clearly perceives this 'myth' to be socially and politically progressive. This view is shared by its producers, its main fan base and a number of other commentators, in both the public and academic spheres.

The gap between the myth and the product (the franchise)

Star Trek's status as a global myth might be confirmed by the way that phrases such as 'Space: the final frontier' and 'Beam me up, Scotty' have become international linguistic currency (see Quinion, 2005). According to most accounts, the various *Star Trek* television series have been shown in over 100 countries and dubbed into dozens of language (*Star Trek History*, 2002: 2). The official Paramount *Star Trek* website offers details of where it is currently being shown, and in 2003, this covered the US, Canada, most of Northern and Southern Europe, parts of Eastern Europe, Israel, Australia, New Zealand and some areas of South and Central America, South East Asia and Africa. Most of these were either showing *Star Trek: The Original Series* (*TOS*, 1966–9) or *The Next Generation* (*TNG*, 1987–94). Some were showing *Voyager* (1995–2001) and *Deep Space Nine* (*DS9*, 1993–99) with only a few showing *Enterprise* (2001–5) (see *StarTrek*.com, 2002).

There are some telling omissions in this list, including the former Soviet Union, China, most of the Arab States and India. However, according to Greenwald, there are five million *Star Trek* fans in Japan and 'loads' in Russia and Pakistan, and in 1997, *TOS* was being repeated on Indian terrestrial television, although only one season of *TNG* was ever aired there, in 1994 (Greenwald, 1997a: 2 and 1997b: 4). The distribution of the *Star Trek* films may be broader and most of the many *Star Trek* spin-off products are available on sale through the web, where there are a number of unofficial fan sites originating from various countries. All of this suggests that from a Euro-American perspective, the reach of *Star Trek* as an export is as 'global' as many things given that descriptor.

Yet, as with many of the academic accounts of globalisation considered above, there is a tendency in analyses of *Star Trek* to downplay or ignore the economics behind (and within) the fictional product. In the preface to their book on *Star Trek*, Michele Barrett and Duncan Barrett refer to an example of the 'dubious business practices' that occurred as part of writer/producer Gene Roddenberry's struggle to put on 'his utopian view of a progressive future' in *TOS*. They continue:

> The contradiction is one that has run through *Star Trek* from that day to this: a profoundly progressive and intelligent dream of an egalitarian future, but one that is now part of an immense financial empire

that owns and controls what is known in the trade as the Franchise.
(Barrett and Barrett, 2001: vii)

As a franchise, *Star Trek* is owned and controlled by Paramount
Television Group, which is now part of Viacom Inc. Viacom is often
described as one of the most powerful, pioneering transnational
multimedia conglomerates, with pre-eminent positions in broadcasting and cable television, radio, outdoor advertising and online
(see Viacom.com website). In 2003, Viacom had a 35% monopoly
of these areas in the US, its profits were expressed in terms of bil-
lions of dollars and its holdings and subsidiaries are too numerous
to mention. However these include many well known brands, such
as CBS Television Network, MTV, Nickelodeon, Blockbuster, and
Simon and Schuster publishers (see Viacom Inc, 2003). Like Viacom
itself, Paramount Television is based in the US but distributes programmes to over 125 countries, in more than 30 languages (see
Viacom Official Website (2001)).

Earth, in *Star Trek*'s fictional world, is apparently *post*capitalist,
and economic considerations seldom if ever motivate the humans or
the majority of other 'advanced' species. However, in terms of the
(actual) context(s) of its production, it would be very surprising if
capitalist values did not inform *Star Trek*'s ideas of democracy and
citizenship. As such, it is interesting that, summing up a visit to
India, Greenwald credits his failure to find 'legions' of *Star Trek* fans
as being due to 'poverty, nationalism and too many reruns', and also
adult Indian's 'addiction to cheesy soap opera and Bollywood
Musicals' (Greenwald, 1997b: 1 and 5). He goes on to quote one
interviewee stating:

> It's simple: the working class here need to come home and relax with
> a drama that they can relate to. *Star Trek* succeeds in societies that
> have already achieved basic levels of satisfaction. Where the food is on
> the table. Where clothes are in the cupboard and the car is outside.
> Then they are willing to watch the next step. *Star Trek* is certainly the
> next step. Our next step is still getting that food on the table.
> (Greenwald, 1997b: 6–7)

Like Greenwald himself, this interviewee appears to accept *Star
Trek* as part of a 'narrative of progress' but suggests a 'discount' in
its reception, apparently based on economics rather than language
or culture. Indeed, arguably, these remarks carry a sense of the
effects of 'cultural imperialism', in terms of embracing North

American values, in so far as car ownership is taken as a signifier of
'*basic* levels of satisfaction'. For this interviewee, at least, *Star Trek*
seems to be related to those values.

It is striking that few of *Star Trek*'s fans, or its academic commentators, many of whom are clearly also fans, touch directly on
the contrast between the economic conditions of its production and
distribution and its (apparently) postcapitalist vision. Beyond the
comment cited above, this includes Barrett and Barrett. This may be
because these analyses focus on textual interpretation or on ethnographic studies of its fan culture, and this culture, like the academic
textual interpretations, is mostly concerned with issues of character,
plot, technical details of the *Star Trek* world and its 'philosophy'.
Authorship of this philosophy is always accredited to Roddenberry,
who is himself frequently mythologised as a visionary or even a
'prophet' (see Porter and McLaren, 1999). Roddenberry retained
creative stamp of approval until his death in 1991, after which
changes in tone were apparent in *Voyager* and *DS9*. Nevertheless,
Roddenberry's estate, the longer-serving members of *Star Trek*'s
production team, Paramount and its fans have all worked to ensure
certain consistencies and continuities in the brand.

Star Trek as mega-text

These continuities have also encouraged discussions of *Star Trek*, as
Daniel Bernardi puts it, as a 'mega-text', a 'continuously unfolding
narrative that is at least relatively coherent across different aspects
of the franchise' (Bernardi, 1998: 7). Yet *as* a franchise, this brand
encompasses a massive number of different commodities, produced
over a period spanning nearly 50 years. This, plus the sheer volume
of primary and secondary material available for analysis, means
that within the mega-text, as with the global, it is possible to find
'local' examples to support a wide range of conflicting and contradictory arguments. For instance, while there is a strict set of guide-
lines for producing the television shows, as Robin Roberts
demonstrates in her book *Sexual Generations* (1999), it is possible
to trace differences in the treatment of ideological concerns between
and across episodes and series, according to the influence of a
shifting stable of writers and directors.

This mix of general continuity and local variation, the fantasy
setting, the presence of nonhuman characters and the way that *Star*

Trek has always drawn intertextually on a wide range of western canonical texts, may contribute to the notion of *Star Trek* as a 'myth' in the classical sense of conveying 'universal human truths'. Such myths operate through metaphor and metonym, parable and parallel, devices which, as Darcee L. McLaren indicates, means that while they may appear coherent, they exist *primarily* in the process of interpretation. This is the basis of their presumed universality (McLaren, 1999: 233). In short, like such myths, as a mega-text, *Star Trek* is a 'producerly' text. Hence, for example, while there is no argument as to the profoundly secular nature of Roddenberry's 'vision', as *Star Trek and Sacred Ground* (1999) indicates, even in the early series, some episodes can be interpreted positively in relation to religious discourse. Bernardi also points to the way that fans often discuss *Star Trek* aliens as metaphors for real-world people and cultures, but with a high level of disagreement over exactly *which* ones (Bernardi, 1998: 163–6).

The same factors that give the *Star Trek* mega-text the semblance of 'universality' simultaneously provide scope for 'resistant reading' by socially situated subjects. This is evinced for example by the body of 'slash fiction writing' that exists around the various series (see Chapter 5). However, as this fiction also demonstrates, *Star Trek*'s assumed universality and progressiveness can be a matter of extrapolation *from* and projection *onto* the texts, rather than what is actually represented within them. For example, in the 1970s, North American fans developed an entire philosophy around on the concept of IDIC (Infinite Diversity in Infinite Combination), from a Vulcan principle mentioned once, in passing, in a *TOS* episode 'Is there no Truth in Beauty' (see Porter and McLaren, 1999). Similarly, in his book *Star Trek in Myth and Legend*, ex Harvard scholar Thomas Richards offers a politcal evaluation of an episode of *TNG* that includes speculation over what *may* have happened on a particular planet *after* the end of the episode (see Richards, 1997: 20–2).

The critique of the *Star Trek* 'philosophy'

In fact, despite its producerly nature, most academic commentators agree that if *Star Trek* is a 'modern myth', it is so in the sense defined by Roland Barthes. That is, it is a 'culturally specific metalanguage', or a discourse within 'which history is transformed into nature' (Barthes, 1973: 140). In these terms, the general consensus is that it offers 'an idealised vision of American society projected into the future' (Roberts, 1999: 7). This myth of a specific national identity is shown not to be without its (human) 'flaws' but is nonetheless represented as the preeminent model for global democracy. While acknowledging this, much recent academic criticism is concerned with this identity in terms of subjectivity, rather than national identity, analysing the mega-text as 'an ongoing investigation of what it means to be human, articulated from a secular, western liberal, humanist perspective' (Barrett and Barrett, 2001: 6). In the 1990s, this prompted feminist and anti-racist critiques of *Star Trek*, such as those produced by Roberts and Bernardi, which, for example, led Bernardi to conclude: 'despite Trek's didactic call for civil rights and its multi-culturalism, despite its moments of beauty and resistance, the mega-text's imagination has been and continues to be, depressingly western and painfully white' (Barnardi, 1998: 180). Similarly, in an essay in *Global Futures* (1999), and as part of a general critique of western discourses of globalisation, Barnor Hesse offers an analysis of Hollywood science fiction that starts by referring to space as 'the final frontier', a phrase associated with *Star Trek* (Hesse, 1999: 122). He then points out how far both these types of fiction *and* many political narratives of globalisation 'recycle and replicate scenarios' such as the '16th century invasion of the Americas, the 19th century conquest of India, Africa and the Pacific', with both being underpinned by a 'distinctly European format of imperialism, which is promoted by an evangelical faith in an apparently self effacing, universal liberalism' (122).

I do not intend to reiterate Bernardi's and similar analyses of (mainly) *TOS* and *TNG* in detail. Suffice to say, commentators have discussed at length the implications of the western, patriarchal, military, or rather naval, traditions that inform Star Fleet. They have also pointed to the ways in which the 'best and highest' human values and qualities are represented by reference to the canonical traditions, artefacts and narratives of mainstream, white, Euro-American culture. They have noted that 'primitive' alien cultures have sometimes been represented in terms which *do* strongly suggest 'other' real-world peoples, such as the Africanesque culture portrayed in *TNG*'s 'Code of Honour', an episode that is, notoriously, a textbook example of racial fetishism.

Even so, like many academic accounts of globalisation, and as indicated by Bernardi's comments above, the majority of these analyses are seldom entirely negative. Most allow that on the level of specific episodes, the *Star Trek* mega-text does raise progressive questions, especially in the context of a popular, commercial television. Hence, Barrett and Barrett argue that 'the values of [western] modernity are examined and challenged, as well as selectively endorsed in *Star Trek*' (Barrett and Barrett, 2001: 11). However, this sometimes moderates into a defensiveness about *Star Trek*'s limitations. For instance, while acknowledging the justice of the sort of view expressed by Hesse above, Richards refers to Roddenberry's 'original intentions' to argue that *Star Trek* 'replays but does not replicate the narratives of colonialism' and was meant as 'a *corrective* to our own bloody history of exploration but not a simple or facile corrective' (Richards, 1997: 14, my italics). Equally, Barrett and Barrett assert that 'there is much good in the values of secular humanism [. . .] which on any scale of real political evil would come fairly low down the list' (Barrett and Barrett, 2001: 9). They later go on to cite Bernardi's work as an example of recent 'heavy handed approaches' to this fiction, arguing that the anti-humanism that informs it 'is simply not shared by either the makers or the audiences of *Star Trek*' (91). While there may be justice in both these statements, I do not see why this should impose limits on critical analysis. Further, Barrett and Barrett themselves proceed to discuss *DS9* and *Voyager* in section 3 of the book under the heading 'The Post-modern Tack', in a way that implies something of a narrative of progress/progressiveness. What is confusing, however, is that they argue that this is not just a matter of style but also of *substance*, in terms of the rejection of some 'key ideas of modernity' (194, my italics). Yet they conclude that the 'style of these series may be post-modern, but the content is definitely not post-human' (197). In fact, as this suggests, these series may more properly be designated as (post)modern, and both continue to maintain certain core elements of the *Star Trek* brand in terms of style *and* substance.

From 'modern' to (post)modern: the *Star Trek* format

In each *Star Trek* series up to and including *Enterprise*, the theme music tends to quote Alexander Courage's 'Bright Galactic Beguine', composed for *TOS*. This piece is reminiscent of the work of the iconic modernist American composer Aaron Copland. Music played under scenes is (still) of a similar genre, where in contrast, for instance, to *Ally McBeal*, it is still used in a conventionally 'realist' or 'illusionist' fashion to heighten emotion and privilege particular readings of the action and characters. As Richards points out, episodes are generally 45 minutes long and have the five-act structure of classic western drama, mainly due to the need to make space for commercial breaks (Richards, 1997: 7–8). This is an interesting point to consider in relation to the potential influence of North America on the development of 'global' television formats. In much popular drama from this source, these interruptions are conventionally followed by a re-establishing shot, in this instance usually an outside view of the space ship or space station. On video, DVD, or noncommercial channels these breaks are experienced as dramatic pauses or punctuation but in either case they slow down the action in ways that may be limiting to the development of certain types of narrative. In fact, as Richards notes, despite the apparent emphasis on action and on props and technology, the primary focus in *Star Trek* on television is on the emotions and relationships of its 'core' crew, who function as a surrogate family (7). In short, it depends on invoking empathetic identification with psychologically motivated characters, who may develop over time but only in relation to essential, established characteristics, rendering them 'predictable'. Equally, while later series show a flexiad tendency towards continuity of some narrative strands across episodes, the majority of instalments remain self-contained narratives, functioning on a disruption/restoration of status quo model. Aside from occasional 'local' excursions into symbolism and expressionism, aesthetically early *Star Trek* operates within established conventions for North American popular television realism.

Richards also suggests that the *Star Trek* universe is essentially comic, with 'tragedy being framed by comedy', so that with rare exceptions, 'No event in the series is final or fatal, not even death', although this *only* covers the 'core' crew(s) (Richards, 1997: 53). As such, this is 'a universe of possibilities and alternatives, in which history is always open and radically unfinished' (54). Yet, as he also notes, however many parallel universes, different dimensions and multiple potential outcomes are invoked, the identity of each character always 'remains integral and whole' (57). History can be rewritten but 'the breakdown of the human individual is the greatest nightmare *Star Trek* has to offer' (57).

Paradoxically, *Star Trek*'s formal 'conservatism' might be seen as enabling it to raise 'progressive' questions, because these 'challenges' are recuperated by a mixture of the 'comic' nature of its universe, the return to status quo at the end of each episode and its focus on characters as individuals.

Whatever their substance, *Voyager* and the first two seasons of *DS9* adhere to all these conventions but Barrett and Barrett also identify evidence of a 'post-modern representational style' in the increasing and self-conscious intertextual references to mid twentieth-century North American popular culture (Barrett and Barrett, 2001: 195–7). In both series this mostly occurs on the 'holodeck', first introduced in *TNG*, a recreational virtual reality facility where the crew can interact with 3D holographic (yet somehow temporarily 'material') characters and environments. In *DS9*, many such episodes occur in Vic Fontaine's 1960s Las Vegas casino, but amongst others, Barrett and Barrett point to the comic *Voyager* episode, 'Bride of Chaotica', where a 'holoprogram' that appears to be a parody of early Buck Rogers and/or Flash Gordon[2] films malfunctions, crew members become trapped in the virtual world and Captain Janeway has to take on a role and improvise to rewrite it from within. A similar plot is explored in a more serious register in 'Worst Case Scenario', and referring to both these episodes, Barrett and Barrat conclude that in *Voyager* 'The captain's function is not only within the *Star Trek* narrative, but as a kind of narrator herself. A postmodern approach to textuality is explicitly aired' (Barrett and Barrett, 2001: 185).

Arguably the device of the 'Captain's Log' that frames episodes of *TOS* and *TNG* always positions *Star Trek* captains as 'narrators'. More importantly, Richards analyses a number of very similar 'trapped in a fiction' narratives from *TNG*, played out both on *and* off the holodeck, and including 'The Royale', 'Ship in a Bottle' and 'Frame of Mind' (Richards, 1997: 100–16). The resolution to 'The Royale' also involved the crew actively becoming narrators and performers in the fiction. However, for Richards, these narratives are part of a *modernist*, neo-platonic discourse, which opposes the dangerous and seductive 'lower' system of stories to the 'higher' and more sustaining system of myths. In *Star Trek*, he claims, 'stories are always close to lies, while myth is always close to truth' (115–16). Further, as Barrett and Barrett acknowledge, *Star Trek*'s 'comic universe' has *always* been inclined toward in-jokes, ironic self-reference and indeed self-conscious intertextuality (Barrett and Barrett, 2001: 195). This again raises the question of the postmodern as a model of reading, in which certain stylistic devices are claimed as 'essentially' postmodern and assumed in advance to create a critical distance that effects an overcoming of realism. In this instance, rather than creating a distance which reflects back on *Star Trek*'s own constructedness as popular fiction or 'lower order of story', these devices might equally interpellate its audience to a position of shared ironic 'knowingness' *about* such stories. In doing so, it remarks *Star Trek*'s (and its audience's) 'cultural capital' and affirms its own 'superior' status as a modern myth, with privileged access to the 'truth'.

These issues arise around 'Shadows and Symbols', a later episode of *DS9*, which Barrett and Barrett use to introduce 'the post-modern tack'. This double episode focuses on Benjamin Sisko (Avery Brooks), the twenty-fourth-century African-American commander of the space station *DS9*. Under the influence of the local Bajoran prophets/wormhole aliens he is 'lost' in a dream in which he is Benny Russell, a science-fiction writer in 1950s America. Russell invents a character, Benjamin Sisko, commander of *DS9*, and his writing in the past increasingly determines Sisko's actions in the future/present. Subject to disturbing 'visions' and to the oppressions of racism, Russell ends up incarcerated in a mental hospital, where his writing increasingly resembles a television script for *DS9*. Russell's narrative is set against the context of the black Civil Rights movement, and as Barrett and Barrett note, 'the entire story is a mass of quotations' (Barrett and Barrett, 2001: 140). These include numerous references to Dr Martin Luther King's celebrated 1963 'I have a dream' speech with, for instance, Russell/Sisko in both 'worlds' being told 'You are the dreamer and the dream'. In a distinctly postmodern fashion, past, present and future, story, myth and historical events overlap and are confused in this narrative. Yet, as Barrett and Barrett suggest, on one level this episode can be read as an analogy for *Star Trek* itself, as a science-fiction series emerging from out of 1950s America with a 'liberal dream' of racial equality (140–1). As such, Russell/Sisko/Brooks is indeed the 'dreamer and the dream', as an African-American lead character/performer on television, of a type that – as the episode remarks – would have been 'unimaginable' in the 1950s. All of this self-reflexivity may remark *Star Trek*'s status as fiction. However, it might equally be seen as a staking an (actual) historical claim, as a 'prophetic vision' of the future that has always been 'close to the truth' and maybe even played a role in achieving (actual) black civil rights in America?

Subjectivity and identity in *DS9* and *Voyager*

In fact, African Americans like Whoopi Goldberg have attested to the influence of Nichelle Nichols as 'Uhura' in *TOS*, in providing a positive role model at a time when television representations of black subjects were either rare and/or based on grotesque stereotypes.[3] The kiss between this character and the white Captain Kirk in 'Plato's Stepchildren' (1968) was also a television 'first'. Nevertheless, as Bernardi and Roberts indicate, while characters in *Star Trek* constantly assert the sexual and racial equality of their world, the dominant subject position in *TOS* and *TNG* is overwhelmingly 'white', and the construction of 'race' within the mega-text has frequently reiterated dubious stereotypes, especially in terms of its articulation in relation to gender and sexuality. The mega-text also often draws on versions of evolution, and later genetic determinism, of a type that has been used to justify 'scientific' racism. In all these terms the representation of Sisko in *DS9* may demand further examination. For example, as the series progresses Sisko gradually comes to be positioned as a 'cultural hybrid' between the human and Bajoran at its most 'other', via his relationship with their prophets/wormhole aliens. However, in the last episodes of *DS9*, he is revealed to be a *genetic* hybrid of human and wormhole alien, so that what appears to be culture is remarked to have always been 'nature'.

Nevertheless, as Barrett and Barrett assert, there are aspects of *Voyager* and especially *DS9* that could be read as reflecting 'the changing perception of rationalism, of gender and of the meaning of human identity', under the influence of postmodern thought (Barrett and Barrett, 2001: 11). They point out that in both series a postmodern 'rupture of the boundary between the irrational and the rational' is indicated in the embracing of religion and mental illness (157). Yet Peter Linford asserts that there is still a marginalisation of religious truth claims in these series (Linford, 1999: 95). Spirituality is also mostly associated with alien forms of exotic 'otherness'. Nevertheless, mental illness, previously in the mega-text a signifier of the dreaded breakdown of the individual, is embraced as part of human (and nonhuman) experience.

Voyager is also captained by the distinctly postfeminist Kathryn Janeway, and on the level of both casting *and* characters, the core crews of *Voyager* and *DS9* are more mixed in terms of gender and ethnicity than *TOS* and *TNG*. In terms of human characters, evidence of 'cultural hybridity' is also portrayed in relation to Sisko, via African artefacts and neo-African clothing, and through Voyager's Chakotay, who practises traditions related to his Native-American ethnicity. However, McLaren and Porter argue that Chakotay is very much 'an imaginary Indian, a white European representation of a native' (Porter and McLaren, 1999: 101). Robin Roberts also analyses *Voyager*'s hybrid Human Klingon, B'Elanna Torres, as a 'tragic mulatto figure', a stereotype which in racist discourse points to the dangers of 'miscegenation' (Roberts, 1999: 129). Although it has a 'happy ending', Torres's narrative arc is indeed one of a traumatically divided self implicitly measured against an ideal of wholeness and unity of (human) identity, mainly represented by Janeway. Torres's 'problematic' fiery Klingon heritage also echoes stereotypes usually associated with the ethnicity suggested by her human surname.

Barrett and Barrett also explore the holographic Doctor and ex-'Borg' Seven of Nine in *Voyager*, in relation to Donna Haraway's conception of hybridity developed around the metaphor of cyborg subjectivity (Barrett and Barrett, 2001: 119–24). Ultimately, they dismiss Haraway's ideas by rather oversimplifying them (see 132). Nevertheless, they acknowledge that Haraway posits a breakdown of all boundaries between identity categories, including that between human and machine, as part of a radical decentring of the western, enlightenment subject. By contrast, the narrative arc of Seven and The Doctor, as with the android Data in *TNG* and aliens in *DS9* such as 'Quark' and 'Odo', is again a journey towards an ideal of human identity, defined very much in terms of this western enlightenment tradition.

For Barrett and Barrett, *DS9*'s Jadzia and Ezri Dax, who both carry the same 'symbiont' which contains the memories and the personalities of previous hosts, can be read in terms of a postmodern identity as a 'multiplicity of selves' (189). However, how far the Daxes' own personalities or the symbiont itself provide a 'core' identity is unclear, and Barrett and Barrett suggest that these characters are most interesting in terms of demonstrating a certain fluidity of gender and sexuality, since previous hosts are of both genders (189–90). Scenarios around Jadzia such as 'Rejoined', however, operate within a framework that strongly allows for recuperation to heteronormativity (see Barrett and Barrett, 2001: 189). Equally, the only time when Ezri evinces unambiguous 'fluidity of sexuality' is in 'The Emperor's New Cloak' in a dystopian alternative universe.

Otherwise, as has always been the case with the mega-text, in *DS9* and *Voyager* heterosexual sex/gender continues to be, in Judith Butler's terms, 'one of the conditions for life' for both humans and aliens (Butler, 1993: 2). As Richards indicates, throughout *Star Trek* 'no species displaying the traits of gender is ever treated as monstrous', even those whose 'aliveness' might otherwise seem to be in question (Richards, 1997: 44). In all series, the overwhelming majority of alien species have two sexes, human secondary sexual characteristics and similar biological and social patterns of reproduction. This is explained in a *TNG* episode, 'The Chase', in terms of most species sharing the same genetic 'roots'. Yet even on the holodeck, potentially a space for playing with 'multiple identities', the roles taken on by core characters seldom if ever cross or confuse boundaries in terms of gender or sexuality. One exception is the *Voyager* episode 'Renaissance Man', when the holographic doctor crosses these boundaries under duress. When taking on the form of Torres, he signals comic disgust at having to express affection to her partner Tom Paris, thereby affirming his 'natural' heterosexuality, and is eventually shown to be relieved to revert to his normal human, white, masculine appearance. By contrast, it is worth considering how far fluidity and multiplicity of identity are attributes of the main 'threat' in *DS9* – 'the founders', who are shape-shifting self-styled gods. The founders also participate in a collective identity, which as in the case of the Borg, who feature in *TNG* and *Voyager*, is represented in turn as dangerously seductive and a source of weakness.

On the other hand, it is undeniable that, on the level of local episodes, the world views of *Voyager* and *DS9* are more troubled and uncertain than those of earlier series. As the series progresses, that of *DS9* in particular becomes increasingly dystopian and touches on ethical and political questions which appear to challenge some of the foundational assumptions of the mega-text's 'idealised' version of North American culture and identity. It is at this point that *DS9* also demonstrates a higher level of narrative continuity across episodes than is normal in *Star Trek*. As Barrett and Barrett indicate, in the last three seasons, the representation of the war with the founders draws intertextually on some of the bleaker and more disturbing (fictional) images and narratives associated with North American engagement in the (actual) Vietnam war. Season 6 also reveals secrecy and corruption at the heart of Star Fleet. As well as its engagement with religion, a number of *DS9*'s narratives also feature *money*, or other forms of currency exchange. It may be that the setting of this series on a space station, in which the Federation has a tactical and peacekeeping role, means that unlike other series, in *DS9* the long-term consequences of intervening in 'other' cultures cannot be 'left behind', or contained within the enclosed family structure of the ship. As a myth of the global, then, *DS9* *might* be seen as rehearsing some of more concrete and challenging aspects of globalisation.

There is, then, some evidence of a postmodern aesthetic in *Voyager* and *DS9* and of changes in the construction and perception of identity since *TNG* and *TOS*. In *DS9* there may even be some evidence of a questioning of the underpinnings of the mega-text's vision of the utopian global. However, most of these changes can be related to discourses of postfeminism and multiculturalism *within* North American national identity and tend to operate primarily on the level of surface and style. *DS9* is also, famously, the least successful of the *Star Trek* television series and unpopular with its Anglophone fan base. Perhaps not surprisingly, then, in its first season initially broadcast in North America in 2001 (and my analysis below relates almost exclusively to this season), *Enterprise* appears as a return to the mega-text's roots in *TOS* in terms of *both* style and substance.

Enterprise: the past of the future

While still set in the future, *Enterprise* takes place several hundred years before *TOS* and a hundred years *after* events seen in the film *Star Trek: First Contact* (1996). In this latter narrative, members of the *Enterprise* crew travel back to the mid-twenty-first century to meet Zefram Cochrane, inventor of the warp engine, and to witness Earth making 'first contact' with an alien species – the Vulcans. As the character Trip Tucker indicates in the *Enterprise* pilot episode, 'Broken Bow', since then, with the help of the technologically more advanced Vulcans, war, disease and hunger have been eliminated on Earth. However, Vulcans are also resented for placing limits on sharing their knowledge and their political interventions into Earth's affairs. In this world, then, the humans are semi-colonised and some technologies taken for granted by Captain Kirk in *TOS* have either yet to be invented or are new and unsophisticated. This includes the *Enterprise* itself, which is the first Earth ship to be capable of the 'warp' speeds necessary for rapid and sustained deep space travel.

The advantage of this setting for *Star Trek*'s producers is that from *TNG* onwards, even if the space being journeyed through is unknown, the established nature of the conventions that govern the diegetic world and the need to maintain continuity with the mega-text's own history increasingly place limits on narrative possibilities. In returning to its own past, then, like *TOS*, *Star Trek: Enterprise* can be a story of 'first time' exploration and a fresh start for both the fictional world and its creators. As a result of this setting there is less reference to previous series than in *TNG*, *Voyager* and *DS9*. However, 'Broken Bow' does feature Kirk's celebrated 'to boldly go speech' which accompanied the credits in both *TOS* and *TNG*, although it is now attributed to Zefram Cochrane. Mentioned in the opening scene and given in its entirety later, in *Enterprise* it appears in *TNG*'s grammatically correct format as 'to go boldly', but this version's politically correct 'where no *one* has gone before' has been changed back to the *TOS* version, 'where no *man* has gone before'. Partly due to the absence of a holodeck, there is also less direct intertextual citation of other fictions than in *TNG*, *DS9* and *Voyager* and there are no hybrid human/alien or cybernetic characters in the core cast.

This setting in the past/future allows viewers familiar with the mega-text the intertextual pleasure of dramatic irony, playing on their pre-existing knowledge of the fictional future. Yet, paradoxically, within *Enterprise* that future – and the past of its own present – is neither fixed nor linear. This is because the pilot episode establishes an ongoing, occasional plot line of a temporal cold war, organised from the future and waged on numerous fronts. This fictional cold war echoes the way that *TOS* was often interpreted as reflecting the 'actual' cold war between North America and Russia.

In production terms this device explains in advance any anomalies that may emerge between *Enterprise*'s depiction of the past, the already seen future and any references to the past in that future. It may even serve, retrospectively, to explain anomalies between past and present already seen in the future, such as the dramatic changes in the physical characteristics of the Klingon species between *TOS* and later series as revealed by the comic nostalgic *DS9* episode 'Trials and Tribble-ations' (see Barrett and Barrett, 2001). More than ever, then, in *Enterprise*, the *Star Trek* universe is one of possibilities and alternatives in which the outcome of any event is never necessarily final or fatal, since history has been suspended in advance. Further, and again paradoxically, *Enterprise* can be understood as demonstrating continuities with previous series, including *Voyager* and *DS9* with their postmodern influences, exactly *because* it invokes *TOS* itself, in ways that could be understood in terms of postmodern nostalgia.

Enterprise as postmodern nostalgia

Lyotard, who understands the postmodern as the radical and progressive within the modern, perceives nostalgia as an aspect of a *modern* aesthetic and as a compensation for loss of the certainties provided by metanarratives (Lyotard, 1979/1984: 79). Frederic Jameson draws a similar conclusion, except for him nostalgia is key trait of a *postmodern* aesthetic, that is symptomatic of late industrial capitalism. Examining this with reference to cinema, he identifies nostalgia or '*la mode retro*' not just in films set in the past but in those set in the present and the future. For example, he describes *Star Wars* as 'reinventing in the form of pastiche the Saturday afternoon serials of the Buck Rogers type', which he describes as 'one of the most important cultural experiences of the generations growing up between the 1930s and 1950s' (Jameson, 1990: 19). He suggests that, for its adult audience, *Star Wars* satisfies 'a deep longing to return to this older period and re-live its aesthetic artefacts once again' (19). Jameson sees this drive to nostalgia as part of an inability to focus on our own present and as 'an alarming and pathological symptom of a society that has become incapable of dealing with time and history' (20). He relates this to a loss of a referent in the real, 'whereby for whatever particular reason, we seem condemned to seek the historical past through our own pop images and stereotypes about that past, which itself remains forever out of reach' (20). In another articulation of this argument, discussing pop music, Paul Stratton defines this nostalgia as an attempt 'to come to terms with loss of time as a linear fixed entity'. The preoccupation with nostalgia, however, is not simply with a return to the past but, 'simultaneously, reworks that past as self conscious representation' (Stratton, 1989: 54).

As a myth of the global, *Star Trek* could be interpreted as *always* having been fundamentally nostalgic in terms of its reworking of the colonial past, in its approach to history, and as the mega-text has unfolded, time has been increasingly portrayed as nonlinear. However, in *Enterprise*, the return to its own fictional past/future might be seen specifically as nostalgia for the period and aesthetic of *TOS* itself and its confident and optimistic vision of a utopian global future, reflecting the certainties of North America's coming to maturity as world superpower. Both a sense of reworking the past and a 'flexible' sense of time and history is evident in the opening credits, including the theme music. While quotes of music from earlier series are discernible, in contrast to all previous *Star Trek* series, this is a lushly orchestrated ballad, strongly suggestive of a contemporary, if slightly outmoded, North American setting, and the words are in the *present* tense, starting with 'It's been a long time getting from there to here'. This plays under a collage of images denoting some key events from the history of travel by sea, air and space from the seventeenth to the twenty-second century. These initially give the impression of linear temporal progression but actually mix and match different periods and original, re-created and fictional footage. So, for example, the sequence opens with shots of images of Earth first taken in 1968 by Apollo 8. These are followed by star charts dating back to Galileo (1609) and Newton (1666) but then move to the Kon Tikki expedition (1945); an engraving of an eighteenth-century schooner named *Enterprize* [*sic*]; the deck of a late twentieth-century aircraft carrier (possibly another *Enterprise*); period footage (?) of a hot air balloon circa 1900; the *Spirit of St Louis* (1927); the NASA prototype space shuttle named *Enterprise* under pressure from *Star Trek* fans (1976); Amelia Earhart (1937) and so on, skipping between images taken from 1947, 1969, 1905 and 1976 respectively, before segue-ing into those of fictional future space crafts and culminating with this current *Enterprise*. Aside from the (debatable) 'original' South American, prehistoric Kon Tikki expedition, the history repre-sented is strictly North American and North European, and images relating to the Russian contribution to the space race are noticeably absent.

A similar temporal confusion is evident in *Enterprise*'s depiction of its fictional world. Historically, the setting is closer to the (actual) present than that of previous series and aspects of its representation draw directly on contemporary North American culture. This is evident in the crew's off-duty clothing and their quarters, which by comparison to all previous series are closer to those afforded by a contemporary naval vessel. Uniforms, sets and lighting are also rendered in military/industrial blue and grey tones, as opposed to, for instance, the warm pastels of *TNG*. 'Replicated' food, the norm on previous/future ships, is available but most of the crew eat hand-cooked, classic North American dishes served in the canteen and the officers' mess. This crew also read 'real' books and attend an on-board cinema. This seems mainly to show films of the 1940s and 1950s, and there are other elements of this world that, from a contemporary perspective, appear nostalgic. The sets sometimes refer back to science fiction of the 1950s and 1960s, including that of *TOS*. On the *Enterprise*, this is mainly evident in the Buck Rogers style warp engine, with its flashing coloured lights, but it is very noticeable on the alien ship featured in 'Unexpected'. This set is based on primary colours, flashing lights, ovoid architecture and furniture, with vegetation growing on walls inset with aquariums. Especially when shown from the distorted point of view of Trip Tucker trying to acclimatise to the environment, this strongly recalls the sort of 1960s futuristic psychedelia that sometimes influenced the visual style of *TOS*. In fact, the fish-eye lens shots used to indicate Trip's physical and mental state, used again in 'Strange New World' when he is affected by a psychotropic drug, were often used in similar fashion in *TOS* and some *TNG*. Such stylistic quotations sometimes seem like an affectionate parody and sometimes a pastiche of *TOS*, and this applies to other nostalgic aspects of *Enterprise*.

The characters and casting of *Enterprise* also recall these of *TOS* rather than later series, although the characters in *TOS* were actually more 'multicultural', albeit in a horribly stereotyped fashion. The *Enterprise* crew is culturally very North American and all characters are heterosexual, the majority of performers are white and there are only two aliens on board: T'pol (Jolene Blalock), a Vulcan female and the ship's science officer, and Dr Phlox (John Billingsley), a Denoblan. Further, this is very much a 'boy's own adventure story', which like *TOS*, is indeed exploring where no (white, western) *man* has gone before.

The 'human' in *Enterprise*

In fact, the pilot episode begins and ends with scenes of Captain Archer (Scott Bakula) as a boy, building and flying a model starship with his father. Thirty years later, he is grown up but accompanied into space by his dog Porthos, named after a character in Alexander Dumas's *The Three Musketeers* (1844), with whom he holds conservations in his cabin. In musketeer fashion, with his best friend chief engineer Trip (who is played by Connor Trineer as a Tom Sawyerish, down-home country boy) and the British security officer, Malcolm Reed (Dominic Keating), Archer is portrayed as throwing himself into the role of explorer, with a boyish sense of adventure, curiosity and wonder. African-American junior officer Travis Mayweather (Anthony Montgomery) is also *sometimes* part of the gang but gets less screentime than the others.

As this suggests, Archer is the most playful and informal of the *Star Trek* captains so far, and military discipline is only lightly observed on the *Enterprise*. On an early away mission in 'Strange New World', Archer participates in the taking of tourist photographs, and in 'Silent Enemy' is shown drinking beer with Trip and Malcolm in a workspace – actions unthinkable in relation to previous captains. The general atmosphere is one of the crew working out the rules as they go along, with an expectation that any aliens they meet will be as pleased and excited by the encounter as they are, and they are puzzled when they meet with hostility and suspicion. The sense of informality and adventure, the scarcity of 'core' alien characters plus the contemporary aspects of the representational style all seem to invite identification with the crew as the most 'ordinary' or 'human' of the mega-text. However, even within the limitations of how the human has been defined from *TNG* onwards, the *Enterprise* version again seems a return both to its *own* fictional past and to the past of the *actual* present.

The early episodes abound with verbal description and definitions of the human, including 'impulsive', 'provincial', 'optimistic', 'impatient', 'volatile' and 'gregarious' – all of which qualities are demonstrated by *male* characters, most especially Archer and Tripp, but *not* by the Asian-American character of Hoshi Sato (Linda Park), the communications officer. Hoshi is presented as the least experienced of the crew in terms of space travel and military training, and, in stark contrast to attitudes expressed by the male characters, is portrayed as cautious, reluctant, pessimistic and openly fearful, especially of undertaking away missions. In 'Flight or Fight', when they encounter a number of dead aliens, in her own words, she screams 'like a 12-year-old girl'. Later on the bridge when the crew's survival depends on her linguistic skills, she panics, is on the verge of tears and only negotiates this crises through Archer's support. In these and other episodes, Archer is shown putting aside his own boyishness to perform the role of indulgent and protective father, who affirms Hoshi's girlishness even as he urges her towards maturity. Although it should be noted that culturally both Travis and Hoshi are firmly Euro-American, this paternalism may be seen as problematic in relation to Hoshi/Park's Asian-American identity, when considered though Edward Said's critique of the way that western colonialist discourse has constructed Asian women (and men) as passive, hyperfeminised and fragile (Said, 1978).

Subsequent episodes suggest that the story arc for Hoshi in the series as a whole is one of maturation, and the same may be said of *all* characters, a point I shall return to presently. Nevertheless, this representation might be less remarkable, if in this first season that of T'pol did not also seem regressive in terms of gender politics. This is complicated but ultimately supported by her alien status, not least that the definitions of the human cited above mostly arise in opposition to her identity as a Vulcan. In previous series, Vulcans, who are characterised by their dedication to rationality and the suppression of emotion, have usually been represented as ethical and trustworthy. However, in *Enterprise*, their role in the affairs of other planets is remarked as 'colonialist' and their spiritual beliefs are linked to their representation as deceitful, manipulative and patronising, in ways that indicate a return to the evangelical secularism of *TOS* and *TNG* (see 'The Andorran Incident').

At the start of the series, then, relations between T'pol and the *Enterprise* crew are antagonistic. As the series progresses she becomes integrated into the work family and, as with many previous *Star Trek* 'alien' characters, undergoes a process of humanisation. In many ways, this character recalls Seven of Nine, notoriously introduced into *Voyager* to boost viewing figures amongst young men. Not being part of Star Fleet, instead of a uniform both characters wear skin-tight body suits that reveal their impressively sculpted figures. Yet, whereas Jeri Ryan played (blonde) Seven as cool and logical, Blalock plays the supposedly logical (brunette) T'pol as sultry and sulky, and seems far more of a sexual object.

This is established from the pilot episode, when T'pol and Trip are shown in their underwear in a decontamination chamber, rubbing gel into their own and each other's bodies. The lighting is soft focus and while they engage in an argument, the camera focuses on parts of T'pol's body as she rubs the ointment on to herself with sensuous gestures. Overall the scene suggests a classic romance narrative, where the 'tension' between these characters might signal attraction. T'pol is also remarked as an object of desire for Malcolm in 'Shuttlepod One' and Ferengi pirates in 'Acquisition', where she also flirts with Archer. In 'Fusion' she is exploited by a male Vulcan, who encourages her to experiment with emotion – expressed as sexual desire. In 'Shadows of P'Jem' she and Archer are captured and tied together, and the action makes much of their enforced physical intimacy as they struggle to escape, with T'pol's breasts 'comically' landing in Archer's face. In these terms *Enterprise* seems a return to the sexual politics of *TOS*, where the primary function of female aliens was often as exotic objects of desire. This tone is also set in the pilot episode of *Enterprise* where, for instance, Malcolm and Trip are shown transfixed by the spectacle of alien female dancers in revealing costumes, gyrating and catching butterflies with their lizardlike tongues.

Diegetically, this objectification of alien 'otherness' may be explained by the fact that aliens are portrayed from the perspective of the human crew, who are encountering them for the first time. As such, there is an effort to render 'strange' 'familiar' species like the Vulcans and the Klingons, and emphasis is placed on failures of understanding through cultural difference. Yet in the incidences of sexual objectification cited above, the camera very much supports this 'male gaze' in a similar fashion to that famously described by Laura Mulvey (1976).

Interestingly, Malcolm's *national* difference is also sometimes remarked, most notably in 'Shuttlepod One', when Malcolm and Trip are trapped in a damaged shuttlepod and believe the *Enterprise* has been destroyed. Aspects of this narrative, such as Malcolm's endless dictating of letters of farewell to his family and friends, suggest a parody of another classic 'boy's own adventure' – that of the (questionably) heroic British failure, Scott of the Antarctic. Malcolm also displays a pessimism and passivity that contrasts with

Trip's optimism, inventiveness and determination to survive. In one scene, Malcolm is reading James Joyce's *Ulysses* and he suggests that if Zefram Cochrane had been European, the Vulcans might have been less reluctant to help humanity, since he says Cochrane (like Trip), probably spent his nights reading about 'cowboys and Indians'. Trip replies, 'Well I don't recall any Europeans figuring out how to build no warp engine, no Brits, no Italians, no Serbo-Croats'. In this enactment of 'old' and 'new' world rivalry, however comic the register, rarely for *Star Trek*, European 'high culture' is opposed to and deemed 'inferior' to North American popular culture and technological inventiveness.

A narrative of maturation: genetic determinism

In 'Dear Doctor', Dr Phlox remarks on the sexual exoticisation of aliens as a sign of the human's 'emotional immaturity'. The same may be implied in Trip's assertion of national identity in 'Shuttlepod One', except his position is validated by the narrative, since their survival depends mainly on Trip's positive 'can do' attitude. In 'Broken Bow', T'pol remarks that it 'remains to be seen whether humanity will revert to its baser instincts', and Archer replies, 'human instinct is pretty strong, you can't expect us to change overnight'. Indeed, the humans are shown to be in the grip of instincts, such as fight or flight, sexual desire, rivalry, etc. This suggests that the first season of *Enterprise* is setting the scene for a narrative of human 'evolution' towards the mega-text's more 'enlightened' future/past. As such, putting aside the sexual objectification of T'pol, Archer's developing relationship with her might suggest a narrative in which they *both* move towards a more 'adult' balance of rationality and emotion. Actually, in later seasons T'pol simply becomes increasingly and often excessively emotional. This aside, however, if in season 1 T'pol is shown to question the behaviour of her own species as colonialists and Archer begins to admit to the cultural and 'political' problems that often arise from the human crew's impulsive actions, he *also* begins to develop an understanding of the Vulcan position in relation to 'less advanced' or 'primitive' cultures.

This is explicitly stated in 'Dear Doctor', which is narrated from the Doctor's point of view, as he considers the theme of 'human compassion'. In this episode, the crew make contact with a planet inhabited by two similar but distinct humanoid species, the more sophisticated Valakians and the Menk, who function as a docile, well cared for servant class. The Valakians are seeking a cure for a disease which is decimating their population but from which the Menk are immune. While slightly concerned about the unequal power relationship between the two species, the *Enterprise* crew devote their resources to finding a cure for the disease. Phlox rapidly discovers that this is a genetic illness, which will render the Valakians extinct in two hundred years. He does find a cure but in studying the Menk's genome, he also discovers that they are evolving and, in a millennium, they might become the dominant species. He urges Archer to withhold the cure on the basis that compassion for the Valakians must not take precedence over ethical and scientific concerns, asserting that they must 'let nature make the choice'. Reluctantly, Archer agrees, also refusing to give the Valakians the warp drive technology which might enable them to seek help from other 'advanced' species. This is because the only safe way they could develop it would be if the *Enterprise* crew remained to supervise, putting themselves in the same position as the Vulcans on Earth, forced into a colonialist position for the 'good' of the colonised. A troubled Archer looks forward to a future when a principle (clearly the yet to be founded Federation's 'Prime Directive') will have been developed as guidance in such dilemmas.

As Richards puts it, since it is based on strict non-intervention, 'Almost any action taken by Star Fleet from tentative exploration to outright colonisation, is by definition a violation of the Prime Directive' (Richards, 1997: 14). In making contact with the Valakians at all and giving them *any* help, the *Enterprise* crew has already 'interfered' with nature. More importantly, there are many assumptions and assertions in this episode that are ethically and scientifically questionable. It is not clear how the Menk are *essentially* less evolved than the Valakians, any more than it is clear how the Valakians are *essentially* less advanced than the humans, except that, as always, this is signified by the invention of the warp engine, presumably understood as a 'natural' stage of evolution. Equally, it is not clear why, in this instance, the 'evolution' of one species should necessitate the extinction of another, except that it is described as 'unusual' for two humanoid species to co-exist on one planet. What actually appears to be at stake is the potential to develop a particular model of social organisation based on specific uses of technology, something that could not be divined from a species genome. In fact, this episode depends on a genetic determinism or genetic essentialism, a discourse which Haraway points out has gained strength in the popular (mis)understanding of the human genome project, in which the genome is seen as 'a master molecule equating [human] beings, in all their social, historical and moral complexity with their genes' (Haraway, 1997: 148).

Doctor Phlox states, 'evolution is more than a theory, it is a fundamental scientific principle'. Even accepting this, the *particular* narrative of evolution favoured in this episode (as elsewhere in the mega-text), with its 'scientific' appeal to nature from a position within a culture that is assumed to be the model for advanced societies, is one that since the enlightenment has been used to provide a pseudoscientific basis for racism and colonialism. Taken as part of a story of progress towards a utopian global future, 'Dear Doctor' could be read as an argument on one hand for 'natural selection' that denies the responsibility of so-called 'developed' nations of the world for providing aid to 'less developed states', and on the other, for colonisation to ensure they develop according to the 'proper' cultural model.

Conclusion

I fear I begin to sound like a 'Trekkie', albeit from one of the mega-text's alternative, dystopian universes. *Enterprise* is, after all, only a popular television show, not a political or scientific treatise. Perhaps my analysis only demonstrates the dangers and the seductiveness of reading too much 'into' single episodes and of taking *Star Trek* representations as metaphors for real peoples and historical events.

After the ambivalences of *DS9*, *Enterprise*'s theme of (temporal) cold war, and its reassertion of a very traditional version of North American cultural identity, might, retrospectively, seem 'prophetic' in relation to subsequent 'real world' events.[4] However, it would be wrong to assume that, because it is an idealised version of North America projected into the future, *Star Trek* might be 'close to the truth', even in terms of representing the beliefs and attitudes of any significant element of this nation's population. In any case, as a popular science-fiction fantasy which depends heavily on various modes of intertextuality *and* is part of a mega-text, *Enterprise* has a certain openness to interpretation. This means that evidence can always be found on the level of the local and the specific to support a number of conflicting and contradictory arguments. However, this openness is always ultimately recuperated to normalise and natur- alise a cultural perspective and set of values. Perhaps how far and in what ways *Enterprise* or any other *Star Trek* product may dis- seminate 'cultural imperialism' and function as a resource for 'new global identities' is open to debate. Yet it cannot be denied that as part of a franchise under the control of Paramount/Viacom, this fiction is very much 'inside' and part of western capitalist processes of globalisation. It is worrying, then, that even from a Euro- American perspective, let alone a global one, *Enterprise* seems a very conservative and inward-looking articulation of the *Star Trek* mythos.[5]

However, in the end I am less concerned with critiquing *Enterprise* or the *Star Trek* mega-text than extending Barnor Hesse's project of indicating the parallels between this set of fictions and other, apparently more 'serious' and 'credible' western narrativisa- tions of the global. To paraphrase Massey, I am concerned with how far these 'visions' might function not so much 'as descriptions of how the world is, but as images in which the world is being made' (Massey, 1999: 36). Amongst other things, I am concerned to indicate how even, and perhaps especially, the most 'postmodern' of these can easily slip from apparently questioning to actually endors- ing the historical values and attitudes of western modernity, '*from* identifying dominance and oppression to always finding a means of redemption' (Morris, 1990: 25, original italics). This occurs, in part, because for good or ill they often work 'within' an implicit meta- narrative of inevitable global dominance of certain modes of western capitalist organisation. As a result, they can induce a sense of loss of agency, a powerlessness to imagine other possibilities for thinking about the global future that might allow for more just and effective ways of negotiating with global diversity and difference. Like *Star Trek*'s style of liberal humanism, the values informing such accounts may 'have much good in them' and 'on any scale of real political evil would come fairly low down the list' (Barrett and Barrett, 2001: 9). However, like this liberal humanism, they are easily appropriated to support and enable other far more reac- tionary and apocalyptic metanaratives of the global, which in their certainty of being close to the truth, offer the greatest threat to the global future.

Notes

1 Some accounts of globalisation now refer to the 'North' and 'South', rather than the 'West', because these terms are seen as more accurate in terms of economic and political divisions and less culturally inflected. However, I have continued to use west and western throughout this book because so many of the works cited still do so.

2 Both Buck Rogers and Flash Gordon were originally created as comic-strip characters in the 1920s. Both have been subject to numerous film adaptations dating from the 1930s onwards and both have also been adapted for television. Flash Gordon is also said to have 'inspired' George Lucas's *Star Wars* films (1977–2005).

3 See, for instance, the entry for Goldberg in www.nndb.com.

4 The final episode of season 2 and the whole of season 3 of *Enterprise* were unquestionably a direct response to the events of 9/11 and very much reflected attitudes expressed within most 'mainstream' North American institutions. In the *Enterprise* narrative, an attack on Earth by a coalition of related species (the Xindi) causes the death of millions and sends *Enterprise* on a mission to discover the identity and location of the attackers and to prevent the creation of an even more devastating 'weapon of mass destruction'. While this narrative has a happy(ish) ending and leads to the founding of the Federation, the optimism and playfulness of season one has entirely vanished. Archer and his crew also engage in ethically dubious behaviour that is beyond the norms of the mega-text's traditional values. While concerns over this behaviour are rehearsed in the diegesis, ultimately they are overruled by the importance of the mission, through reference to Earth's murdered dead.

5 In 2005 Paramount/Viacom announced the end of *Enterprise* after four seasons, with no future plans for either further *Star Trek* television series or films. For many this signals an 'end of an era' and this decision itself is open to a variety of interpretations.

Only human nature after all? Romantic attractions and queer dilemmas (*Queer as Folk*)

As I noted in the introduction, in 1998 Michael Jackson, the controller of Channel 4, used *Queer as Folk* (1998) to imply a narrative of progress in that channel's representation of 'minority groups'. A similar narrative of progress, specifically in relation to gay and lesbian subjects, is also suggested by the article which appears on the pages of the BBC website devoted to *Tipping the Velvet* (2002), a historical drama focused around a lesbian character and based on the novel of the same name by Sarah Waters (BBC, 2003). Summarising the history of the representation of gay men and lesbians on (mainly) British and American television since the 1970s, the piece ends on a hopeful note in regard to the more 'enlightened approach to sexuality' on our screens in the last decade. This optimism would appear to be justified by the rising numbers of lesbian and gay characters across a wide range of popular television drama productions, to the extent that *The Genre Book* includes a subsection entitled 'Gay and Queer Sitcom' (Feuer, 2001: 70–1).

Yet the *Tipping the Velvet* article also indicates that Andrew Davis, who adapted the novel for television, had to defend the 'lesbian sexual content' ahead of the drama's broadcast and that *Queer as Folk* produced a 'storm of controversy' (BBC, 2003). This storm gathered, partly, because the first episode contained scenes showing sexual intercourse between a 15-year-old boy and a 29-year-old man. This was screened while a bill seeking an amendment to the Sexual Offences Act to lower the age of consent for homosexual sex from 18 to 16 years old was being debated in parliament. The fact that, despite resistance from the House of Lords, this bill was eventually forced through by the House of Commons in 2000, becoming law in 2001, and was followed later by the repeal of the notorious 'Section 28' of the Sexual Offences Act (2003), can in itself be seen as a sign of progress in attitudes to sexuality.[1] Nevertheless, its timing rendered *Queer as Folk* especially controversial amongst a number of groups, including members of the lesbian and gay community. Even without this specific issue, as one of Britain's 'first' gay drama series on broadcast television, it was inevitable that this drama would carry an especially heavy burden of representation.

Before considering this series in detail, however, I want to explore how the the use of the term 'queer' in the title may, in itself, be a signal for controversy within the lesbian and gay community, with some reference to the representation of gays and lesbians in other television dramas.

Defining queer

The difficulty with the concept of queer is that if, within the academy, it is frequently associated with Judith Butler's work on the performativity of gender, in terms of its usage both inside and outside that sphere it can itself be described as 'performative', in the sense outlined by J. L. Austin (see Butler, 1993: 13). By this I mean that the term queer tends to enact and produce that of which it speaks and is generally understood to speak of confrontation and resistance, including, crucially, resistance to single or stable definition. To put it simply, there is a proliferation of sometimes opposing and contradictory meanings for this term, so that, to continue to cite Butler, while it may be considered a 'subversive repetition' of a derogatory term that opens up an identity category as a site of contestation, there is no guarantee that it always signifies in a progressive fashion for everyone, whatever their sexuality (see Butler, 1990: 146 and 1993: 220–3).

Queer in the public sphere

Indeed, for Stephen Farrier in his essay on 'queering soap opera', to start by defining queer as performative and thereby locating it within academic discourse might be seen as contributing to the process whereby it is distanced from the 'public arena' and loses its 'radical edge', becoming present 'only as high theory' (Farrier, 2000: 90).

While Farrier does go on to offer examples of definitions from the academic sphere, he commences his exposition of the concept by quoting a flier distributed in a Manchester club in 1991. This document asserts that queer is not about who, how, when or if you have sex with, but rather:

> What you fuck
> Fuck boundaries
> Fuck gender
> Fuck the lesbian and gay community
> Fuck labels

Farrier offers this as an early definition of queer on this side of the Atlantic that affirms it status as 'a rambunctious radical idea in the public arena' (90). Yet, if queer 'fucks' boundaries, this might be said to include the boundary between the public arena and high theory. In fact, it is almost impossible to explore the implications of this quote without reference to academic discourse.

The concept of 'queer' is said to have emerged from US-based activist groups such as ACT-UP (the AIDS Coalition to Unleash Power), founded in the late 1980s, and Queer Nation, founded in 1990. However, discussing ACT-UP, Tim Edwards asserts that:

> Its ideas are not only premised on the identity and community politics of the 1970s, it also supplements these with a more academic post-structuralist emphasis upon representation and meaning, and places a centrality on the plurality of identity that comes from the work of Foucault, Lacan and Derrida, as well as a whole host of other postmodernists and poststructuralists. (Edwards, 1994: 134)

This suggests a permeability of theory and practice around the notion of queer from the start, although ACT-UP was primarily a militant, direct action group. Its activities included public acts of civil disobedience and demonstrations undertaken in a deliberately confrontational, flamboyant 'camp' aesthetic. Part of the intention was to combat representations in the media and elsewhere, which reflected and consolidated the homophobia and other modes of prejudice that characterised the treatment of many people with HIV/AIDS medically, socially and on the level of government. One slogan of this movement was 'everywhere and in your face', and this work was carried out across various arenas, including academic publications.

ACT-UP's status as a *coalition* also suggests the unification of diverse groups around a common cause. The term queer, then, signified a self-conscious, political identification that acknowledged and embraced differing identities in the gay and lesbian community but could also extend to groups at risk from HIV/AIDS who might suffer discrimination by dint of ethnicity, economic status, class or gender, as well as/and/or sexual orientation (Edwards, 1994: 150). Therefore, Farrier argues that queer has grown from 'notions of gayness' but has changed to 'include all of those people who are marginalised in some way, and can even encompass those people who call themselves straight' (Farrier, 2000: 92). Yet Farrier conditions all those marginalised through the subclause 'those whose sexuality doesn't work within the gender imperative' (92). How far queer *always* encompasses those marginalised by dint of factors other than/as well as gender and sexuality is open to question.

Queer is also sometimes perceived as generational, signifying younger gays' and lesbians' rejection of the strategies both of assimilationist, conservative sectors of the community and of the more radical 1970s liberation movement. For some, queer stands in a similar relation to gay and lesbian liberation as postfeminism does to feminism. In fact, there has always been significant crossover between these movements, although adherence to 'old' feminism was sometimes a point of division. Like some feminism(s), gay and lesbian liberation was committed to challenging marriage, the family and gender roles, and like some feminism(s) was, according to Mary McIntosh, 'traditionally and intrinsically anti-capitalist' (McIntosh, 1997: 234). Like feminism, gay and lesbian liberation is often characterised as overly politically correct, puritanical, repressive and as being based on a white, middle-class definition of homosexuality. As both McIntosh and Medhurst indicate, this was evinced in an ambivalence towards, if not outright disapproval of, certain types of sexual practices and identifications, such as lesbian butch/fem play, gay, camp queening and sadomasochism, all of which were thought to replicate the unequal power relations within normative gender roles (see McIntosh, 1997: 244 and Medhurst, 1997: 278).

By contrast, in principle, queer is an inclusive term embracing people who are bisexual, transgendered, transvestites, butches, fems, queens of all types and so on. Yet in practice, despite insisting that queer is not synonymous with gay, Farrier suggests that, as a grassroots definition, queer has sometimes become a 'label', having been 'turned from a political slant to a type of queer (the politico queen) that fits into other types (the clone, the acid queen, the ice queen). In effect, queer at this level has become hegemonised by the dominant gay identity and all that goes along with being a "real gay" ' (Farrier, 2000: 91).

Based on Farrier's examples, this identity may disturb gender distinctions but appears to do so primarily in relation to gay men. How far, even within this category, it embraces differences of 'race', age and class is open to debate. For instance, writing in 1995, Lawrence Knopp commented:

> The largely urban based, predominantly white, and male dominated gay social and political movements [. . .] have taken their own alternative coding of space out of the closet and into the public sphere, but usually within racist, sexist and pro-capitalist discourses. (quoted in Taylor, 1997: 11–12)

Further, while Simon Watney decries the 'old self styled Marxists' for their puritan dislike of the thriving, commercial gay scene of the 1990s, for some, this scene signals the translation of the aesthetics of ACT-UP into a emphasis on (life) style over political substance (see Watney, 1997: 373). As such, Farrier quotes Chris Woods' assertion that 'queer can constitute a process of identification by commodification' (quoted in Farrier, 2000: 91).

As with postfeminism, in the early 1990s Madonna was frequently an iconic figure in both academic and popular queer commentaries and cited as disturbing polarities of gender *and* sexuality. For others, her quoting of gay and lesbian subcultural practices in her videos and her performance of bisexuality constituted a mode of 'sexual tourism' and an appropriation of queer as a 'spectacle for mainstream consumption' (Andermahr, 1994: 38–9). As Ruth Goldman also points out, in the video of *This is not a Love Song*, which includes butch/fem play, the fems are Asian and portrayed in a manner that could reinforce the same colonialist discourse I discussed in relation to the character of Hoshi in *Enterprise* (Goldman, 1996: 175). This might suggest that it is not only in the academic arena that queer can lose its radical edge, and McIntosh seems to imply that in fact it is in the *public realm* that 'Queer theory too has taken on bourgeois clothing, with its focus on consumption rather than production, style rather than content' (McIntosh, 1997: 245).

Theoretically queer

Yet this view runs counter to those expressed by many academics contributing to anthologies of queer and/or lesbian, gay, bisexual and transgender studies. Most use the term queer in lower case, either alongside gay and lesbian, or to displace them altogether. However, many also use Queer in upper case when referring to theory and agree with Farrier's assessment of its deradicalisation within the academy.

Criticisms levelled at academic Queer theory echo those directed against postmodern feminism, with which it shares a number of theorists and methodologies. Medhurst cites Donald Morton's argument in *The Material Queer* that 'dominant parameters of Lesbian and Gay Studies have become so enveloped in poststructuralist abstractions that they have ceased to maintain any connection with political commitment' (Medhurst, 1997: 288–9). In the late 1990s, Simon Watney also argued that Queer theory had created a generation of queer scholars with no interest in or knowledge of issues relating to HIV/AIDS, 'except as seen though the binoculars of arcane literary theory' (Watney, 1997: 369). As Medhurst and Munt note, then, 'in spite of its originally inclusive agenda, Queer theory has come to be associated with elitism and has manifested its own exclusions, becoming a minority discourse institutionalised within academic and performance/art contexts' (Medhurst and Munt, 1997: xi).

The genealogy of Queer theory is usually traced back to Foucault's *History of Sexuality* (1979) and Derrida's work on deconstruction, deployed in relation to Freudian and Lacanian psychoanalytical theory, and developed by thinkers such as Teresa de Lauretis, Eve Kosofsky Sedgwick and Leo Bersani. However, Queer theory at some point is nearly always linked to Judith Butler's work on gender performativity. As such, clearly referencing Butler, Moe Meyer states: 'What "queer" signals is an ontological challenge that displaces bourgeois notions of the Self as unique, abiding, and continuous, while substituting instead a concept of Self as performative, improvisational, discontinuous, and processually constituted by repetitive and stylised acts' (Meyer, 1994: 2–3). In theory, then, Queer signifies a rigorous anti-essentialism and the deconstruction of the sex/gender system and therefore the notion of sexuality as an expression of the 'truth' of identity. These concepts are posited as historical 'regulatory fictions', which function to naturalise and normalise a social structure based on patriarchal heterosexuality. In this context, Queer signals a refusal of the term homosexuality, historically defined as the inferior, excluded other to heterosexuality, and of the perception of *both* terms as denoting single, stable categories. Similarly, 'gay' and 'lesbian' are rejected as reiterating gender categories, and the concept of a community set up in opposition to the straight world simply reaffirms the heterosexual/homosexual binary. While Queer may represent a reversal and a reclamation of a derogatory term, then, it looks forward to a 'third stage' of deconstruction, or as Halprin puts it, it refers to an 'identity in a state of becoming, rather than as a referent for an existing form of life' (quoted in Farrier, 2000: 91). As such, it is less an inclusive term than one which seeks to exploit weaknesses in the signifying system(s), whereby the process of defining or describing a norm always produces a proliferation of categories apparently outside the norm on which it is actually fundamentally dependent for its meaning. Further, since in order for a norm to be established it must be repeated, and a repetition cannot be the thing itself, this produces further differences within the norm. As Butler argues, the process of reiteration produces the possibility, indeed the inevitability, of unfaithful or subversive repetitions. This at once reveals the norm to be a shifting social and historical construct rather than fixed, stable and natural, and creates the possibility of confusion between the norm and its foundational, internal exclusions (Butler, 1990 and 1993).

This mode of thinking is not exclusive to Butler or Queer theory, but as noted in Chapter 2, Butler's particular contribution is her bringing together of various strands of thought, so as to argue that there is no access to biological sex, except through gender, and that gender can be understood as 'performative' (see Chapter 2). Further, as already indicated, when Butler gives examples of the ways in which sex/gender is open to 'subversive repetition', she starts with a discussion of gay and lesbian crossdressing and drag and other strategies which use a 'camp aesthetic', based on exaggeration, irony, parody and pastiche, and makes direct reference to ACT-UP (see Butler, 1990: 136–9 and 1993: 232–3).

While there may be problems and limitations with Butler's own writings, much of the criticism of Queer theory is directed at those who took up the ideas in *Gender Trouble* with more enthusiasm than intellectual rigour. Indeed, her later book *Bodies that Matter* was partly a response to those who took the concept of gender as performative to suggest that it could be equated with performance and be put on or taken off in a 'single act' (Butler, 1993: 12 and 232–4). Equally, Butler never suggested that drag and crossdressing, or any other use of parody, irony and pastiche, whether in the context of queer subculture or elsewhere, were always and 'inherently' subversive (see Butler, 1990: 139). Indeed, as so many have pointed out, such repetitions can easily signify in ways that support misogyny and/or homophobia. Yet certain modalities of Queer theory and postmodern feminism do sometimes seem to imply that the sex/gender system has been (performatively) abolished by such analyses, ushering in a 'post identity' era, so that there is 'no longer any hierarchy for the disenfranchised to undermine' (Medhurst, 1997: 283). In short, as Medhurst asserts, some Queer theorists appear to have 'lost sight of the everyday contexts in which gender is experienced', ignoring the fact that 'Sexual inequality did not evaporate simply because an elite phalanx of academics decided identity was passé. Gender polarities may be considerably less fixed than they once were [. . .] but gender hierarchies still persist' (283).

This is perhaps why in *both* the public and academic arenas, according to Medhurst and Munt, 'Queer is not claimed by the majority of Lesbian and Gay men', many of whom continue to identify with these categories as possible sites of resistance, a basis for collective political activism and indeed for a sense of community (Medhurst and Munt, 1997: xi). Queer theory can also operate to privilege sex/gender hierarchies at the expense of those relating to ethnicity, class and age or national cultural identities. As Medhurst (1997), Goldman (1996) and Vivian Ng (1997) indicate, this can make it problematic for instance in relation to racism, from which the gay and lesbian community is no more immune than any other sector of white-dominated, western culture. This issue emerged strongly in the early 1990s in debates around the images of African-American men produced by white, queer photographer Robert Mapplethorpe. Referring to this debate, Ng discusses Kobena Mercer's recanting of his earlier position on these images as perpetuating 'racial fetishism', and his subsequent argument that it was possible to read them, 'not as a repetition of racist fantasies but as a deconstructive strategy that lays bare psychic and social relations of ambivalence in the representation of race and sexuality' (quoted in Ng, 1997: 227). Ng was not convinced, stating that, 'when exposure to Queer Theory can lead to a dramatic re-vision of Mapplethorpe's racist photographs, I fear there is little room for anti-sexist, anti-racist work in the queer academy' (229). As Goldman indicates, paradoxically, there can be a 'homogenising tendency in Queer theory' (Goldman, 1996: 172). This may be connected to its relationship to postmodernism, and especially the relationship between 'camp' and postmodern aesthetics.

The camp aesthetic and postmodernism

Speaking in the early 1990s, Joseph Arroyo states that queer films could be seen as a 'prime example of postmodern aesthetics' (Arroyo, 1997: 79). Similarly, Medhurst notes, 'the camp aesthetic can easily be confused with a postmodern one', acknowledging that in the earlier 1990s he himself had publicly (and, he says, camply) declared that 'postmodernism is only heterosexuals catching up with camp' (Medhurst, 1997: 290). In 1997, however, he makes the distinction that, while camp grows from a specific subcultural identity, 'postmodern discourse peddles the arrogant fiction that specific cultural identities have ceased to exist' (290). Equally, Arroyo distinguishes the 'new Queer Cinema' from a general postmodern one, on the basis that the former was closely related to 'AIDS as a socio-political and discursive context' (79).

Both Medhurst and Arroyo, then, primarily make distinctions between camp and postmodern aesthetics through subcultural history and sociopolitical discursive context. Yet, at times, Medhurst seems to come close, as others have done, to claiming a camp aesthetic as *essentially* related to a *male* gay sensibility, which has been appropriated and commodified by mainstream culture. This approach is evident in Moe Meyer's work on camp, which embraces historical as well as recent examples of a camp aesthetic. He claims *all* of these examples as queer through reference to Butlerian notions of gender performativity and goes on to state that 'there is only one kind of camp and it's queer', arguing that 'the unqueer do not have access to the discourse of Camp, only to derivatives constructed through the acts of appropriation' (Meyer, 1994: 1). The difficulty arises that while it may be possible to identify some precise instances of 'unqueer appropriation' of gay and lesbian subcultural practices, as noted above, one of the fundamental propositions of Queer theory is that, as a discursive production, homosexuality is not *outside* of heterosexuality but functions as a foundational *internal* exclusion. One of the projects of gay and lesbian studies has been to chart the history of queer interventions *within* the heterosexual mainstream, and it is this 'working within' that is the presumed basis of a camp aesthetic's power to reveal heteronormativity as a construct. Moreover, even within Meyer's own work, this aesthetic is championed as breaking down boundaries and confusing distinctions between the heterosexual norm and its supposed homosexual imitation or derivative. As such, the very concept of queer puts into question the idea of an aesthetic entirely distinct from a heterosexual 'derivative'. Hence, in fact, a confusion between a generalised postmodern aesthetic and a camp one could be seen as evidence of successful queer subversion and resistance.

Defined *against* 'straight', queer reaffirms the identity categories of homosexual and heterosexual as 'essential'. However, as simply part of a general postmodern subjectivity, queer can undergo a process of reversal and substitution in which, in the words of the song that accompanied the end credits of *Tipping the Velvet*, it turn out to be 'only human nature' after all. As Judith Roof argues:

> Queer may well permit thinking beyond modernist categories, but because it is appended to these categories in their performative dislocation, it sometimes has a tendency to come full circle, not enabling a wholesale rejection of sex/gender categories, but in finally enfranchising even heterosexuality as queer. While this might come as, in some ways, a desirable result, it also represents a levelling of queerness and its return to the status quo. (Roof, 1997: 180)

In short, divorced from, as Medhurst puts it, 'the historical, palpable raw material of gay men's cultural experiences' (or lesbian, or queer, cultural experiences) and defined in abstract terms, camp becomes *purely* a matter of style (Medhurst, 1997: 290). In these terms, a camp or queer aesthetic can easily become 'one of the chic trademarks of a broadening sex/gender market [. . .] within the larger logic of global capital' (Roof, 1997: 181). In short, like postmodern feminism, or notions of diasporic cultural hybridity, it can easily either fall into pure relativism, or by means of a reversal and substitution take on the status of a 'new' universal truth of all identity. In this instance, a camp aesthetic simply functions as a new mode of realism, even while it supposedly retains a radical edge by its association with marginalised identity categories.

Television, queer reading and the camp aesthetic:
from *Star Trek* to *Tipping the Velvet* via *Buffy*

These same problems and contradictions occur around the notion of 'queer reading' of texts. While taken up as a concept in the academic sphere in the late 1980s and early 1990s, and involving the reading of texts through Queer theory, this form of 'resistant reading' is actually an established lesbian and gay subcultural practice, which predates *both* the reclamation of queer *and* the popularisation of the notion of resistant reading in the postmodern academy.

As with other marginalised groups, historically, representations of queer characters in popular, dramatic fiction have been strictly limited. Like those of black subjects, when these do occur they have tended towards stereotypes of (usually) gay male characters and male to female transvestites as hopeless figures of fun, or both gay men and lesbians as, at worst, corrupt and evil and at best, doomed and self-loathing. Moreover, as Doty notes, even when 'positive' or complex representations do occur, queer characters have almost always been 'narratively positioned as secondary to, or on the margins of, some more centrally important heterosexual plot' (Doty and Gove, 1997: 88).

As a result, queer reading does not depend on the presence of overtly queer characters, hence *The Genre Handbook* includes both *Absolutely Fabulous* (1992–) and *Frasier* (1993–2004) under the category of 'queer sitcom' (see Feuer, 2001: 71). Texts can be queered by reading for signs of lesbian and/or gay desire or subcultural coding in the production and performances, based on extratextual knowledge of the sexual orientation of those involved. This is not necessarily a matter of 'authorial intention' or 'essential' sexual identity, since such readings can be based on the *rumoured* rather than the *known* sexuality of those involved. More importantly, such reading can occur around any text and involve the queering of any fictional narrative, character or actor's performance, based on a *perceived* sexual ambiguity, often related to camp exaggeration or theatrical excess. This is the basis for the queer reading of the character of Frasier and his brother Niles, although within the diegesis, any ambiguity in the representation of their masculinity may be accounted for in terms of snobbery and class aspirations. Something similar holds true for *Absolutely Fabulous*, although this text's 'campness' is largely a matter of its joyous transgression of the social norms for middle-aged femininity. As these examples indicate, queering has historically embraced (apparently) heterosexual characters from dramas as diverse as *The Avengers* (1961–69), *Coronation Street* (1960–), *Dallas* (1979–91), *Dynasty* (1981–89) and *Xena: Warrior Princess* (1995–2001). *Star Trek* probably offers the best-documented example, initially starting with *TOS* with fans creating and disseminating 'slash fiction' fantasies, in which Spock and Kirk engage in often sadomasochistic, homosexual relations, but this practice continues around both male and female characters in more recent *Star Trek* series (see Penley, 1997). It may be significant that, like *Xena: Warrior Princess* and *The Avengers*, *Star Trek* is already marked generically as 'fantasy', although as noted in the last chapter, this does not prevent it from being interpreted as conveying 'universal human truths'. However, a queer reading can potentially be performed around any genre, where two characters of the same sex, who are not (usually) closely related, are portrayed in terms of a loving bond or a tension between them. Borrowing from conventional romance plots, in this framework even apparent antagonism can be read as a sign of repressed desire, since, according to Farah Mendlesohn, within such narratives, 'only where there is tension can there be real love' (Mendlesohn, 2002: 45).

Interestingly, the problematic of the burden of representation can create a *preference* for appropriating apparently straight characters and narratives, rather than identifying with overtly queer ones. As both Whatling and Doty point out, this is partly because what may be a positive or negative representation at any given time is complicated by the fact that, as queer theory indicates, the categories homosexual or gay and lesbian are not homogenous groups, so that what may be positive for some, may for others may be, in Doty's words, 'bland, saintly, desexualised, mainstream figures who might as well be heterosexual' (Doty and Gove, 1997: 87). Discussing 'fantasising lesbians in film', Whatling also asserts that, due to their scarcity, overt representations of lesbians may carry a raft of social and political anxieties for a lesbian spectator. By contrast, the 'covert representation of lesbianism, as for example platonic friendship, at least allows us to make what we want of them' (Whatling, 1997: 89).

This is evident in Farah Mendlesohn's reading of *Buffy the Vampire Slayer* (1997–2003), in which she critiques the overt lesbian relationship of Willow and Tara as 'neutralising', arguing: 'On one hand this is lesbianism for the male gaze, and on the other, there is a clear sense that the producers were trying to avoid this route, but its very openness and innocence desexualises and removes the erotic tension crucial to a queer reading of the text' (Mendlesohn, 2002: 58). Instead, Mendlesohn prefers to focus on the platonic relationship between Willow and Buffy, identifying tensions in their friendship that offer queer possibilities. These comments also indicate the problem of the too easy recuperation of representations of lesbian desire as a spectacle for the heterosexual male gaze.

Significantly, *Buffy* is frequently described as employing a postmodern aesthetic, as part of which it parodies and pastiches the horror genre. Again this is a fantasy genre and one often perceived as intrinsically camp, partly because, within psychoanalytical discourse, it is associated with sexual transgression and its monstrous yet seductive figures, such as vampires and witches, connected to the disavowal of queer desire. As Whatling indicates, such interpretations occur *both* as part of homophobic discourse that constructs queers as 'abject', damned or doomed, but also in positive terms, as a queer appropriation and reclamation of the horror genre. She notes that this latter may signal 'nostalgia for abjection' and the internalisation of homophobia on the part of the queer subject. However, as a site of covert representation, the horror gender also allows a play of sexual fantasy and desire that does not necessarily reflect upon 'reality' (Whatling, 1997: 93–4). Similarly, the fact that such figures also appear highly seductive for heterosexual viewers may indicate, as Judith Mayne suggests, that cinema can act as a 'safe zone', in which homosexual as well as heterosexual desires can be 'fantasised and acted out' in ways that problematise the categories heterosexual versus homosexual, albeit only in a fashion that leaves basic assumptions intact (quoted in Whatling, 1997: 130).

This 'safe zone' may be more easily activated in relation to fantasy genres like *Star Trek* and *Buffy*, which in Thomas Richards's terms can be said to construct 'comic universes of possibilities and alternatives' (Richards, 1997: 53–4). The same can apply to historical costume drama, a nostalgic genre where 'historical distance' allows for the safe representation of transgressive sexual 'romps'. *Tipping the Velvet*, of course, belonged to this genre and this drama had many indicators of a postmodern/camp aesthetic in its visual style, clearly marking it as a return to the past that 'simultaneously, reworks that past as self conscious representation' (Stratton, 1989: 54; see Chapter 4). Yet it also had strong potential for foregrounding gender as performative, since the central character Nan (Rachael Stirling) and her first love Kitty (Keeley Hawes) are cross-dressing music-hall entertainers, and Nan is also supposed to be a 'Tom' who passes as male on the street. However, the gender confusion signalled by these characters remains a matter of costumes and short hair, since neither Stirling's or Hawes's physical performances, make-up or the way in which they are filmed ever depart from the conventions for the normative representation of femininity, or those of psychological realism within this genre. The gender confusion Nan supposedly produces within the diegesis is, then, purely a matter of the viewer's willing suspension of disbelief, and is therefore readily recuperable to heteronormatvity. The only female performances that *do* encroach on the codes for masculinity are of figures characterised in strictly negative terms, by dint of age, appearance and sexual excess, so that normative sex/gender assumptions can remain firmly intact.

However, Whatling asserts that 'queer reading of popular culture [. . .] need not be limited to those who publicly identify as queer'. She goes on to argue, 'It is, however, frequently premised upon the subcultural desire to infiltrate the dominant through one order or another' (Whatling, 1997: 129). Hence, perhaps, the sado-masochistic nature of the *Star Trek* slash fiction, which is often created by *female* viewers around *male* authority figures. Doty agrees that queer reception can embrace 'those who identify as straight' but insists that queer readings are *not*, as I suggest in relation to some readings of *Star Trek* in Chapter 4, 'alternative readings, wishful or wilful misreading, or reading too much into things. They result from the recognition and articulation of the complex range of queerness that has been in popular culture texts and their audiences all along' (Doty, 1993: 16). As such, he argues that, while it may go beyond 'conscious real life sexual identities and cultural positions, as a practice, queer reading does not stand outside of personal and cultural histories, so that politically queer reception (and production), can include everything from the reactionary to the radical to the indeterminate' (15). This is not least because Doty asserts that straight culture 'uses queerness for pleasure and profit without admitting to it' (xi).

All of this raises the question of how to distinguish radical or progressive queer reception and production from reactionary or indeterminate modes. In terms of production, in *The Genre Handbook*, as already noted, Jane Feuer includes series like *Frasier* under the heading queer sitcom, but distinguishes this subgenre from *gay* sitcom with reference to *Will and Grace* (1998–). This is on the basis that *Will and Grace* demonstrates a camp aesthetic or 'queer humour' 'which embraces both identification and parody [. . .] it combines into one sensibility the most extreme feelings of empathy and the bitchiest kind of detached amusement' (Dyer quoted by Feuer, 2001: 72). On this point, it is worth noting that the *British* gay sitcom *Gimme, Gimme, Gimme* (1999–2001) actually tends far more to bitchiness than empathy, and arguably this might indicate fairly common national differences in the articulation of the genre as a whole. However, this aside, Feuer goes on to state that this queer sensibility, 'long cherished by closeted gay men, has now become part of mainstream American humour' (72). As such, Dyer's definition of camp bears a significant similarity to Jim Collins' description of the alternation between emotional identification and ironic distance in *Twin Peaks* and '*all* other forms of postmodern hyperconscious popular culture' (Collins, 1992: 347, my italics, see Chapter 1). In these terms, it is notable that the last twenty years have seen a sharp rise in the range of television programmes presented and *received* as ironic or camp, and as such often understood to be in some way 'subversive'. Discussing this with reference to 'camp readings' of talk shows like *Jerry Springer* (1991–), Kay Richardson and Ulrike H. Meinhof argue that 'the logic which equates excess with irony, and irony with critical function is flawed', going on to quote Jane Shattuc: 'If nothing is to be taken seriously, then nothing needs to change [. . .] the camp aesthetic stops the questioning' (Richardson and Meinhof, 1999: 130–1).

Stephen Farrier argues that *radical* queer reading or production must leave a 'residue or trace', presumably either in the viewer or in the general discourse of television, that continues to trouble the relationship between categories of sex/gender and sexuality (Farrier, 2000). However, I would argue that if this occurs it is not solely a matter of aesthetics, since like the feminine and diasporic hybridity, the camp aesthetic works on a dialectic between imposition and dissidence, subversion and recuperation, difference and repetition (Sinfield, 2000: 106). Rather, while it may embrace aesthetics, it is also a matter of a relationship to specific positionalities, subcultural practices and sociohistorical contexts – all of which can be seen to be in play in the British version of *Queer as Folk*.

Case study: *Queer as Folk*

Filmed on location in and around Canal Street, the centre of Manchester's 'gay village', *Queer as Folk* focuses on three white, male, gay characters. Stuart (Aiden Gillen) is a wealthy accounts director in advertising, Vince (Craig Kelly) is a supermarket supervisor and Nathan (Charles Hunnam) is a 15-year-old schoolboy. Stuart and Vince have been best friends since their teens and are now both approaching 30. While Vince is very much 'out' to his family he is closeted at work, with the reverse holding true for Stuart. The series opens on the night of Nathan's first visit to Canal Street and his sexual encounter with Stuart. This night also sees the birth of Stuart's son Alfred, the result of sperm donation to a lesbian couple, Romey and Lisa. Key events in the first series include the death of Vince's friend Phil from a heroin-induced heart attack; Vince's relationship with a new boyfriend, Cameron; Nathan's obsession with Stuart and his coming out to his family and at school. The drama also portrays varying degrees of parental acceptance of their son's sexuality, from Vince's mother Hazel's engagement with all aspects of his life, to the outright rejection of Vince's 'camp' friend Alexander by his parents. While *Queer as Folk 2* continues to develop many of the same themes and storylines, there is a change of register, with some key events being Stuart's coming out to his family and his revenge on Alexander's homophobic mother, Mrs Perry, in which he blows up her car.

Controversy within the gay and lesbian community

While most of the controversy produced by the series concentrated on the explicit sex scenes between Nathan and Stuart in the first episode, there was much else in *Queer as Folk* that made it potentially provocative. As Peter Billingham puts it, 'from the opening scenes it offers a rampant collage of desire and sexuality, depicting a love that far from daring to speak its name, positively screams its mobile telephone number, like some outrageous queen, at the viewer' (Billingham, 2000: 121). Actually, it should be noted that of the main characters in the drama only Alexander 'acts out' as an outrageously camp queen, and when he introduces Alexander and Phil in episode 2, Vince feels the need to apologise for this. The series then eschews the 'positive' representation of a wide range of queer identities, in favour of an unabashed and sometimes celebratory depiction of a particular type of gay lifestyle, based around bars and clubs, casual drug taking and one-night stands.

Aiden Gillen's ferociously physical and uninhibited performance in the sex scenes is also in stark contrast to previous limited representations of gay eroticism in mainstream television drama, which even so, have often been declared shocking by the tabloid press (see BBC, 2003). Moreover, while references are made to HIV/AIDS, especially in relation to Stuart's promiscuity, unlike the North American version of the series, British *Queer as Folk* does not state a clear and unambiguous 'safe sex' message. As Billingham suggests, then, if *Queer as Folk* was 'calculated provocatively to disrupt both right field homophobic positions and centralist tolerance of homosexuality – it clearly fulfilled its aim' (Billingham, 2000: 121).

It is not surprising, then, that the Independent Television Commission received more complaints about *Queer as Folk* than it has for any other made for television drama (see Billingham, 2000: 122). Nor is it surprising that it was pilloried by the tabloid press and that the brewer Becks withdrew its sponsorship of the series. Yet, its writer Russell T. Davis did appear to be surprised by the negative criticism of the show from within the gay and lesbian community, concerned that the series would confirm homophobic prejudice. This included complaints from public figures such as pop singer Boy George and spokespeople from the political association Stonewall. There were also complaints from gay men who felt this drama misrepresented them and from lesbians over the marginal, and in the case of Lisa, negative, representation of the lesbian characters (see *Queer as Folk*, DVD, 'Special features').

Yet in the interviews and features that accompany the definitive collector's edition DVD of *Queer as Folk*, both Davis and the show's co-producer Nicola Shindler constantly stress that the series was not concerned with issues. In an article in *Attitude* magazine, Davis expanded angrily:

> When all this began in 1997, no one told me there was an agenda. Because there must be an agenda – every gay politician, spokeswoman

and militant, has shouted at me for not following it. I'd love to see it, this set of rules, as unwritten as the British constitution and as rigid, dictating what, how and why a gay writer must write. The creation of the series was entirely personal. (quoted in Billingham, 2000: 184)

Ironically, the debate generated within the gay and lesbian community might indicate, as Billingham asserts, that 'no such homogenous grouping actually exists' (185). Yet, for Billingham, *Queer as Folk* did have an agenda and one very much *for* the gay and lesbian community, in so far as he suggests it 'enacts a struggle within the between the liberal/left strategy of disciplined resistance leading towards equality and assimilation, and the confrontational postmodern queer discourse of 'We're queer were here and were not going away' (185). I would argue that it also enacts the conflicts and contradictions *within* as well as *between* these positions, as I rehearsed above.

This is in accord with Billingham's characterisation of the representation of Canal Street in the series as a 'gay heterotopia' (119). He takes this notion from Foucault via Affrica Taylor, referring to a 'kind of effectively enacted utopia in which real sites, all the other real sites that can be found within the culture, are simultaneously represented, contested and inverted' (Taylor, 1997: 8). Such sites are then at once real and imagined, playing on the boundaries between fact and fiction, representations and lived experience, fantasy and reality.

Eclecticism of form and visual style: shifting identifications

Yet, Billingham tends to analyse *Queer as Folk* primarily in terms of a postmodern aesthetic understood as a loss of reference to 'the real'. As a result, for instance, he is critical of the ending of part 2, where Stuart and Vince are translated into myth, for its 'postmodern transcendence of material conditions' (Billingham, 2000: 123). Significantly, he describes aspects of this scene as 'self dramatising, camp bravura, and as uncomfortably sentimental in the context of a series that has striven to sustain an uncompromisingly honest account of sexual desire and identity, within an urban city context' (123). These remarks actually suggest elements *both* of referential realism and of camp in the whole, which as Billingham demonstrates elsewhere, is not *always* a matter of 'self dramatising bravura'.

Further, as Billingham's detailed discussions of the main protagonists clearly indicate, in terms of the representation of character this is primarily a (post)modern drama, in that rather than showing identity to be multiple and discursive, for the most part it repeats the conventions of psychological realism and of depth models of identity. However, as I have argued, *Ally McBeal* gives the illusion of suspending all reference to the real, while implicitly reaffirming a hegemonic understanding of reality. In contrast, in *Queer as Folk* there is a tension operating between referential or mimetic realism, naturalism and camp or postmodern self-referentiality, parody and pastiche, that corresponds to the play of resistance and containment, assimilation and challenge within the concept of queer itself.

In fact, some of the controversy the series provoked within the gay and lesbian community may have arisen due to the *realism* of its setting in Manchester's 'gay village'. Situated literally within the centre of Manchester, like the neighbouring Chinatown, this area has historically functioned as a 'ghetto', a place of refuge and community but also of marginalisation and symbolic exclusion. Yet it is also now advertised as one of the city's 'tourist attractions', which may signify increasing social acceptance of queer identities within a dominant heterosexual culture but perhaps only as 'chic trademarks of a broadening sex/gender market' (Roof, 1997: 181). This complex and contradictory signification of Canal Street as a 'real' place is very much a theme in *Queer as Folk* and in terms of its representation this location is clearly remarked as *both* real and fantasy.

Interestingly, the producer Nicola Shindler identified *Ally McBeal* as a model for the visual style of the series, in the use of a dominant colour in every scene, and in the softening effect produced on the background by the use of long lenses (Channel 4, 2001). These techniques are used to give many of the locations a heightened glossy glamour but are especially in evidence in depictions of Canal Street, which is rendered as an exaggeratedly dazzling, neon-lit 'fun palace' and a place of magical possibility. This visual style is enhanced by extensive use of mobile steadicam and this plus the bustle of extras, dialogue given on the move, the theme music with its dynamic beat punctuated by ecstatic 'whooping' sounds, mixed with a soundtrack of club and classic disco and gay anthems, all provide pace and excitement. Canal Street is figured as a place of fantasy, desire and pleasure, then, but also, as Billingham indicates, of 'conspicuous consumption', emphasised in the narrative by the constant use of mobile phones and other expensive and fashionable items (Billingham, 2000: 185). As a representation of a queer space and a queer identity, this could be read as one robbed of its radical edge through a focus on surface and style, recuperated as 'wearable tradable marks within the larger logic of global capital' (Roof, 1997: 181).

This conspicuous consumption is particularly marked around the character of Stuart, with his trendy jeep, high-concept warehouse flat(s) (he seems to move between parts 1 and 2) and designer wardrobe. His activities are also lit and filmed in ways that recall expensive adverts or glossy soft porn. As Billingham notes, Stuart's transgressive lifestyle is dependent on his high economic status and he might be understood to treat his sexual partners as 'endlessly replaceable, fetishised commodities' (Billingham, 2000: 126). However, the representation of Stuart's character and lifestyle is constantly contrasted both positively and negatively with those of the other protagonists, who are situated within a range of class and economic backgrounds, and both they and their 'home' environments are often presented in ways that are closer to traditional television realism(s) and naturalism(s). As this suggests, then, despite some continuities indicated above, *Queer as Folk* can indeed be defined as postmodern, in so far as it is eclectic and fragmented, employing differing stylistic techniques according to aspects of the narrative, character, scene or segment of action.

Part 1 can be loosely divided into two halves with episodes 1–4, directed by Charles McDougall, introducing the main characters but focusing far more on establishing the milieu and on action. This section is especially 'MTV' in style, using a high proportion of swooping, sweeping and spinning shots, split screen, wipes and freeze frames at climatic scene endings. Yet within this, there are traces of a naturalistic documentary technique in the use of fade to black to indicate the passing of time or as a mode of punctuation. The series also opens with three direct-address monologues by Vince, Nathan and Stuart, reminiscent of those used at the beginning of Jimmy McGovern's drama documentary *Hillsborough* (1996), to authenticate the drama. This device also prefigures the existence of different perspectives and narrative strands in the series, which although chiefly interpellating the viewer as a white gay man, provoke shifting identifications. These perspectives and the different styles of shooting sometimes cohere and sometimes function dialectically.

For example, towards the end of episode 3, Vince, Phil and Alexander are shown on the balcony at a club looking down longingly at two attractive men and Vince comments, 'Sometimes you see these men and you think that's it, that's him. You don't even talk to him, you never see him again, he doesn't even know you exist but you think about that man for the rest of your life'. This impels a wickedly grinning Stuart into action and soon he is dancing suggestively with both desirable strangers. Asked what Stuart says to these men, Vince replies he doesn't know, 'but if we knew that . . . if we knew the magic words . . . but whatever he says – he says it for all of us'. Indeed, Stuart very much plays this scene to and for Vince, and the action is initially shown mainly from Vince's point of view, focusing on his responses, later opening to embrace those of Nathan, with both their faces showing admiration, pleasure and delight. However, this sequence ends with a shot of Stuart dancing and looking intensely at the camera to include the viewer in his gaze, which is simultaneously seductive and narcissistic. This cuts to a shot of the dancers from above, with Stuart and his conquests still looking up into the lens. The camera pulls back, the image spins and the music builds and swells, until the shot pans up to the smoke-filled ceiling of the club and the image fades to white in a manner that suggests 'heaven'. This is a celebratory and extremely seductive scene, which positions the viewer first to identify with Stuart *through* Vince and Nathan, then directly *with* him, so that he is subject and object, the hero whom we are encouraged to identify with *and* desire, and who has the power to act out a fantasy of sexual excess for all of us, regardless of our sex and gender in 'reality'.

Yet, this is immediately followed by a collage of intercutting scenes that show a variety of outcomes for such casual sexual encounters, each in a different aesthetic register. Stuart's subsequent threesome is depicted as a confusion of beautiful bodies in glamorous surroundings, bathed in golden, soft porn, soft focus. In Vince's darker, downmarket flat, a more social realist/ironic mode is used to further the established running gag of Vince's disastrous sexual encounters, when it turns out that his pick-up is suffering from an exotic anal parasite. In a camp, comic-horror scenario, Alexander and his friend Dean, also looking for a threesome, find themselves in a nightmarish gothic bedsit with a ghoulish morgue assistant. Finally, in something close to a naturalist documentary mode, Phil is shown going to his middle-class house with the ordinary seeming 'Harvey', who gives him the drugs which kill him. Harvey panics and runs off, stealing some money, and the scene closes with a fade to black on Phil dying on the kitchen floor. When this death is revealed to Vince by phone in a bar, the episode ends with Vince's appalled expression as a drunk or drugged Stuart, unaware of the news, laughs beside him, suddenly rendered grotesque. Soft porn celebratory fantasy is contrasted with, in turn, ironic social realism, camp gothic parody, naturalism and finally the grotesque, as a seductive identification with Stuart's behaviour moderates into parody, disidentification and implied critique.

However, Phil's death is not the defining or determining action of the drama, but functions as part of the setting up of themes pursued in the second half of part 1, directed by Sarah Harding. While these episodes sometimes reprise techniques and types of shots from earlier scenes, the pace is slower and less fragmented. This reflects an expansion that opens up ethical and political questions of what ageing, mortality, parenthood, friendship, community and taking responsibility might mean – not within 'universal' terms, or those of the entire lesbian and gay community, but to a very particular gay lifestyle. These episodes underline the way that, if as a fantasy figure Stuart appears to be celebrated as a 'postmodern queer subject; an expression of unconstrained sexuality without a centre', in terms of referential realism he also constitutes a 'potential ethical and ideological anxiety regarding that expression' (Billingham, 2000: 125).

Characterisation and the performance of identity

In fact Stuart, Vince and Nathan *all* tend to be represented in ways that provoke some play between emotional identification and ironic detachment. Described by all other characters as selfish and narcissistic, Stuart is also portrayed as having moments of conscience and generosity. Equally, while mainly depicted as irritatingly self-dramatising and immature, Nathan is allowed vulnerability and even heroic status. This occurs when he publicly outs fellow schoolboy Christian Hobbs as a bully and a homophobe when Hobbs makes a 'tourist' visit to a Canal Street bar. Conversely, while mostly regarded and portrayed as sensitive and sympathetic, Vince is shown lying unconvincingly to his sexual partners, and at Phil's funeral shows little evidence of grief. Indeed he is concerned to deny that Phil was his friend at all. In line with the norm of television realism, in *Queer as Folk* the camera usually offers a sense of privileged access to characters' actions, thoughts and emotions, so as to allow these sorts of 'contradictions' to be resolved in terms of 'coherent' psychological motivation. However, this is not always the case. For instance, while Vince's behaviour at Phil's funeral can be 'made sense of' in relation to the drama's broader themes of the fear of ageing, death and loneliness, this is left very much to the viewer to interpret. This impedes empathetic identification with Vince as subject to these fears, and in these scenes he appears far more selfish and narcissistic than Stuart, who does eventually show *some* sensitivity towards Phil's family in his own way. On this point, it is illuminating to compare the characters in this series to those within the longer-running North American version (2002–5), which is closer to soap opera in its aesthetic. In this version the protagonists seldom appear ambivalent because as well as 'telling' reaction shots, comments and back stories are constantly provided to 'explain' their less admirable actions. By comparison, this points up the gaps in the psychological 'coherence' of their counterparts in the more condensed British version. As a result, if both versions can be said to employ a camp or queer aesthetic, the North American version is again balanced far more towards empathy and the British to detached amusement.

There is also a far higher level of specifically televisual, intertextual reference in the British version. In the American version Michael (Hal Sparks) is a fan of superhero comic books, while his counterpart Vince is a committed fan of the children's science fiction series, *Dr. Who* (1963–88). Vince shares a passion for the soap *Coronation Street* with Rosalie, a co-worker. He also mentions the 1980s police series *Juliet Bravo* (1980–85) in his first monologue. All of these texts have a certain 'camp' cult status in Britain. In the opening episode, Vince also compares the events of the night to soap opera, in terms of having a birth and death in the same episode. This convention is (almost) fulfilled when Nathan steals flowers from the bedside of a dying man to give to Romey, the mother of Stuart's baby. Soap opera is also a constant point of reference for Nathan, who cites soap scenarios to dramatise his own experiences. In the first episode Stuart also initiates an enactment of the 'top of the world' speech from the film *Titanic* (1997) on the hospital roof, with him in the Leonardo Di Caprio role and Vince as Kate Winslet.

The world Stuart is 'on top of' at this point is literally and figuratively that of Canal Street, and his identity as 'hero' of this space is signified in Gillen's performance by a swaggering walk and an intense smouldering gaze. The theatrical excess of this behaviour emerges most strongly from the manner in which Nathan is shown to model his identity as a gay man on Stuart, mimicking his bodily style and copying his lines socially and sexually. In part 2, Nathan eventually inherits Stuart's role on 'top of the world' of Canal Street, and this is shown via a series of still photographs in which Nathan bears a resemblance to Di Caprio. All this might begin to signal a queer understanding of identity as 'performative'.

Romance narratives and queer as folk reading

This is complicated, however, by the overarching framing of the series as a story of unrequited love between Vince and Stuart, which has many of the traits of the classic romance narrative. As Lynne Pearce and Jackie Stacey remark in their introduction to *Romance Revisited*, this usually involves a quest that demands 'the overcoming of obstacles, or rather the conquest of barriers in the name of love, and perhaps by extension, also in the name of truth, knowledge, justice or freedom' (Pearce and Stacey, 1995: 15–16). Usually perceived as 'universal' and linked to discourses of rites of passage and maturation, such narratives also tend to reaffirm social norms for gender and sexuality. They work towards closure in the shape of monogamous sexual relationship and/or marriage – or in the case of 'inappropriate' or 'deviant' object choices, through loss and death.

In this understanding of *Queer as Folk*, Stuart is a kind of 'late twentieth century gay metropolitan Byronic hero, with many of the signs of Romantic masculine transgression' (Billingham, 2000: 123–4). This includes an inability to admit to or be aware of his 'true' feelings. Expressions of (feminine) emotion are then the territory of Vince, who like Ally McBeal, appears to be looking for 'the one'. Like her, he is portrayed as rejecting a series of men who fail to live up to his ideal 'first love', in her case Billy, in his Stuart. From this perspective, Stuart's dedicated promiscuity is an obstacle to be overcome along with Nathan's obsession with Stuart and Vince's relationship with Cameron, who is also looking for a committed, monogamous relationship. Stuart's higher economic and social status is also typical for heroes of romance narratives, as is the sometimes sadomasochistic dynamic between Stuart and Vince.

Other characters constantly remark on their relationship in Lisa's sarcastic words as 'the greatest love story never told'. There is also significant pressure either for them to consummate the relationship, or for Stuart to end the friendship to allow Vince to 'find happiness' with someone else. This prompts Stuart to make a classic romantic gesture of self-sacrificing renunciation, when he arranges Vince's thirtieth birthday party, so as to drive Vince away and into Cameron's arms. When the plan succeeds, typically for such narratives, Stuart finds himself lost, lonely and even robbed of his legendary power to seduce. In the classic romance narrative, this episode should effect the hero's transformation into 'an emotional being with a heart, who declares his love for the heroine' (Pearce and Stacey, 1995: 16). A version of this does occur in a café scene in episode 9, although Stuart's feelings are still expressed in oblique and ironic terms. As importantly, thematically, this series of events causes Stuart to reflect on the smallness of the world he is 'on top of', pointing to the double status of Canal Street as a ghetto – a space of escape and refuge but also of containment and exclusion.

This narrative might be seen as part of an assimilationist discourse, in which growing up and taking responsibility entails leaving the ghetto and conforming to heterosexual models for identity, lifestyle and relationships. However, where such relationships exist, in the case of Romey and Lisa, or have the potential to exist, as with Vince and Cameron, the narrative foregrounds how far, like the institution of marriage, they are bound up with 'property rights' that embrace ownership of both goods and people. Further, it is significant that the crisis in the relationship between Stuart and Vince is engineered around Vince's closeted status at work, where his attempts to pass include laughing along with homophobic jokes. Moreover, the subcultural context of the drama's setting opens up the romance narrative self-reflexively so that it can be understood through the practices of queer reading. The tension between Stuart and Vince exactly mirrors that of characters in heterosexual narratives appropriated to such readings and the exaggerated nature of Stuart's representation as 'Byronic hero' may point to the campness and potential queerness of all such representations of Romantic masculinity. As such, it is interesting that apparently 50% of viewers of *Queer as Folk* were women, presumably a proportion of these being heterosexual (see Madden, 2000). Romance has traditionally been designated as a 'feminine' form, and so this figure may indicate that the series simply repeated such narratives by other means, reaffirming for these viewers a normative discourse of feminine subjectivity via an identification with a feminised Vince. Equally, it might indicate a potential 'infiltration of the dominant', through the order of masculinity, a pleasurably queer confusion between identification with and desire for, between being and having, that might be a subversion of the normative gender positions within a phallic economy as articulated by Lacan.

Importantly, in terms of resistance, even though the obstacles to their relationship seem to be removed in part 1, the resolution of the tension between Vince and Stuart is refused. Breaking off with Cameron, Vince states that he *chooses* unrequited love, saying 'it's fantastic, it never has to change, never has to grow up and it never has to die'. He runs off to join Stuart in a club and as friends, not lovers, they dance together on a podium with the scene ending in a crane shot that swoops up above them as the music swells. In its setting and shooting, this scene reprises the celebratory club scene of episode 3 discussed above, and there is an implication that Vince chooses not so much unrequited love as a relationship and a lifestyle that reject heterosexual narratives. Yet, while this ending is affirmative, it is immediately preceded by Vince arriving at the club just in time to prevent Stuart from going off with Harvey, who brought about Phil's death. This could be read romantically as Vince 'saving Stuart from himself' but it also potentially operates as a distancing device, reprising a source of anxiety over the lifestyle Vince chooses. The refusal of the traditional closure of the romance narrative resists an assimilationist discourse, but this ending also resists a simple 'happy ending' for the ethical and political questions around this lifestyle the series has opened up.

Queer as Folk part 2: abandoning realism

Part 2 also resists closure in a way that is still linked with the practice of queer reading and the exploration of assimilationist versus politicised queer positions, but it also gradually abandons referential realism altogether in favour of postmodern fantasy. Directed by Menhaj Huda, there are consistencies with the visual style of part 1, but Huda also adds the use of a naturalistic documentary style in

the bar scenes in which the characters swap stories of their conquests. In this instance, this use of naturalism is very much part of
a flexiad (post)modern aesthetic and these sequences are edited at
an extremely fast pace. They are also set alongside large-scale, cinematic set pieces, performed to a soundtrack in which the original
theme music is remixed into a more sombre orchestral composition.

These shifts in style coincide with a transformation of Stuart as
hero that is emotional, but mainly in so far as the personal is political and the romance narrative becomes as much concerned with the
'conquest of barriers in the name of truth, knowledge, justice or
freedom' as in the name of love (Pearce and Stacey, 1995: 16). The
first series contained two notable 'political' scenes, the confrontation between Nathan and Hobbs cited above and a scene where
Stuart drives a jeep through a car showroom window in response to
a homophobic remark from a salesman. In part 2, Nathan once
again takes a public stand at school against Hobbs, his gang and a
teacher who supports their homophobic behaviour, but it is Stuart
who emerges most strongly as a radically queer character. When, at
a family gathering, Stuart's nephew Thomas attempts to blackmail
him by threatening to 'out' him to his family as a pervert, Stuart
instead outs himself, launching into a long list of increasingly
derogatory terms for homosexual, 'Because I'm queer, I'm gay, I'm
a poof, I'm a bum boy, batty boy, backside artist, bugger, I'm bent,
I am that arse bandit, I lift those shirts, I'm a fudge packing uphill
gardener' and so on, until he ends with 'But I am not a pervert. If
there is one twisted bastard in this family, it's that little blackmailer,
so congratulations Thomas, I've just outed you'.

As Billingham remarks, 'at the core of this speech lies the angry
radicalism that informs the reclamation of the derogatory term
queer, an expression of uncompromising, politicised reaction to the
dominant reactionary value set' (Billingham, 2000: 124–5). Yet the
impact of this speech is undercut by Stuart's mother pointing out in
its aftermath that Thomas is an 8-year-old child. The inappropri-
ateness of directing this anger at a child is partly mitigated by the
way that during most of this speech the camera remains focused on
Stuart, allowing it to become a statement within the drama as a
whole. Nevertheless, even in political mode Stuart is never an
entirely positive character.

Less ambivalent, however, is a scene that takes place at the
hospital, where Vince and Stuart accompany Alexander to visit his

estranged father, who is dying. Instead, they are waylaid by his hostile, homophobic mother whose only concern is that Alexander should sign away any legal right to inheritance. As the three men walk away from Mrs Perry, Stuart suddenly turns. In a serious and threatening manner, he mimes pointing a gun at her head and the force of his anger produces a reaction of genuine fear. Alexander's subsequent suicide attempts provoke Stuart into blowing up Mrs Perry's car. This scene, shot at night and showing a triumphant Stuart in slight slow motion and framed against the spectacular background of the burning vehicle, strongly recalls portrayals of anti-heroes in Hollywood action and/or road movies.

The obstacle to Vince and Stuart's union is now no longer Stuart's promiscuity but rather his politicised anger and confrontational behaviour. Vince is shown as having gained a promotion at work and scenes at his half sister's wedding underline his desire to be accepted with the dominant, heterosexual culture. He therefore refuses to support Stuart's actions with Mrs Perry both at the hospital and in blowing up the car, asking why he doesn't 'just tell her to fuck off, you're always telling them to fuck off'. Stuart responds by saying, 'It's not enough anymore', calling Vince a coward and later 'a straight man who fucks men'. In his defence, Vince cites the financial responsibility he has for his mother Hazel and her family of gay lodgers and again the grandeur of Stuart's gesture of blowing up the car might be seen as relating to his confidence in his economic status.

However, when Stuart is about to leave Manchester without him, it is through Hazel's intervention that Vince also decides that 'It's not enough any more'. After a set piece involving a host of drum majorettes, a car chase and a fight with the police, and with both of them (for different reasons) 'on the run', he joins Stuart on Canal Street. Stuart says he doesn't want to be part of a married couple and 'I'm not settling down, ever'. Vince counters this with reference to fantasies derived from *Dr. Who*, suggesting that they can 'just go and keep on going'. They are then joined by Nathan for a scene filmed in a series of wipes in which magically, day turns to night and the empty glowing street is populated and filled with music. Speaking against and virtually in time with 'important'-sounding piano music which evolves into lush, cinematic orchestration, Stuart defines Canal Street for Nathan as 'This ghetto, always stinking of piss, beggars in every doorway, straights and students coming to look at the freak show', but also as 'the middle of the world because on a street like this, every single night, anyone can meet anyone'. Vince chimes in, 'It's all yours now, all of them, the poofs, the dykes and all the people in between', adding 'Just stick with your friends and you'll be fine'. At this point Stuart's jeep becomes a 'tardis',[2] spinning on its axis, and in a display of flashing lights and special effects, takes off to land on a long straight road cutting through a desert. This is the territory of the Hollywood road movie and the following scene, set at an American gas station and where Stuart uses a gun to threaten a homophobic, redneck truck driver, confirms it as very much the world of *Thelma and Louise* (1991). This is again a text that has a cult status in terms of queer reading and one that might also be an intertextual reference for the blowing up of Mrs Perry's car.

Although there is a hint that Vince and Stuart *may* sexually consummate their relationship, this remains open and they depart into a cinematic fantasy world not as a romantic happy couple but as mythic 'queer avengers'. The references in these scenes then are not only to other fictions but to other fictions *already* filtered through the practice of queer readings. As such, as Billingham argues this ending may be seen to deploy a camp aesthetic to 'foreground the heightened, generic construction of the series as a whole', including the heightened generic construction of character as representations that refer back to previous representations, and therefore as performative (Billingham, 2000: 123). Yet, as he also argues, it could equally be seen as a depoliticised, postmodern 'transcendence of material conditions', a wish-fulfilment strategy in which the complete suspension of reference to everyday material reality divorces it from the 'historical, palpable raw material of gay men's cultural experiences', in ways that stop the questioning (Medhurst, 1997: 290).

Moreover, there is a segment just before the end credits where two silhouetted figures that might be Stuart and Vince appear to be leaping off into space. This recalls the end of *Thelma and Louise* where the heroines drive off into a canyon and also the ending of the 'original buddy movie' and classic subject for queer reading, *Butch Cassidy and the Sundance Kid* (1969), where the heroes are caught in freeze frame as they run out of hiding to certain death. In political terms, these references might be seen as exhibiting 'nostalgia for abjection' and an internalisation of homophobia. In both films the 'tensions' between the characters and their various transgressive acts are resolved through their deaths as a romantic gesture of doomed resistance against a culture that, literally, has no place for them. As such, the ending may simply repeat the traditional closure of the romance narrative where the object choice is inappropriate, potentially allowing the straight viewer to retreat to a 'safe zone' that may well function to problematise the categories heterosexual versus homosexual, but only in so far this remains firmly marked as *outside* of real lives and social identities.

Conclusion

I would agree with Billingham that the ending of part 1 of *Queer as Folk* is in many ways more radical than that of part 2, in that it genuinely leaves the questions raised in the text open. However, I would argue that it is when the series remains alternating between referential realism and postmodern/camp, between fantasy and specific subcultural location, distance and identification that it is at its most radically queer and/or resistantly postmodern. Hence, in part 2, paradoxically, Stuart's threat to Mrs Perry with an 'imaginary' gun in the hospital has far more political impact than his threatening of the redneck with a 'real' gun in the later fantasy scenes. Similarly, Nathan's self-dramatising act of resistance at school has more impact than Stuart's spectacular, cinematic, blowing up of the car.

It seems to me, then, that the aesthetic of *Queer as Folk* is indeed performative, in that this drama not only explores but embodies some of the tensions and contradictions around the concept of queer/Queer. This includes the way that, ultimately, it focuses on a relatively privileged white, male, gay identity in ways that offer little serious challenge to class and gender norms. Moreover, its representation of 'race' and ethnicity is problematic. Donna, Nathan's best friend in part 1, counters one of his self-dramatising complaints by saying, 'Well, I'm black and I'm a girl, try that for a week', but she is a supporting character defined primarily in relation to Nathan and disappears without trace in part 2. One of Stuart's casual pick-ups is black and the two series include a gay, non-English-speaking, Japanese prostitute as part of a comic subplot, a black British homophobic teacher and an African postgraduate student Romey plans to marry to ensure him a visa. This character becomes violent when arrested by immigration authorities, a point underlined by Hazel to indicate the ill-advised nature of the arrangement. Some of this may actually constitute an attempt at representing a range of ethnicities within the drama, but if so it is a tokenism that backfires, since some of these minor characters come close to repeating racial stereotypes. This is ironic, because referring to the complaints about the way *Queer as Folk* focused on a very particular type of queer indentity, Russell T. Davis responded in the *What the Folk* documentary, by stating 'No good drama ever comes out of representation' (Channel 4, 2001). I will take up this point in the conclusion.

Notes

1 Section 28 of the Sexual Offences Act came into force in 1988. It was designed to prevent 'the promotion of homosexuality by local authorities', including schools. Outrage at this homophobic amendment to British law prompted the forming of a number of campaigning groups, including 'Stonewall' (1989), seeking equality and justice for lesbian, gay men and bisexuals (see Stonewall.org.uk).
2 'The tardis' is the name given to Dr Who's interdimensional, time/space travel ship, which is camouflaged as an old-fashioned British police phone box.

Conclusion: beyond (simple) representation? *Metrosexuality* and *The Murder of Stephen Lawrence*

The context of Russell T. Davis's remark, 'No good drama ever comes out of representation', cited at the end of Chapter 5, suggests that he is referring to simple, positive representation but also to the notion of 'representation' in terms of attempting to speak for, to and about a specific group as a whole.

In this conclusion, I want to use this comment as a starting point for exploring two pieces of television drama. *Metrosexuality* (2000) and the drama documentary *The Murder of Stephen Lawrence* (1999), each of which provides a different perspective on the question of 'simple' representation. In a sense, these analyses also indicate a return to where I started in the introduction, with Michael Jackson's remarks on the representation of such groups. As indicated in Chapter 1, it is also a return to some issues highlighted in my discussion of Robin Nelson's *TV Drama in Transition* (1997), a work which I used, in part, as a means of defining my own approach in this book.

Ethics and the question of 'good drama'

As I have already indicated, I very much agree with many of Nelson's arguments and approaches. Like Nelson, in this book I have been concerned to contest ideas, in circulation within modernism and gaining increasing currency within some postmodernisms of the 1990s, that certain aesthetic strategies can be regarded as 'monolithic', and/or can be assumed in advance to be 'inherently' progressive or reactionary. Like Nelson, I also wish to critique tendencies towards relativism that often occur in both celebratory and pessimistic accounts of the postmodern. As part of all this, like Nelson, I have also been concerned to challenge the notion that the 'context of postmodernity', for good or ill, is *necessarily* a defining one in television, on the level either of production or of reception (Nelson, 1997: 5 and 111). However, as I also noted, none of this is to suggest that aesthetics do not play a role in the signifying process within television, or that the context of capitalist postmodernity can be ignored in considering what is, after all, primarily a commercial medium. In short, like Nelson, I acknowledge that various factors, ranging from the general, the abstract and the contextual to the particular and the textual, must be taken into account in assessing the political implications of any given television production. Nevertheless, my primary interest is in interrogating the relationship *between* the general and the 'local', explored on the level of the specificity of representations.

In Chapter 1 I also noted two related differences between Nelson's approach and my own. He carefully maps out the *ethical* position from which he judges some dramas as being more or less 'serious' than others, in terms of 'generating meanings of greater social and political use value' (Nelson, 1997: 232). Yet he tends to identify his own *political* position mainly in negative terms, in opposition to the aesthetic practices and values associated with capitalist postmodernity. As a result, this political position remains largely implicit, rather than being explicitly stated. This leaves open questions as to the sort of 'social change' being envisioned and, equally importantly, as to the definition and implications of the notions of 'the human' that feature in his discourse. In fact, as I noted in Chapter 1, this discourse seems to operate very much within the Marxist-socialist tradition, and therefore within the values and assumptions that, in the past, have been closely associated with the type of critical realist aesthetic he favours for progressive television drama. By contrast, my own project not only focuses on, but is explicitly articulated through, political perspectives drawn from feminism, anti-racism and queer, and as developed *within* rather than in opposition to postmodernity. Part of my project has been to interrogate and problematise these perspectives, as well as affirm them, and the same applies to the various aesthetic strategies that have come to be associated with them. Even so, my political identification(s) with these positions means that, while I may hold that no aesthetic strategy is 'inherently' progressive or reactionary, ultimately I do tend to lean towards the privileging of certain types of aesthetic strategies over others. These are often (but not always) closer to Nelson's notion of 'critical post-modernism' than his 'critical realism'. However, for me, this is once again, to paraphrase Butler, a matter of the necessity of provisionally instating a position, while attempting at the same time to open it up 'as a permanent site of contest' (see Butler, 1993: 222).

Nevertheless, in foregrounding these political alignments, in comparison to Nelson, I might sometimes have neglected certain *ethical* considerations. That is I have not (self-reflexively) interrogated how far some of the political and aesthetic judgements I have made in this book may be filtered through the less conscious identifications and investments that result from my own construction as a socially situated subject. If I have avoided this, it is partly because, as Sara Ahmed points out in relation to feminism, a concern for the ethics of speaking 'about', to or for others can sometimes end in silence or relativism or produce works primarily about 'the impossibility of speaking at all', or those which focus on self-reflection at the expense of the supposed object of study (Ahmed, 2000: 166). Instead, in areas where the issue of my own social positioning might be most at stake, I have attempted to address this concern by drawing heavily on voices more 'authorative' than my own. Even so, I am aware that in the course of some of my textual analyses, I have often referred to some of the more general criteria for judging 'dramatic quality' in circulation in and around television. These include high (expensive) production values, the casting of well-known performers, how far a drama approaches the cinematic in terms of design and visual style, as well as issues of authorship and literary, high-culture associations. Yet, unlike Nelson, I have not *directly* pursued this question of dramatic quality, on the understanding that it is one that is 'inevitably imbricated with aesthetics and politics' and therefore is already in play in my discussion (Nelson, 1997: 225). Nonetheless, *because* these issues are imbricated with one another, in failing to directly address 'dramatic quality', some of my *explicit* judgements about politics and aesthetics might be affected by *implicit* assumptions that arise from my own social and cultural positioning.

Of course, this really only underlines the fact that there is no such thing as a 'view from nowhere', no means of speaking from an objective place 'outside' of social and cultural discourse, and no amount of self-reflection alters this. Further, this late in the day, I have no intention of engaging with the theoretical debates circulating around notions of dramatic quality and television. Yet if I am touching on this topic in my conclusion, it is because looking back over this book, it struck me that if the various (explicit and implicit) political and aesthetic judgements I make about the texts I have discussed were pieced together to make a 'blueprint' for politically progressive television drama, it might look something like *Metrosexuality*. Ironically, and inevitably, this text opens up a number of questions concerning the relationship between politics and aesthetics, *and* between these things and questions of ethics and of 'dramatic quality'. Arguably, it does so as much as, and perhaps even far more than, any of the other texts I have discussed so far.

Metrosexuality as a postmodern, feminist, culturally hybrid, queer text

Metrosexuality was commissioned by Channel 4 and broadcast in Britain in 2001, after which it was shown at gay and lesbian film festivals in Britain, North America and elsewhere. It was created, written and directed by Rikki Beadle-Blair, who also played 'Max', one of the pivotal roles in the production.[1] Consisting of six half-hour episodes, it was shown in a late-night slot. The opening scenes of the first episode introduce a teenage boy, Kwame (Noel Clarke), and are centred around his relationship with his girlfriend Asha (Rebeca Varney) and his attempts to reunite his 'two gay dads', Jordan (Karl Collins) and Max (Rikki Beadle-Blair). Although Kwame initially operates as a narrator figure and his story frames the whole, *Metrosexuality* draws on the structure of soap. Like soap, it focuses on a community based around a clearly defined locale, different stories are given more time and weight in each episode, and not all plot lines are entirely resolved by the closure of the series. The focus of these storylines and the emotional registers in which they are portrayed are often reminiscent of soap, although there is also a strong tendency toward self-conscious irony.

The locale is a version of London's Notting Hill, which like *Queer as Folk*'s portrayal of Canal Street, is revisioned as a 'queer heterotopia', except in this instance the fantasy aspect of this space dominates the referential. The community it embraces also includes a far wider spectrum of queer identities than *Queer as Folk*, encompassing those 'who call themselves straight' but whose 'sexuality doesn't work within the gender imperative' and those marginalised for other reasons (Farrier, 2000: 92). In the early 2000s, the term 'metrosexuality' was in circulation in some of the more fashion-conscious print media. In this arena it was related to dandyism, and was used to refer to straight men, like British footballer David Beckham, said to be in touch with and not afraid to express their 'feminine' side. As such, it is interesting that while within *Metrosexuality* the 'sensibility' evinced by the majority of its *male* characters, both gay and straight, confuses the boundaries of traditional masculinity and femininity (as with other shows discussed), the female characters tend only to have mobility *within* the genre of femininity. Therefore, while *Metrosexuality* offers itself for discussion in terms of subversive repetition that reveals gender as performative, the problems and limitations of the manner in which this theory has been taken up are still apparent.

On the other hand, and perhaps more importantly, this is also a multi-ethnic, diasporic community. Kwame's mother is white northern British but his two dads (Jordan and Max), Max's lesbian sister Cindy (Carleen Beadle) and Jordan's new boyfriend Jonno (Silas Carson) are all African Caribbean British and the other characters embrace South and South East Asian and Jewish British identities. While the main focus of the piece is on issues of sexuality, the 'hybridity' of these positionalities is also remarked within various aspects of the drama. In addition, the cast includes Mat Fraser, whose work for the stage and television has constantly challenged the normative discourses which construct and determine the category of 'people with disabilities'.[2] His casting in *Metrosexuality* refuses this categorisation and he plays Monty, whose defining features are that he is a 'cool', tough, sexually opportunistic, straight drug dealer and user. He is also older brother to Dean (Paul Keating), a sensitive gay teenager who hero worships Monty. This narrative strand focuses around Dean and includes their meek Catholic mother's attempted murder of their abusive, drunkard father. Monty is also involved in a storyline featuring Pablo (Gavin Delaney) and Peggy (Lisa Harmer), who are ex-junkies trying (and failing) to resist the resumption of former habits. These storylines are the more sombre of the series but are still treated with some irony and their weight is countered by other aspects of the drama.

Formally, *Metrosexuality*'s most striking features are its sometimes extremely fast-paced editing, its explosive use of colour and its employment of an extraordinarily eclectic range of technical and visual devices that further the fragmentation already created by its flexi-narrative structure. While there are some continuities throughout, even more than in *Queer as Folk*, visual style seems to have been matched to content on a scene by scene basis, rather than in terms of a unifying strategy. For example, 'fish eye lenses', black and white footage, naturalistic documentary look and direct address are all used to express Dean's mother's mental state. These devices *only* appear in this storyline and although other scenes use direct address to camera, this is in the register either of 'dramatic monologue' or of the theatrical 'aside', rather than the documentary address. Mostly, however, action remains within the frame and the majority of scenes are shot using a mobile single camera and often feature rapid pans and staggered 'shotgun' zooms. Edits between scenes are often achieved by intrusive comic-book wipes and cartoon sound effects, and a range of other highly contrived special effects are used, such as heart-shaped 'thought bubbles' and day-glow captions and/or inserts placed in various parts of the frame to signal locations or point up details. A musical soundtrack features heavily throughout and there are points when characters sing along direct to camera in ways that blur the distinction between the intra- and extra-diegetic. The same self-conscious eclecticism extends to costume, make-up, hair and interiors, all of which vary from high camp kitsch to a conceptual postmodern art aesthetic, embracing on the way retro styles such as 1950s chintzy, 1970s Afrocentric, 1980s new romantic/punk/gothic, 1990s 'new age' and a sort of *Barberalla* (1968) meets *Mad Max* (1979) futuristic style. This is all rendered in dazzling technicolour and lighting includes a striking use of UVA. A large number of sequences are also shot through different coloured filters, which wash scenes in primary tints.

The visual style, then, places the emphasis on high design, fantasy, pleasure and overt display and, as with *Queer as Folk*, all this suggests a certain level of conspicuous consumption, and once again fashionable cars and mobile phones play significant roles in the action. However, this is a far more 'bohemian' and 'artistic' community than that of *Queer as Folk*, with much of its style suggesting creative bricolage rather than passive consumerism. Jobs are distinctly 'non mainstream' and include drug dealing, running a skateboard rink, being a local telephone therapist, a gay male prostitute, a 'sexual revolutionary' fashion designer and a D.J. In virtually all respects, then, *Metrosexuality* appears to offer an almost textbook example of camp and/or postmodern and even diasporic cultural aesthetic(s) and it goes out of its way to embrace a wide range of socially marginalised identity categories. So is this my ideal for politically correct television drama?

Critical reception: the question of 'dramatic quality'

Metrosexuality was potentially as controversial as *Queer as Folk*. It depicts graphic scenes of drug taking and again a sexual relationship between a teenage boy and an older man – although in this instance the boy was 17. However, critical reaction focused not on 'content', or its representation of the gay and lesbian community, but on its qualities as a drama. This dominated reviews in the 'mainstream' quality press, with Gareth McLean in *The Guardian* describing it as 'tiresome predictable pap' (McLean, 2001: 1) and Charlie Skelton in *The Observer* as 'the most beautiful and the worst programme on television' (Skelton, 2001: 2). In the same paper, Kathy Flett felt moved to offer extracts from her unedited notes, which included the word 'crapness', in order to demonstrate that she got 'quite angry watching it'. These notes referred to it as 'over styled, under written, yoof orientated' and 'like something made for a far-flung cable outpost as a local community project', 'unfathomably plotless and vapid', and finally 'without any doubt easily one of the worst pieces of drama ever to be commissioned by a terrestrial channel' (Flett, 2001: 4).

Reviews in the British gay and lesbian press focused positively on content, with Lee Hudson in *Now* praising its 'inclusiveness' as 'different races and sexual orientations sit alongside each other effortlessly', and *AXM* commending it for dealing with an issue 'that still remains a lump in many people's throats – homosexuality and black people' and in a manner that was not 'boring and politically correct' (quoted in The Knitting Circle, 2003: 1). However, in *OutUk*, while Rodney Breen praised its 'good intentions', he also stated that 'No amount of good intentions can overcome the need for serious character development and subtle exposition. There's some serious overacting here. And in its eagerness to avoid stereotypes, the show creates some stereotypes of its own; Asian-Lesbian, Black-Gay, Straight-White etcetera' (Breen, 2001). The response to showings at North American gay and lesbian film festivals seems similarly 'mixed' and this is summed up by an article in New York's *Gay City News* by Gary M. Kramer. Kramer refers to the show's 'relentlessly breathless style, which may scream young hip and trendy', and suggests that 'the show is either irresistible or irritating depending on one's point of view' (Kramer, 2002: 2). In short, in the gay and lesbian 'community', while *Metrosexuality* was welcomed and widely supported in terms of the politics of its representation, questions were raised as to its status as 'good drama'.

What is striking is how far the negative judgements made about the show still appear to be based on definitions of quality, tied up with the same sort of notions of 'literacy' and psychological 'depth' suggested by some 1980s definitions of 'quality' on television (see Feuer, Kerr and Vahimagi, 1984: 56). The problem seems to be that the show moved too far from the traditional structures of 'realism' in terms of character and performance. Yet, Feuer et al. also include 'stylistic complexity' in their list of markers of quality, and you cannot actually *get* much more stylistically complex than *Metrosexuality*. In fact, in the abstract, *Metrosexuality* demonstrates many of the same aesthetic qualities as the critically acclaimed *Twin Peaks* (see Chapter 1). Unlike most other shows that have been compared with *Twin Peaks*, this includes an (apparent) absence of psychologically motivated characterisation. One of the differences between them is that, if *Metrosexuality* is actually closer to Nelson's concept of postmodern flexiad drama than to *Twin Peaks*, it is because for the most part its references are televisual and popular. By contrast, *Twin Peaks* draws on the popular but overall remains closer to the styles of art-house cinema. It also plays upon the psychoanalytical theories that have traditionally fascinated the avant-garde, and which played a major role within twentieth-century criticism in according film the status of 'art'.

In short, the sort of postmodern blurring of boundaries that occurs when the avant-garde borrows from the popular (a practice traceable back to the modernist avant-garde) still has far higher cultural status than those that might occur when the 'popular' borrows from the avant-garde. This is disguised by the manner in which academics such as John Fiske draw on theories developed in relation to the avant-garde and *apply* them to popular television. While this may have allowed a form like soap, to take one example, to be 'valued' in terms of popular pleasures and certain 'modes of ironic or camp reading', it has not necessarily allowed soap (at its best) to be valued as a form of 'good' drama *on its own terms*. Despite the supposed postmodern breaking down of boundaries, then, 'quality' on television, may still often be, as it was in the 1980s, a matter of how far texts refer or can be referred to forms (literary, theatrical, cinematic) *outside* of television as a 'popular medium'.

The comparison between *Twin Peaks* and *Metrosexuality* also raises questions of authorship. Some of Beadle-Blair's previous work has been in 'art house' queer British film making and in experimental performance but he is simply not as famous within (white) intellectual and avant-garde circles as David Lynch. Does this issue of authorship, along with its primarily 'popular' references, explain why *Metrosexuality* was not understood as experimental postmodern television drama in a similar vein to *Twin Peaks*? Or was it that in contrast to *Twin Peaks*, *Metrosexuality* deploys a radical queer or diasporic or postmodern feminist aesthetic, which is actually more *successful* in subverting the 'depth' models of identity that still dominate most television representations?

Political correctness and over-representation

These issues cannot be discounted and unquestionably on the level of the representation of marginalised identity categories, *Metrosexuality* shows up the 'conservatism' of *Twin Peaks*. Nevertheless, I would argue that such factors do not entirely account for the questions raised about the quality of *Metrosexuality* as a drama. Significantly, taking into account Flett's criticism, *Metrosexuality* did apparently start as a 'community' film project (see 'Pinktink', 2001). This might explain a tendency in *Metrosexuality* towards *over*-representation. By this I mean that, in the first instance, its visual elements often operate to illustrate and underline the verbal text. This creates overstatement and refuses 'distance' from the material in a manner which *limits* the range of readings that might be produced from it. In the second instance, it operates a strategy of inclusive and 'positive' representation that attempts to speak to, about and for so many different constituencies at once, including the white heterosexual mainstream, that it verges on reducing these differences to the 'same'. In short, its aesthetic and political challenges are recuperated from within by its own political correctness.

Indeed, the majority of the *Meterosexuality* community are themselves portrayed as relentlessly politically correct and also charmingly eccentric, wise, generous and supportive and/or 'cool', witty, sexy and/or simply extraordinary and gorgeous. Max, who occupies the 'matriarch' role, traditionally at the 'heart' of soap opera, has *all* these qualities. As such, he functions as an idealised figure, not only for unconditional parental and familial love and community spirit, but also for radical queer and anti-racist politics, romantic and sexual desire and camp/postmodern stylishness. His only 'problem' is that he is *too* empathic and emotionally generous. This means that there is absolutely no tension or contradiction between these various identities and the different discourses that construct them. Further, although within the fiction *as* a character, he is capable of some level of 'camp' self-reflexivity, it is not clear how far, if at all, this characterisation is intended to be taken ironically, since all other characters and narratives appear to take him at 'face value'.

Characters who do demonstrate antagonistic or conflicted behaviour tend to be 'redeemed' in the narrative through emotional empathy. So, for example, Jordan's 'straight-acting' boyfriend Jonno is initially an outsider in the community, partly by dint of (as he puts it himself) his 'fashionably politically incorrect' views, which include a strongly expressed prejudice against 'feminine' gay men such as Max. This excessive investment in the signs of masculinity is explained through reference to his experiences as a black gay man in the army, and is overcome through his love for Jordan. Significantly, Jonno's eventual acceptance by the community is symbolised by a scene in which he breaks down and cries in front of Max (thereby getting in touch with *his* 'feminine' side), and is taken to Max's bosom. While not all the narrative strands have such straightforward 'happy endings', one way or another they all drive towards a similar resolution based on the power of love (whether sexual, romantic, familial or between friends), which is portrayed as a unifying force that can transcend social, political and cultural difference. In an indirect fashion, this even embraces Dean's violent, misogynistic and homophobic father. This is signalled by the climax of this storyline, which is a soft-focus flashback/fantasy sequence, in which Dean remembers/imagines his parents as a happy, romantic couple in evening dress, dancing together in the hallway of their home, previously the setting for violence and trauma.

In short, if, as Dyer asserts, a camp aesthetic 'embraces both identification and parody, [. . .] it combines into one sensibility the most extreme feelings of empathy and the bitchiest kind of detached amusement', in *Metrosexuality* bitchiness and detached amusement are overwhelmed by extreme empathy (Dyer quoted in Feuer, 2001: 72). While characterisation and performances may work in terms of theatrical overstatement, there is little evidence of critical distance. As a result neither is there a foregrounding of the paradoxes and contradictions that occur as a result of the construction of identity by multiple and shifting discourses. These are the things on which a *radical* camp/feminist or culturally hybrid aesthetics *actually* depends and which render the representation of character as 'complex' without simply repeating the model of psychology that informs traditional modes of realism and naturalism. In this instance, rather than being remarked as the product of deep-rooted social and historical discourse, the differences between these characters are signified as purely a matter of surface and style that conceals a universal human 'essence', and so are easily resolved and transcended. In these terms, *Metrosexuality*'s fragmented, formal eclecticism might actually be understood as a mode of 'expressionism', aimed at revealing the emotional human 'truth' behind each scene. No wonder that, as many critics pointed out, the acting can appear 'bad', since it seems to me that the performers struggle to find a register to portray characters conceived of as 'types', as if they were written in terms of deep 'interior' psychological motivation.

All of the above means that *Metrosexuality* can appear both sentimental and overtly didactic. It may be these qualities that made Kathy Flett identify the piece with 'community' and 'yoof' drama, as much as the way its aesthetic recalls MTV and pastiches the iconography of comic-book teenage romance. A whole raft of key characters – Kwame, Asha, Dean, Bambi, Jaye and April – are also in their early teens. Combined together, all these factors mean that despite the 'adult' nature of some of its images and its late-night slot, this drama does often seem to interpellate viewers as superficially sophisticated but fundamentally naive teenagers who are in the process of exploring their social and sexual identities.

From political correctness to family values

In these terms, like much 'youth television', *Metrosexuality* seems preoccupied with treading a line between appealing to teenagers and providing reassurance for their parents that issues are explored in 'responsible fashion' and within a clearly defined 'moral' framework. Hence, in contrast to the lustiness of *Queer as Folk*, the portrayal of sexual activity in *Metrosexuality* tends to be either romantic or comic in tone, and mostly functions to make some sort of 'point', political, moral or educational. Casual sexual activity, divorced from a 'serious' and monogamous (if serially monogamous) loving relationship, is portrayed as an empty and unsatisfying experience. For example, in the final episode the film is treated to look like decayed Super 8 to reflect Bambi's (Davie Fairbanks) yearningly nostalgic memories of lovemaking with Robin (Michael Dotchin), whom he wishes to marry. In contrast, the visual style of a 'casual' sex scene between Pablo and Robin uses a cold and unappealing 'realist' style and neither is able to reach a climax because, as Pablo puts it, 'they are both in love – but not with each other'. Similarly, when Bambi (heartbroken by Robin's refusal to marry him) and Dean (a virgin and unrequitedly in love with Max) go 'cruising' in a dark alley, this is shot in sombre style and with a sense of threat, and Bambi comes to his 'senses' and 'rescues' Dean at the last minute. It is Jonno's preparedness to 'share' Jordan by means of a sexual threesome that persuades Max that Jonno loves Jordan far more than he does. This sex act is therefore constructed as a 'sacrifice' which might reluctantly be made out of 'true' love. Finally, when apparently 'streetwise' young lesbian Jaye first goes to bed with April, this devolves into a heavy handed comic episode concerning Jaye's embarrassed ignorance about dental dams and her rushing out of the house to find one, while pretending to April that she is using the bathroom. This sequence is pointedly designed as a corrective to the way that lesbians have so often been ignored in the delivery of 'safe sex' education.

Similar attitudes are evident in relation to drug use. While Phil's death in *Queer as Folk* might be seen as conveying an anti-drugs message, this death was part of larger themes in the drama, and at other points drug taking is associated with social and sexual pleasure. This latter is never the case in *Metrosexuality*. At one point, Kwame, Bambi and Dean attempt to take ecstasy but Monty gives them sleeping pills instead and the maintenance of their 'innocence' is underlined by a shot of a Kwame sucking his thumb in his sleep. This contrasts sharply with disturbing and unpleasant images involving Pablo, Peggy and Monty, some of which, such as Pablo injecting heroin into his tongue, appear to serve no dramatic purpose other than to show the horrors and dangers of drug abuse.

Overall, then, despite the transgressiveness of some of its images, the 'radical' nature of its form and its apparent inclusiveness, *Metrosexuality* might be seen as rejecting some of the more 'troubling' aspects of the sort of queer lifestyle represented by Stuart in *Queer as Folk*. This is not necessarily problematic but, instead, it seems to favour exactly the same liberal humanist 'family values' that circulate in most mainstream television soap. Paradoxically, I would argue that this is the result of its own 'good intentions' and its ambition to offer positive, politically correct representations of a broad spectrum of identity categories and to address as wide an audience as possible. Ultimately, however, its fantasy of an idealised, polymorphously perverse, multi-ethnic community sidesteps the politics of difference(s) and ends up by reducing the complexity of the historical, the social and the political to a position that reaffirms the status quo.

Equally, while formally much of *Metrosexuality* is striking, innovative and beautiful its eclecticism often functions as overstatement and seems to indicate a desire to appeal to a wide range of different viewers, in ways that close down the potential for production of 'alternative' meanings. Significantly, all this may reflect something of the production process, in which Beadle-Blair took on the roles of writer, director *and* star. While within the collective processes of film and television this sort of multi-tasking may ensure a high degree of 'authorial control', it is also notorious for promoting a lack of critical distance.

The Murder of Stephen Lawrence (beyond representation)

The topics of authorship and process are also relevant to the final drama I want to consider in terms of representation and the question of 'good drama'. As a drama documentary, *The Murder of Stephen Lawrence* again brings me back to where I started in Chapter 1 with the MacCabe/McArthur/Caughie debate, which influenced thinking on 'progressiveness' and television drama beyond this specific genre for some time. This is because, as Derek Paget puts it, 'The form and the debates on it highlight questions about the nature of the real and the limits of representation, about television itself and its access to reality' (Paget, 1998: 92). By the same token, this genre and the debates on it also foreground the imbrication of aesthetics, ethics and politics in the field of television drama.

While I want to make some cross reference between *Metrosexuality* and *The Murder of Stephen Lawrence* (hereafter *Stephen Lawrence*), I am not suggesting that they are actually 'comparable', aside from the way that they might be used to reflect on the problematic of 'good drama' and political correctness. One is a mainly comic, utopian fantasy and the other is a sober and serious exploration of some of the actual events surrounding the murder of a black British teenager and the subsequent police investigation. As the Macpherson report confirmed, these events exposed how profoundly the discourse of 'race' influences behaviour and attitudes in the police force and other major British institutions. From the start, then, as a drama *Stephen Lawrence* is involved in an entirely different set of problematics around the issue of 'representation' to those raised by *Metrosexuality* and indeed all the other dramas I have considered so far.

Form and critical reception

In terms of form, *Stephen Lawrence* uses an extreme mode of 'naturalism', or the 'documentary look', often employed within this genre. It is entirely shot on location, using a single hand-held camera and natural light and sound, so that both visibility and audibility are subject to a high level of interference. The camera follows and 'finds' the action and its view is frequently obscured by people and objects moving in front of it and by its own 'shake', panning and refocusing. Captions are used to indicate locations and time passing, and this latter is also signified by scenes being cut to black, a device that also highlights the edited nature of the material and the discontinuous nature of the scenes. In the abstract, then, there is some very slight formal similarity between *Metrosexuality* and this drama- documentary in so far as they both incline towards 'fragmentation'.

However, *Stephen Lawrence* was generally far better received critically than *Metrosexuality*, signified by its winning of a Bafta award in 2000 as best single drama. Yet despite this industry classification as a drama, negative critiques focused on its short-comings as a documentary and its failure to adequately represent all perspectives on events, especially those of the police and the suspects in the investigation. Charlotte Raven in *The Guardian*, for instance, complained that the piece recounted events from the perspective of the Lawrences, with the suspects being presented as 'ciphers' and the police being taken at 'face value', 'as thick and insensitive'. She goes on, 'this might have been OK – if the programme had announced itself as fiction' but she argues that by using the 'grammar of documentary', *Stephen Lawrence* deliberately obscured the 'partial nature' of its account (Raven, 1999). These comments on the 'misleading' nature of the form and on bias repeat time-honoured complaints made about the genre from the 1960s. As Julian Petley points out, this view patronisingly assumes an audience who, *unlike* the critics themselves, are easily confused when it comes to distinguishing between factual and fictional programmes (Petley, 1996: 17). Further, although they use the 'grammar of the documentary', *mockumentaries* like *The Office* never directly 'announce' themselves as drama, whilst in fact *Stephen Lawrence* clearly did so in a disclaimer at the start of the programme. This is because all dramatic reconstructions of actual events on television are legally required to do so (which as a TV critic Raven should know).

Further, much of what Raven identifies as weaknesses in this work as a 'factual account' can be seen as its strengths as a dramatic one. Hence, if *Metrosexuality* has a tendency to *over*-representation in terms of both its aesthetics and its politics, I would argue that the impact of *Stephen Lawrence* as a political drama is due to a deliberate strategy of *under*-representation. I would also suggest that this operates as part of an aesthetic which is 'performative', in so far as it 'enacts' or comments on the politics and ethics of its own representation, in ways that *also* implicate the viewer in these concerns, and without using the conventions of 'ironic' self-reflexivity.

This is not a matter of form in general. As noted in Chapter 1, while this 'naturalistic' aesthetic might have once been understood in Brechtian terms to be progressive, in so far as it draws attention to the means of reproduction, it is now used in a range of dramatic genres and has become simply another (post)modern, realist convention. As such, as is clear from *The Office*, it can give the illusion of revealing the inner 'truth' of a character. The effect of this form, in the instance of *Stephen Lawrence*, then, depends on its particular articulation in relation to 'content' and this, in turn, relates to its particular production process.

The ethics of production

Both writer/director Paul Greengrass and producer Mark Redhead have stated that they started the *Stephen Lawrence* project with an acute awareness of being white film makers, dealing with events that came to symbolise the racism experienced by black British subjects (Redhead, 1999: 2). Their first move was to ensure that they had the approval and co-operation of Stephen's parents, Doreen and Neville Lawrence. This led to the deliberate decision to focus on the Lawrences' perspective, in the awareness that as drama rather than as journalism it would be impossible to cover all aspects of these complex and far-reaching events. A crucial aspect of the Lawrences' perspective was that 'for most of the past five years the Lawrences were told virtually nothing'. The aim then was to reproduce this experience and create a drama which would 'never let the audience know any more than they did', so that like the Lawrences, 'we will never quite have the perfect view' (Redhead, 1999: 2). If, as Raven suggests, this drama treats the suspects in this case as 'ciphers', it is because the Lawrences had no direct contact with them outside of court. Similarly, if it does not break down the 'facades' of the police, this again reflects the Lawrences' experience. Yet equally, there is no attempt to define the police *individually* as 'villains', as seen, for instance, in the overdetermined portrayal of the senior officer in charge of the football ground in Jimmy McGovern's drama documentary *Hillsborough* (1996).

Greengrass and Redhead also worked in close collaboration with the performers. These included (as Neville) Hugh Quarshie, an actor whose career spans both the Royal Shakespeare Company and *Star Wars: The Phantom Menace* (1999), and (as Doreen) Marianne Jean Baptiste. This was Jean Baptiste's first major acting role in Britain since her nomination for an Oscar for her role in Mike Leigh's film *Secret and Lies* (1996), and she has been outspoken about her experiences of institutional racism within the British film and television industry (see Glaister, 1997). Although Greengrass is credited as both writer and director, this collaboration included achieving dialogue and performances through improvisation with the performers.

This again is not uncommon in drama documentary, which favours a naturalistic style and tends to result in dialogue closer to the texture of everyday speech and an acting style that, as Paget puts it, is 'ratcheted down' from that of most mainstream television drama (Paget, 1998: 115). In this instance, the lack of polished rhetoric and the understated performances it achieves give a sense of 'ordinary' people struggling to respond to a painful and bewildering experience. However, there is no attempt in the diegesis to determine or define this 'ordinariness'. An empathic identification is invited with the Lawrences' *situation*, but the camera acts as 'witness' within the drama. In this 'role', and in contrast to the vast majority of modern and (post)modern television drama, the camera has no privileged access to the Lawrences' 'inner thoughts and feelings', or to the 'truth' of events. The 'look' of the camera in *Stephen Lawrence* is therefore neither that of the privileged observer with an overview of the action, which allows viewers to 'know' more than the protagonists, nor is it aligned with that of the protagonists so as to give the illusion of being able to 'know' them as psychologically motivated individuals. Instead, the camera engages the viewer in the same process the Lawrences undergo, that of trying to 'make sense' of unexpected traumatic events with restricted information.

Between (*un*-ironic) distance and (*in*-complete) identification

The first few scenes, which cut between Neville and Doreen at home and Stephen and his friend Dwayne Brooks just before Stephen's murder, have something of the inevitability of classical tragedy. However, the scenes of the murder itself and its immediate aftermath are a sudden, shocking blur of confused, badly lit, out of focus images and sounds, from which details emerge but which never cohere into an authoritative version of events. Thereafter, the camera is constantly shown focusing and refocusing, trying and failing to get a clearer picture. Many scenes are shot through doorways, using mid-shots or wide-shots, with very few full-face close-ups or reaction shots. Even in 'key' scenes, Doreen and Neville are shown in profile or partly obscured by others, and due to the lack of light they are also often literally 'in the dark' or in silhouette against windows, with their features hard to make out.

Instead, a sense of the protagonists' responses to events is suggested via the *mise-en-scène*. For example, in one sequence the

Lawrences and their two surviving children are shown having a conversation in their small kitchen. This is shot from the adjacent living room which is overflowing with people from support organisations, engaged in setting up a campaign around Stephen's death. As a family, the Lawrences appear both trapped and 'sidelined' by the tide of events in their own home. Similarly, in a sequence dealing with the inquest, the Lawrences and their supporters literally have their backs against the wall, while the suspects take up middle benches in the room. If Dwayne Brooks appears to become progressively isolated and increasingly vulnerable as the drama unfolds, this is partly due to Joseph Kpobie's stunning performance which portrays a teenager overwhelmed by nightmare circumstances. However, this is also due to the way that, after the murder, he is always shown alone or with people crossing distances to speak to him and then departing. Especially moving is the scene just after the civil case brought by the Lawrences, in which his evidence is rejected as untrustworthy. The camera shows him in mid-shot profile, hurrying alone along the street, socially, physically and emotionally isolated, his head bent, weeping and apologising to Stephen for failing him.

Emotional identification is not refused and is in fact invoked more powerfully because emotion is suggested or caught in passing, seldom fully 'performed' for the sake of the camera. As Doreen breaks down on hearing that her son is dead, she moves out of shot, coming back into view only to have her face hidden in her husband's shoulder. Equally, when she visits the spot on the street in Eltham where Stephen was killed, the lighting is so poor and the traffic noise so loud that her anguish and anger at finding racist graffiti on the site can barely be seen or heard – but this only increases the painful intensity of the moment. When Neville returns from making his first press statement about Stephen's murder, his home is over-run with friends, council workers and representatives of anti-racist organisations. Retreating upstairs, he finds Doreen in tears on the bathroom floor. He goes in to her and closes the door, not just on the noise and confusion downstairs but also, decisively, on the camera. This moment of potential self-reflexivity signals more than a (by now) conventional willingness of television drama to expose its own constructedness. Rather, it is one of the ways that *Stephen Lawrence*, as a drama, engages with the ethics and politics of its own representations, remarking the camera's tendency to voyeurism and objectification and refusing to make a 'spectacle' of the Lawrences' grief, even *as* a dramatic reconstruction. Significantly, there is only one 'major' speech in the whole of *Stephen Lawrence* where any one *explains* their emotions and private thoughts. This sequence, of Neville alone by Stephen's grave in Jamaica, is filmed mainly in mid-shot and the speech is full of pauses, gaps, hesitations, unfinished sentences and repetitions. This is partly the effect of improvisation, but this technique in itself is part of a strategy that attempts to avoid reducing the Lawrences to the status of transparent 'characters'.

It is part of their 'ordinariness' that, in the early scenes after the murder, the Lawrences are shown as having no expectation of encountering racism. They place their trust in the police investigation and are confident in the expectation of justice. Neville appears to be puzzled by a reference at a press conference to the British National Party and this puzzlement extends to the representatives of anti-racist groups in his living room, who are at first ignored and even resented by Doreen, caught up as she is in her grief. The Lawrences are shown only to have a dawning realisation that if, as Dwayne Brooks has witnessed, their son was 'interpellated' and reduced to a racist stereotype in the last moments of his life by the words 'what, what nigger', then after his murder, both they and Stephen continue to be perceived and defined through a discourse of institutional racism. As Doreen states at the inquest, it is *they* who are constructed as somehow being 'criminal'.

I would suggest that the aesthetic of this drama documentary constitutes an attempt to resist the processes of definition and objectification that are part of the violence of racism, and to reject the closures of representation that render 'others' as always already known and knowable. Its devices produce a 'distance' from its protagonists, even as they promote an emotional identification with their situation, implicating the viewer in making sense of events in ways that draw on both abstract and embodied knowledges, the rational and the emotional. This is not an 'ironic' distance but an *ethical* one and, as such, this is an identification which remarks the impossibility of its own completion. In Sara Ahmed's terms, the piece allows the viewer to 'get close' to the Lawrences, to identify with them but only in so far as to be 'touched by that which simply cannot be got across', to be witness to their trauma and loss but 'without being able to assume such witnessing is the presenting or ownership of the truth' (Ahmed, 2000: 157–8). If *Stephen Lawrence* uses self-reflexivity, it is not as a suspension of reference to material reality. Rather, it remarks what is beyond the 'limits' of its own representation, its inability to speak with authority for or about the Lawrences as specific and complexly constructed subjects, or to pronounce on the truth of the events it portrays. As such, it not only seeks to 'activate' the viewer in terms of making 'meanings' in relation to a particular dramatic text but, to borrow from Bill Nichols, 'it produces [. . .] a sense of suspended closure, of partial knowledge, the sense of incompleteness, and the need for retrospection to look *beyond the text*, at the larger text of [British] society' (Nichols, 1994: 147, my italics).

As such, I would argue that this drama constitutes a genuinely '*critical* postmodern drama'. This means that its representations of subjectivity and identity, and its mode of interpellating the viewer, do not simply repeat either the hierarchical structures of enlightenment liberal humanism or the indifferences of postmodern relativism. Instead it interpellates us, its viewers, as witnesses but ones who necessarily have a stake in these events due to our intersociality, our intersubjectivity, our fundamental interconnectedness in which 'we' are all different in our specificity and yet part of the same. However, I am *not* offering *Stephen Lawrence* as a general model for progressive television drama, nor even as one for progressive drama documentary. Indeed, I am not even suggesting it as a model for progressive drama documentary *on this subject*, since one of the questions raised 'beyond' this text is the reason why this drama or others similar to it could not have been made by a black British producer and director? Nor am I offering it as a model for 'quality' television drama. Rather my point is that it is the very *specific* relationships between process, form and substance, politics, ethics and aesthetics that make *Stephen Lawrence both* politically progressive in its representation of subjectivity and identity *and* good drama.

Yet, it also has to be acknowledged that this work demands a level of sustained intellectual and emotional engagement which, whatever the myths about active reception or 'interactive' TV, few people are prepared to give to television drama *all* of the time. I have discussed *Stephen Lawrence*, then, mainly because I wanted to end on a positive note by exploring strategies for representing marginalised identity catgeories within television drama, beyond either simple positive representation, or the 'more complex', psychologically motivated characterisation of social realism, or postmodern strategies that depend heavily on the subversive potential of irony, parody and pastiche. Again, this is not to say that dramas that employ these strategies always stop the questioning and/or are necessarily 'reactionary', because where there is repetition there is also always difference and the possibility of new meanings. However, I don't think this, in itself, is reason to celebrate the progressive potential of the vast majority of television drama. It is important to remember that 'beyond' these representations and the investments and identifications viewers might or might not make in relation to them, is a massively powerful, primarily commercial institution. No one working in this institution has been democratically elected to represent the 'people', subordinate or otherwise, and not all the 'people' are necessarily represented in its decision-making structures. This is all the more reason that it should be subject to rigorous and searching criticism from clearly defined political (and ethical) positions.

Notes

1 Beadle-Blair is a writer, actor, director, musician and performance artist. He also wrote the screenplay for the award-winning film *Stonewall* (1997).
2 Mat Fraser's work in British theatre includes his one-man theatre show *Sealboy/Freak* (2002). He been a presenter on the series concerned with issues relating to disability *Freak Out* (1999) and has created television documentaries such as *Born Freak* (2004).

References

Adkins, L. (2001) 'Cultural Feminisation: Money, Sex and Power for Women', *Journal of Women in Culture and Society*, 26:3, pp. 669–97.

Ahmad, A. (1995) 'The Politics of Literary Postcoloniality', *Race and Class*, 36:3, pp. 1–20.

Ahmed, S. (1998) *Differences that Matter: Feminist Theory and Postmodernism*, Cambridge: Cambridge University Press.

Ahmed, S. (2000) *Strange Encounters: Embodied Others in Post-Coloniality*, London and New York: Routledge.

Alexander, J. M. and Mohanty, T. C. (2001) 'Geneologies, Legacies, Movements', in K.-K. Bhavnani (ed.), *Feminism and Race*, Oxford: Oxford University Press.

Andermahr, S. A. (1994) 'A Queer Love Affair: Madonna and Lesbian and Gay Culture', in D. Hamer and B. Budge (eds.), *The Good the Bad and the Gorgeous: Popular Culture's Romance with Lesbians*, Pandora: London.

Ang, I. (2001) 'I'm a Feminist but . . . "Other" Women and Postnational Feminism', in K.-K. Bhavnani (ed.), *Feminism and Race*, Oxford: Oxford University Press.

Appaduria, A. (1993) 'Disjuncture and Difference in the Global Cultural Economy', in P. Williams and L. Chrisman (eds.), *Colonial Discourse and Postcolonial Theory*, London: Haverster Wheatsheaf.

Armstrong, I. (2000) *The Radical Aesthetic*, Oxford: Blackwell.

Arroyo, J. (1997) 'Film Studies', in Medhurst and Munt (eds.), *Lesbian and Gay Studies*.

Asians in Media (2003) 'Channel 4: *Second Generation* a Boost for British Asian Talent', www.asiansinmedia.org/news/article.php/television/133, accessed October 2004.

Aziz, R. (1997) 'Feminism and the Challenge of Racism: Deviance or Difference?', in H. S. Mirza, (ed.), *Black British Feminism*, London: Routledge.

Bakare, I. (2000) 'A Journey from the Cold: Rethinking Black Film

Making', in K. Owusu (ed.), *Black British Culture and Society*, London and New York: Routledge.

Bakare-Yusef, B. (1997) 'Raregroove and Raregroovers: A Matter of Taste, Difference and Identity', in H. S. Mirza (ed.), *Black British Feminism*, London: Routledge.

Barker, C. (1997) *Global Television: An Introduction*, Oxford: Blackwell.

Barker, C. (1999) *Television, Globalisation and Cultural Identities*, London: Open University Press.

Barrett, M. and Barrett, D. (2001) *Star Trek: The Human Frontier*, Cambridge: Polity Press.

Barthes, R. (1973) *Mythologies*, London: Paladin.

Barthes, R. (1977) 'The Death of the Author', *Image, Music, Text*, trans. S. Heath, London: Fontana.

Baudrillard, J. (1988) *Jean Baudrillard: Selected Writings*, ed. M. Poster, Cambridge: Polity Press.

Baudrillard, J. (1993) *The Transparency of Evil: Essays on Extreme Phenomena*, trans. J. Benedict, London: Verso.

BBC (2003) 'Get this Filth off Our Screens', *Tipping the Velvet*, www.bbc.co.uk/drama/tipping/article2.shtml, accessed January 2004.

BBC News (2002) '*BabyFather* Author Furious with BBC', http://news.bbc.co.uk/1/hi/entertainment/tv_and radio_/2367643.stm, accessed October 2004.

Bellafante, G. (1998) 'Feminism: It's All About Me!', *Time Magazine*, 151:25, www.geocities.com/TelevisionCity/Set/8532.allymbealefiles28.html, accessed July 2001.

Bernardi, D. (1998) *Star Trek and History: Race-ing Towards a White Future*, London and New Jersey: Rutgers University Press.

Bhabha, H. K. (1986) *The Other Question in Literature, Politics, Theory*, London: Methuen.

Bhabha, H. K. (1990) 'The Third Space' in J. Rutherford (ed.), *Identity: Community, Culture, Difference*, London: Lawrence and Wishart.

Bhabha, H. K. (1994) *The Location of Culture*, New York and London: Routledge.

Bhabha, H. K. (1998) 'Cultures In Between', in S. Hall and P. du Gay (eds.), *Questions of Cultural Identity*, London: Sage.

Billingham, P. (2000) *Sensing the City through Television*, Bristol: Intellect.

Biltereyst, D. and Meers, P. (2002) 'The International Telenovella Debate and the Contra Flow Argument: A Reappraisal', *Media Culture and Society*, 24:4, pp. 396–429.

Bordo, S. (1995) *Unbearable Weight: Feminism, Western Culture and the Body*, Berkeley, Los Angeles and London: University of California Press.

Brah, A. (1996) *Cartographies of Diaspora: Contesting Identities*, London: Routledge.

Brandt, G. W. (1981) *British Television Drama*, Cambridge: Cambridge University Press.

Brandt, G. W. (1993) *British Television Drama in the 1980s*, Cambridge: Cambridge University Press.

Braxton, G. (1999) 'Colorblind or Just Plain Blind?', *Los Angeles Times*, www.geocities.com/TelevsionCity/Set/8532/allymcbealefiles40.html, accessed July 2001.

Brecht, B. (1987) *Brecht on Theatre: The Development of an Aesthetic*, trans. J. Willet, London: Methuen

Breen, R. (2001) 'Outspoken *Metrosexuality*', *OutUk: The UK Gay Man's Guide*, www.outuk.com/content/news/metro, accessed April 2004.

Brunsdon, C. (1982) '*Crossroads*: Notes on Soap Opera', *Screen*, 22:4, pp. 32–7.

Brunsdon, C. (1987) 'Men's Genres for Women', in H. Baeher and G. Dyer (eds.), *Boxed In: Women and Television*, New York: Pandora.

Brunsdon, C. (1994) 'Pedagogies of the Feminine: Feminist Teaching and Women's Genres', in J. Storey (ed.), *Cultural Theory and Popular Culture: A Reader*, London: Harvester Wheatsheaf.

Brunsdon, C. (1998) 'Structure of Anxiety: Recent British Crime Fiction', *Screen*, 39:3, pp. 223–43.

Brunsdon, C., D'Acci, J. and Spigel, L. (eds.) (1997) *Feminist Television Criticism: A Reader*, Oxford: Oxford University Press.

Butler, J. (1990) *Gender Trouble: Feminism and the Subversion of Identity*, New York and London: Routledge.

Butler, J. (1993) *Bodies that Matter: On the Discursive Limits of 'Sex'*, New York and London: Routledge.

Carrington, B. (2000) 'The Black British Athlete', in K. Owusu (ed.), *Black British Culture and Society*, London and New York: Routledge.

Carson, B. and Llewellyn-Jones, M. (2000) *Frames and Fictions on Television: The Politics of Identity within Drama*, Bristol: Intellect.

Cashmore, E. (1994) *And Then There was Television*, London and New York: Routledge.

Caughie, J. (1981) 'Progressive Television and Documentary Drama', in T. Bennett, S. Boyd-Bowman, C. Mercer and J. Woollacott (eds.), *Popular Television and Film*, London and Milton Keynes: British Film Institute/Open University Press.

Caughie, J. (1990) 'Playing at Being American: Games and Tactics', in P. Mellencamp (ed.), *The Logics of Television: Essays in Cultural Criticism*, Bloomington: University of Indiana Press.

Chadha, K. and Kavoor, A. (2002) 'Media Imperialism Revisited: Some Findings from the Asian Case', *Media Culture and Society*, 24:4, pp. 416–29.

Channel 4 (2001) *What the Folk* (documentary), *Queer as Folk*, DVD, the definitive collectors' edition.

Collins, J. (1992) 'Postmodernism and Television', in R. C. Allan (ed.), *Channels of Discourse Reassembled*, London: Routledge.

Corcoran, F. (2002) 'Globalisation, Television, Education', *Circa 89: Art Education Supplement*, www.recirca.com/backissues/c89/supp_corcoran.shtml, accessed November 2002.

Dahlgren, P. (1995) *Television, the Public Sphere, Citizenship, Democracy and the Media*, London: Sage.

Derrida, J. (1978) *Writing and Difference*, trans. A. Bass, London: Routledge.

Derrida, J. (1981) *Dissemination*, trans. B. Johnson, London: Athlone Press.

Derrida, J. (1994) *Spectres of Marx: The State of the Debt, the Work of Mourning and the New International*, trans. P. Kamuf, London and New York: Routledge.

Doty, A. (1993) *Making Things Perfectly Queer: Interrogating Mass Culture*, Minneapolis: University of Minnesota Press.

Doty, A. and Gove, B. (1997) 'Queer Representation in the Mass Media', in Medhurst and Munt (eds.), *Lesbian and Gay Studies*.

Dowmunt, T. (ed.) (1993) *Channels of Resistance: Global Television and Local Empowerment*, London: British Film Institute.

Edgar, D. (1979) 'Ten Years of Political Theatre', *New Theatre Quarterly*, 32: Winter, pp. 25–32.

Edwards, T. (1994) *Erotics and Politics: Gay Male Sexuality, Masculinity and Feminism*, London and New York: Routledge.

Elam, D. (1994) *Feminism and Deconstruction: Ms en Abyme*, London: Routledge.

Faludi, S. (1992) *Backlash: The Undeclared War Against Women*, London: Chatto and Windus.

Fanon, F. (1986) *Black Skin, White Masks*, London: Pluto Press.

Farrier, S. (2000) 'Ga(y)zing at Soap: Representation and Reading-Queering Soap', in Carson and Llewellyn-Jones (eds.), *Frames in Fiction on Television*.

Fenton, N. (2000) 'The Problematics of Postmodernism for Feminist Media Studies', *Media, Culture and Society*, 22:6, pp. 723–41.

Feuer, J. (2001) 'Gay and Queer Sitcom', in G. Creeber (ed.), *The Television Genre Book*, London: British Film Institute.

Feuer, J., Kerr, P. and Vahimagi, T. (eds.) (1984) *MTM: Quality Television*, London: British Film Institute.

Fiske, J. (1991) *Television Culture*, London and New York: Routledge.

Flett, K. (2001) 'Tell Me You're Joking', *The Observer*, http://observer.guardian.co.uk/screen/story/0.6903,44257,00.html, accessed March 2003.

Foucault, M. (1979) *The History of Sexuality*, Vol. 1, trans. R. Hurley, London: Allen Lane.

Foucault, M. (1991) 'What is an Author?', in P. Rabinow (ed.), *The Foucault Reader*, London: Penguin.

Frankenberg, R. and Mani, L. (2001) 'Crosscurrents, Cross Talk: "Race", Postcoloniality and the Politics of Location', in K.-K. Bhavnani (ed.), *Feminism and Race*, Oxford: Oxford University Press.

Franklin, S., Lurie, C. and Stacey, J. (2000) *Global Nature, Global Culture*, London: Sage.

Gamman, L. (1988) 'Watching the Detectives', in L. Gamman and M. Marshment (eds.), *The Female Gaze*, London: The Woman's Press.

Geraghty, C. (1991) *Women and Soap Opera: A Study of Prime Time Soap*, Cambridge: Polity Press.

Gergen, K. (1994) *Realities and Relationships*, Cambridge, MA and London: Harvard University Press.

Giddens, A. (1994) 'Living in a Post-traditional Society', in U. Beck, A. Giddens and S. Lash (eds.), *Reflexive Modernisation: Politics, Tradition and Aesthetics in the Modern Social Order*, Stanford: Stanford University Press.

Gillespie, R. (2004) 'Television Channels are Failing Black Talent, says Bafta Seminar', *The Stage Online*, www.thestage.co.uk/news/newsstory.php/sid=509, accessed November 2005.

Gilroy, P. (1993) *The Black Atlantic: Modernity and Double Consciousness*, London: Verso.

Glaister, D. (1997) 'Oscar Actress Hits Out at "Old Men" of British Film Industry', *The Guardian*, 15 May, www.filmunlimited.co.uk/News_Story/Guardian/0,4029.68705,00.html, accessed November 2001.

Goldman, R. (1996) 'Who is that Queer Queer? Exploring Norms of Sexuality and "Race"', in B. Beemyn and M. Eliason (eds.), *Queer Studies: A Lesbian, Gay and Bisexual Reader*, New York: New York University Press.

Greenwald, J. (1997a) 'Bullet Train to the Stars: Why the Japanese Love *Star Trek*', Planet *Star Trek* series, *Salon Magazine* 21, http://archive.salon.com/feb97 /21st/startrek970206.html, accessed December 2001.

Greenwald, J. (1997b) ' "No Time for *Trek*": in India, Poverty, Nationalism and too Many Reruns Conspire to Ground *Star Trek* Fandom', Planet *Star Trek* series, *Salon Magazine* 21, http://archive.salon.com/feb97/21st/startrek970220.html, accessed December 2001.

Griffiths, T. (1986) 'Interview with Misha Glenny', 1985, in *Judgement Over the Dead*, London: Verso.

Hall, S. (1981) 'The Whites of Their Eyes: Racist Ideology and the Media', in G. Bridge and R. Brunt (eds.), *Silver Linings*, London: Lawrence and Wishart.

Hall, S. (1992) 'New Ethnicities', in J. Donald and A. Rattansi (eds.), '*Race*', *Culture and Difference*, London: Sage.

Hall, S. (1994) 'Notes on Deconstructing the Popular', in J. Storey (ed.), *Cultural Theory and Popular Culture*, London: Harvester Wheatsheaf.

Hall, S. (1998) 'Aspiration and Attitude . . . Reflections on Black Britain in the Nineties', *New Formations*, 31, pp. 38–47.

Hall, S. (1998a) 'Who Needs Identity', in S. Hall and P. du Gay (eds.), *Questions of Cultural Identity*, London: Sage.

Hall, S. (2000) 'Cultural Identity and Diaspora', in N. Mirzoeff (ed.), *Diaspora and Visual Culture*.

Haraway, D. (1990) 'A Manifesto for Cyborgs: Science, Technology, and Socialist Feminism in the 1980s', in L. J. Nicholson (ed.), *Feminism/Postmodernism*, London and New York: Routledge.

Haraway, D. (1997) *Modest_Witness@Second_Millenium: FemaleMan©_Meets_OncoMouse™*, London and New York: Routledge.

Havens, T. (2000) 'The Biggest Show in the World: Race and the Global Popularity of *The Cosby Show*', *Media Culture and Society*, 22:4, pp. 371–93.

Hesse, B. (1999) 'Reviewing the Western Spectacle: Reflecting Globalisation through the Black Diaspora', in A. Brah, M. J. Hickman and M. Mac an Ghaill (eds.), *Global Futures: Migration, Environment and Globalisation*, London: Macmillan.

Hill Collins, P. (2001) 'The Social Construction of Black Feminist Thought', in K.-K. Bhavnani (ed.), *Feminism and Race*, Oxford: Oxford University Press.

hooks, b. (1992) *Black Looks: Race and Representation*, Boston: South End Press.

Jameson, F. (1990) 'Postmodernism and Consumer Society', in E. A. Kaplan (ed.), *Postmodernism and its Discontents*, London: Verso.

Jenks, C. (1986) *What is Postmodernism?*, London: St Martin's Press.

Kaplan, A. E. (1992) 'Feminist Criticism and Television', in R. C. Allan (ed.), *Channels of Discourse Reassembled*, London: Routledge.

Kramer, G. (2002) 'Love to Love You', *Gay City News*, www.gaycitynews.com/GCN13/lovetolove.html, accessed March 2004.

Lee, J. (1988) 'Care to Join me in an Upwardly Mobile Tango? Postmodernism and the New Woman', in L. Gamman and M. Marshment (eds.), *The Female Gaze*, London: The Women's Press.

Linford, P. (1999) 'Deeds of Power: Respect for Religion in *Star Trek: Deep Space Nine*', in Porter and McLaren (eds.), *Star Trek and Sacred Ground*.

Lyotard, J. F. (1984) *The Postmodern Condition: A Report on Knowledge*, trans. G. Bennington and B. Massumi, Manchester: Manchester University Press.

MacCabe, C. (1981) '*Days of Hope* – a response to Colin McArthur', in T. Bennett, S. Boyd-Bowman, C. Mercer and J. Woollacott (eds.), *Popular Television and Film*, London and Milton Keynes: British Film Institute/Open University Press.

McGrath, J. (1977) 'TV Drama: The Case Against Naturalism', *Sight and Sound*, 46:2, pp. 100–5.

McIntosh, M. (1997) 'Class', in Medhurst and Munt (eds.), *Lesbian and Gay Studies*.

McKinson, F. (2003) 'How Black is my TV', *Precious*, www.preciousonline.co.uk/features/may03/tv.htm, accessed October 2004.

McLaren, D. (1999) 'Understanding the *Star Trek* Phenomenon as Myth', in Porter and McLaren, *Star Trek and Sacred Ground*.

McLean, C. (2001) 'I Just Can't Get Enough', *The Guardian*, www.guardian.co.uk/tv_and-radio/story/0,3604,441206,00.htm, accessed March 2003.

McLuhan, M. (1969) *Understanding Media: the Extensions of Man*, London: Sphere Books.

Macpherson, W. (1999) *The Stephen Lawrence Inquiry*, www.archive.official-documents.co.uk/document/cm42/4262/4262.htm, accessed October 2004.

Madden, J. (2000) 'Queer as Friends', *The Guardian*, 7 February, www.guardianunlimited.co.ukwomen/story/0,237588,00html, accessed March 2003.

Massey, D. (1999) 'Imagining Globalisation: The Power Geometries of Time–Space Compression', in A. Brah, M. J. Hickman and M. Mac an Ghaill (eds.), *Global Futures: Migration, Environment and Globalisation*, London: Macmillan.

Maynard, M. (2001) ' "Race", Gender and the Concept of Difference', in K.-K. Bhavnani (ed.), *Feminism and Race*, Oxford: Oxford University Press.

Mayne, J. (1997) '*L. A. Law* and Prime Time Feminism', in Brunsdon, D'Acci and Spigel (eds.), *Feminist Television Criticism*.

Medhurst, A. (1997) 'Camp', in Medhurst and Munt (eds.), *Lesbian and Gay Studies*.

Medhurst, A. and Munt, S. R. (eds.) (1997) *Lesbian and Gay Studies: A Critical Introduction*, London: Cassells.

MED-TV (1999) 'UN World TV Forum', www.ib.be/med/med-tv/sterka/issue03/un_w_tv.htm, accessed October 2002.

Mendlesohn, F. (2002) 'Surpassing the Love of Vampires, or Why (and How) a Queer Reading of the Buffy/Willow Relationship is Demanded', in R. Wilcox and D. Lavery (eds.), *Fighting the Forces: What's at Stake in Buffy the Vampire Slayer*, Oxford: Rowman and Littlefield.

Meyer, M. (1994) *The Politics and Poetics of Camp*, London: Routledge.

Mirza, H. S. (1997) 'Black Women in Education: A Collective Movement for Social Change', in, H. S. Mirza (ed.), *Black British Feminism*, London: Routledge.

Mirza, H. S. (2000) 'Race, Gender and IQ: The Social Consequences of Pseudo. Scientific Discourse', in K. Owusn (ed.), *Black British Culture and Society*, London and New York: Routledge.

Mirzoeff, N. (2000) *Diaspora and Visual Culture: Representing Africans and Jews*, London and New York: Routledge.

Modleski, T. (1991) *Feminism Without Women: Culture and Criticism in a 'Post-Feminist Age'*, London and New York: Routledge.

Modleski, T. (1997) 'The Search for Tomorrow in Today's Soap Operas', in Brunsdon, D'Acci and Spigel (eds.), *Feminist Television Criticism*.

Morris, M. (1990) 'Banality in Cultural Studies', in P. Mellencamp (ed.), *The Logics of Television: Essays in Cultural Criticism*, Bloomington: University of Indiana Press.

Mulvey, L. (1975) 'Visual Pleasure and Narrative Cinema', *Screen*, 16:3, pp. 6–18.

Nelson, R. (1997) *Television Drama in Transition*, London: Macmillan.

Nelson, R. (2000) 'Performing (Wo)manoeuvres: The Progress of Gendering in TV Drama', in Carson and Llewellyn-Jones (eds.), *Frames and Fictions on Television*.

Ng, V. (1997) 'Race Matters', in Medhurst and Munt (eds.), *Lesbian and Gay Studies*.

Nichols, B. (1994) *Blurred Boundaries: Questions of Meaning in Contemporary Culture*, Bloomington: Indiana University Press.

Paget, D. (1998) *No Other Way to Tell It: Dramadoc/Docudrama on Television*, Manchester: Manchester University Press.

'Palefella' (2003) 'Gene Rodenberry's Dream is on Fire', http://palefella.com/sticky/Sept/sept11.html.

Pearce, L. and Stacey, J. (1995) *Romance Revisited*, New York and London: New York University Press.

Penley, C. (1997) *NASA/Trek: Popular Science and Sex in America*, New York: Verso.

Perlmutter, T. (1993) 'Distress Signals: A Canadian Story and International Lesson', in Dowmunt (ed.), *Channels of Resistance*.

Petley, J. (1996) 'Fact Plus Fiction Equals Friction', *Media Culture and Society*, 18:1, pp. 11–27.

Pieterse, J. (1995) 'Globalisation as Hybridisation', in M. Featherstone, S. Lash and R. Robertson (eds.), *Global Modernities*, London: Sage.

Pines, J. (1995) 'Black Cops and Black Villains in Film and TV Crime Fiction', in D. Kidd-Hewitt and R. Osborne (eds.), *Crime and the Media*, London: Pluto Press.

'Pinktink' (2001) 'Rikki Beadle-Blair on *Metrosexuality*', interview, http://pinktink.250X.com/misc/rikkiBB.htm, accessed March 2004.

Poole, M. and Wyver, J. (1984) *Powerplays: Trevor Griffiths in Television*, London: British Film Institute.

Porter, J. E. and McLaren, D. L. (1999) *Star Trek and Sacred Ground: Explorations of Star Trek, Religion and American Culture*, Albany: New York: State University Press.

Probyn, E. (1997) 'New Traditionalism and Postfeminism', in Brunsdon, D'Acci and Spigel (eds.), *Feminist Television Criticism*.

Quinion, M. (2003) 'Beam Me Up, Scotty: The Lingustic Legacy of Star Trek', WorldWide Words, www.worldwidewords.org/articles/startrek.htm, accessed June 2005.

Rassool, N. (1997) 'Fractured or Flexible Identities? Life Histories of "Black" Diasporic Women in Britain', in H. S. Mirza (ed.), *Black British Feminism*, London: Routledge.

Raven, C. (1999) 'The Lawrence Case in Black and White (and Nothing in Between)', *The Guardian*, 23 February, www.guardianunlimited/Columnist/Column/0,238283,00.html, accessed September 2004.

Redhead, M. (1999) 'The Justice Game', *The Guardian*, 15 February, www.guardianunlimited.co.uk/Archive/Article/0,4273,3821913,00.html, accessed June 2003.

Richards, T. (1997) *Star Trek in Myth and Legend*, London: Millennium.

Richardson, K. and Meinhof, U. H. (1999) *Worlds in Common: Television Discourse in a Changing Europe*, London and New York: Routledge.

Roberts, R. (1999) *Sexual Generations: Star Trek: The Next Generation and Gender*, Urbana and Chicago: University of Illinois Press.

Robertson, R. (1995) 'Globalisation: Time–Space and Homogeneity', in M. Featherstone, S. Lash and R. Robertson (eds.), *Global Modernities*, London: Sage.

Robins, K. (1991) 'Tradition and Translation: National Culture in its Global Context', in J. Corner and S. Harvey (eds.), *Enterprise and Heritage: Crosscurrents of National Culture*, London: Routledge.

Roof, J. (1997) 'Postmodernism', in Medhurst and Munt (eds.), *Lesbian and Gay Studies*.

Rosenthal, P. (1988) 'It's Only TV Insists Star of *Ally McBeal*', www.geocities.com/TelevsionCity/Set/8532/allymcbealefiles40.html, accessed November 2001.

Said, E. (1978) *Orientalism*, New York and London: Routledge.

Shalit, R. (1998) 'Ally, Dharma and Ronnie, and the Betrayal of Postfeminism', www.geocities.com/TelevisionCity/Set/8532.allymbeale files12.html, accessed November 2001.

Shohat, E. and Stam, R. (1994) *Unthinking Eurocentricism: Multiculturalism and the Media*, London: Routledge.

Sinfield, A. (2000) 'Diaspora and Hybridity: Queer Identities and the Ethnicity Model', in Mirzoeff (ed.), *Diaspora and Visual Culture*.

Skelton, C. (2001) 'Come on Damian and Tracey – Look at Yourselves and Laugh', *The Observer*, http://observer.guardian.co.uk/reveiw/story/0, 6903,462509,00,html, accessed March 2003.

Skirrow, G. (1985) '*Widows*', in M. Alvarado and J. Stewart (eds.), *Made for Television: Euston Films Limited*, London: British Film Institute.

Spronk, B. (2002) 'Globalisation, ODL and Gender: Not Everybody's World is Getting Smaller', www.cade-aced.ca/icdepapers/spronk.htm, accessed November 2002.

Stam, R. and Spence, L. (1985) 'Colonisation, Racism and Representation: An Introduction', in B. Nichols (ed.), *Movies and Methods, Volume II*, Berkeley: University of California Press.

Star Trek.Com (2002) 'Viewing Stations', Paramount, the Official *Star Trek* Website, www.startrek.com/information/ad.html, accessed June 2002.

Star Trek History (2000) Paramount press release (1994), online at http://pages.prodigy.com/nadel/history.htm, accessed June 2003.

Stratton, J. (1989) 'Beyond Art: Postmodernism and the Case of Popular Music', *Theory Culture and Society*, 6:1, pp. 31–57.

Straubhaur, J. D. (1997) 'Distinguishing the Global, Regional and National Levels of World Television', in A. Sreberny-Mohammadi, D. Winseck, J. McKenna and O. Boyd-Barrett (eds.), *Media in the Global Context: A Reader*, London: Edward Arnold.

Street, J. (1997) 'Across the Universe: Globalisation and Popular Culture', in A. Scott (ed.), *The Limits of Globalisation*, New York and London: Routledge.

Strummer, C. (1993) 'MTV's Europe: An Imaginary Continent', in Dowmunt (ed.), *Channels of Resistance*.

Taylor, A. (1997) 'A Queer Geography', in Medhurst and Munt (eds.), *Lesbian and Gay Studies*.

The Knitting Circle (2003) 'Popular Culture: *Metrosexuality*', press cuttings, http://myweb.isbu.ac.uk/-stafflag/metrosexuality.html, accessed April 2004.

The Plain Dealer (1998), www.geocities.com/TelevisionCity/Set/8532/ allymcbealefiles99.html, accessed January 2001.

Travis, A. (2000) 'How Hague Mugged Macpherson', *The Guardian*, 15 December, www.guardian.co.uk/macpherson/article/0,2763,411596,00. html, accessed July 2003.

Viacom Official Website (2001) 'Viacom Inc, the facts', www.viacom/the facts.tin, accessed January 2003.

Viacom Inc (2003) 'Securities and Exchange Commission Washington form 10K' [online] www.Viacom.com./pdf/form10k, accessed April 2004.

Walter, N. (1999) *The New Feminism*, London: Virago.

Watney, S. (1997) 'Lesbian and Gay Studies in the Age of AIDS', in Medhurst and Munt (eds.), *Lesbian and Gay Studies*.

Wayne, M. (1998) 'Counter-Hegemonic Strategies In Between the Lines', in M. Wayne (ed.), *Dissident Voices: The Politics of Television and Cultural Change*, London: Pluto Press.

Whatling, C. (1997) *Screen Dreams: Fantasising Lesbians in Film*, Manchester: Manchester University Press.

Williams, R. (1977) 'A Lecture on Realism', *Screen*, 18:1, pp. 61–74.

Young, L. (1996) *Fear of the Dark: 'Race', Gender and Sexuality in the Cinema*, London and New York: Routledge.

Young, S. (1988) 'Feminism and the Politics of Power', in L. Gamman and M. Marshment (eds.), *The Female Gaze*, London: The Women's Press.

Index

Absolutely Fabulous 148–9
ACT-UP 140, 142, 144
affect 11
Ahmad, Aijaz 101
Ahmed, Sara 15–19, 39, 46–7,
    68, 101, 171, 187
AIDS 54, 140–3, 146
Alexander, J. 106, 111
Ali, Tariq 50, 53
Allen, Jim 10–11
Ally McBeal 32, 34, 48, 53–64,
    119, 156, 161
Althusser, Louis 18
Andermahr, S.A. 142
Ang, Ien 36–7, 46
Anthony, Susan B. 34
Appaduria, A. 100, 103
Armstrong, Isobel 45
Arroyo, Joseph 146
Atkins, Lisa 40–1, 47–8
Aubrey, Juliet 82
Augustus, Patrick 95
Austin, J.L. 139
authorship 26, 75, 177
The Avengers 149

Babyfather 95, 97
Bakare, Imruh 71–4, 108
Bakare-Yusef, B. 70
Bakula, Scott 130
Baptiste, Marianne Jean 184

Barker, Chris 23–6, 103–10
Barrett, Duncan 113–25, 136
Barrett, Michele 113–25, 136
Barthes, Roland 18–19, 22, 26,
    116
Baudrillard, Jean 3, 17–18, 21,
    23, 28, 30, 41, 102–3, 108
Beadle, Carleen 173
Beadle-Blair, Rikki 172, 177, 181
Beckham, David 173
Becks (company) 154
Bellafante, Ginia 53–4
Bellows, Gil 57
Bernardi, Daniel 100, 115–18,
    122
Bersani, Leo 143
Bhabha, Homi K. 12, 21, 71–5,
    84–5, 108
Bhaji on the Beach 97
Big Women 50–3
The Bill 66, 76, 90–4
Billingham, Peter 153–61, 164–7
Billingsley, John 129
Biltereyst, Daniel 105
Biswas, Neil 96
'black' as a political
    category 68–71
Blalock, Jolene 129, 132
Bleasdale, Alan 10
'Bollywood' films 75
Bordo, Susan 22, 38–9, 46, 105

Boulton, Nicholas 50
Boy George 154
Brah, Atvar 67, 70–1, 89, 94, 111
Brecht, Bertolt 9–13, 17, 183
Breen, Rodney 175–6
British Broadcasting Corporation (BBC) 94–5, 138
British National Party 187
Brooks, Avery 121
Brunsdon, Charlotte 34–7, 42–3, 66, 78–9
The Buddha of Suburbia 96
Buffy the Vampire Slayer 32, 149–50
Burke, Simon 96
Butch Cassidy and the Sundance Kid 166
Butler, Judith 37–9, 44, 47–8, 65, 71, 124, 139, 143–6, 171

Cagney and Lacey 41–2
Camilleri, Anya 48
camp aesthetic 144–7, 150–2, 179
Canada 105
capitalism 22–3, 46, 74, 100–1, 105–6, 111, 114, 127, 136
Carby, Hazel 36
Carrington, Ben 86, 88
Carson, Bruce 96
Carson, Silas 173
Cashmore, Ellis 76, 105
Cattrall, Kim 49
Caughie, John 11–12, 21, 24, 181
Chadha, Kalyani 105
Chadwick, Maureen 48
Channel 4 Television 1, 94, 138, 172
Chekhov, Anton 11
Chicago Hope 53
China 105, 113
Chisholm, Melanie 44
Cixous, Hélène 36
Clarke, Noel 172

CNN 105
cold war 126
Collins, Jim 29–32, 59, 152
Collins, Karl 91–2, 172
'colonial mimicry' 74, 84
Commission for Racial Equality 95
complexity theory 110–11
Copland, Aaron 118
The Cops 91
Corcoran, Farell 103–4
Corday, Barbara 41
Coronation Street 31, 95, 149, 160
Cosby 107
Country 11
Courage, Alexander 118
Crimewatch 24
cultural hybridity 6, 72–5, 93, 108–9, 122, 147
cultural imperialism 7, 102, 105–6, 109–15, 136
Currie, Edwina 46

D'Acci, J. 34
Dahlgren, Peter 105
Dallas 149
Davis, Andrew 138
Davis, Russell T. 8, 154–5, 168, 169
Days of Hope 11
deconstruction 14–15, 65, 67–9, 72, 103, 143–4
Delaney, Gavin 173
Derrida, Jacques 13, 18, 22–4, 28, 36–7, 140, 143
Di Caprio, Leonardo 160–1
diaspora aesthetics 6–7, 66, 73–6, 94–7
Diawara, Mantia 47–8
disavowal 85
Dr Who 160, 165
Dotchin, Michael 180
Doty, A. 148–52

Dowmunt, T. 105–6
drama-documentary 24, 182–5, 188
dramatic quality 171–2, 177
dramatic reconstructions 24
'dual address' concept 79, 84
Dynasty 149

Earhart, Amelia 128
Eastenders 31
Eco, Umberto 19
Edgar, David 11
Edwards, Tim 140
Elam, Diane 28–9
Eliot, George 27
emotional identification 32
epic theatre 9–10
ethnicity 68, 75

Fairbanks, Davie 180
Faludi, Susan 34, 44–5
Fanon, Franz 12, 85–6
Farrier, Stephen 139–43, 152
feminine aesthetic 36, 38, 43
femininity 14, 42, 47, 50, 163
feminisation 6, 41–2, 47–8, 64
feminism 13, 22, 29, 34–44, 70–3, 117, 170–1;
 media image of 40
 postmodern 37–8, 44, 143–7
 on television 41–4; *see also* postfeminism
Fenton, Natalie 39–40
Feuer, Jane 152, 176
Fielding, Helen 53
Fiske, John 18–28, 42–3, 58, 105, 108, 176–7
Flannery, Peter 27, 50
Flett, Kathy 175, 177, 179
flexi-narratives and flexiad drama 27–8, 31–2, 57, 76, 83–4, 95, 119, 164, 176
Flockhart, Calista 34, 54

Foucault, Michel 13, 18, 22, 26, 37–8, 45–6, 71, 75, 140, 143, 155
Frankenberg, Ruth 39, 108
Franklin, S. 99–100
Fraser, Mat 173
Frasier 148, 152
Freudian analysis 61–2, 143
Friedan, Betty 34
Frow, John 68
fundamentalism 111

Galileo 128
Gamman, Lorraine 41
Gangsters 77
gay identity 138–44
Gaynor, Gloria 60
gender 38
The Genre Handbook 138, 148, 152
Gergen, K. 23
Germann, Greg 55
Gibson, Mel 83
Giddens, A. 103
Gillen, Aiden 153–4, 161
Gilroy, Paul 67–8, 71–2, 108
Gimme, Gimme, Gimme 152
Gless, Sharon 41–2
globalisation 7, 99–102, 106–13, 117, 125, 136
Glover, Danny 83
Goldberg, Whoopi 122
Goldman, R. 142, 145–6
Goodness Gracious Me 97
The Governor 78–9
Grant, Sherry 44
The Green Wing 32
Greengrass, Paul 184
Greenham Common 51
Greenwald, Jeff 112–14
Griffiths, Steve 80
Griffiths, Trevor 10–11, 27
Gulati, Shobna 95

Habelstram, Judith 47
Hague, William 93
Haley, Alex 69
Hall, Stuart 13, 18, 22, 25, 77–8,
    85–6, 108
Hamer, Lisa 173
Haraway, Donna 37, 39, 102,
    123, 135
Harris, Mel 112
Harris, Susan 57
Havens, Timothy 107–8
Hawes, Keeley 151
Hesse, Barnor 117–18, 136
Higgens, Anthony 80
Hill Collins, Patricia 69
Hill Street Blues 24, 76–7, 90
Hillsborough 157, 184
Hollyoaks 90
homosexuality 14, 87–8,
    138–9; *see also* queer
hooks, bell 36, 46, 75
Huda, Menhaj 163–4
Hudson, Lee 175
human genome project 135
humanism 118, 136, 181, 188
Humphries, Barry 62
Hunnam, Charles 153
Hutcheon, Linda 16–17
hyperrealism 17, 21, 28, 54,
    102

Ibsen, Henrik 11
identity 13–15, 23, 33;
    transnational 107–9;
    see also gay identity
Independent Television
    Commission 154
India 105, 113–14
interdisciplinarity 3
International Monetary Fund 100
intersubjectivity 32, 188
intertextuality 20, 26, 51, 57, 97,
    115–16, 120–1, 125, 135

Irigaray, Luce 36
irony 32, 84, 152, 183, 189
It Ain't Half Hot Mum 77

Jackson, Michael 1, 138, 169
Jameson, Frederic 127
Japan 113
Jarrold, Julian 96
Jenks, Charles 16, 48
Jerry Springer 152
Joyce, James 133
Juliet Bravo 160

Kaplan, Anne E. 19, 26, 46
Kavoor, Ananndan 105
Keating, Dominic 130
Keating, Paul 173
Kelly, Craig 153
Kelly, David E. 53, 58, 63
Kennedy-Martin, Troy 10
Kerr, P. 176
King, Martin Luther 121
King, Rowena 49–50
King, Stephen 31
King Lear 96–7
Kingdom Hospital 31
Knopp, Lawrence 142
Kon Tikki expedition 128
Kpobie, Joseph 186
Krakowski, Jane 63
Kramer, Gary M. 176
Kristeva, Julia 36
Kureishi, Hanif 96

LA Law 42, 53, 57
La Plante, Lynda 41, 66, 78–80,
    89
Lacan, Jacques 12, 36–7, 140,
    143, 163
Lauretis, Teresa de 143
Lawrence, Doreen and
    Neville 184–8
Lawrence, Stephen 6; *see also*

[*The*] *Murder of Stephen Lawrence*
Lee, Janet 40, 46
Leigh, Mike 184
lesbianism 138–9
Lethal Weapon 83
Life and Loves of a She Devil 51–2
Linford, Peter 122
linguistic theory 12
Loach, Ken 10–11, 27
Lorde, Audre 36
Love Thy Neighbour 77
Lui, Lucy 63
Lurie, C. 99–100
Lynch, David 29, 177
Lyotard, J.F. 13, 16–18, 127

MacArthur, Colin 11, 181
MacCabe, Colin 11–12, 19, 181
MacDonald, Peter 80
McDougall, Charles 157
McDowell, Linda 47
Macfayden, Angus 49
McGovern, Jimmy 157, 184
McGrath, John 10–11
McIntosh, M. 141–2
McKinson, Fiona 94–7
McLaren, Darcee L. 116, 123
McLean, Gareth 175
McLuhan, Marshall 101–3
MacNicol, Peter 56
Macpherson Report (1999) 6, 90–4, 182
Madonna 21, 26, 43–6, 142
Manchester 156
Mani, Lata 39, 108
Mapplethorpe, Robert 145–6
Martin, Jesse L. 63
Marx, Karl 22, 74
The Mary Tyler Moore Show 57
Massey, Doreen 99–101, 136
Maynard, Mary 66–70

Mayne, Judith 41–2, 150
Medhurst, A. 141–7
MED-TV 103–4
mega-text 100, 115–18, 122–30, 133–5
Meinhof, Ulrike 32, 104, 152
Mendlesohn, Farah 149–50
Mercer, Kobena 75, 145
metanarratives 110–11, 136
Metrosexuality 92, 169, 172–83
Meyer, Moe 143, 146–7
Miami Vice 77
Middlemarch 27
Mind Games 80
Mind Your Language 77
Mirza, Heidi Safia 63
Mirzoeff, Nicholas 74
Modleski, Tania 39, 43, 45
Mohanty, Chandra Talpade 106, 111
Montgomery, Anthony 130
Morris, Meaghan 43, 68, 21–2, 109–10, 136
Morton, Donald 143
MTV 104, 106, 114, 157, 179
multiculturalism 68, 125, 129
Mulvey, Laura 12, 21, 42, 132
Munt, S.R. 143, 145
The Murder of Stephen Lawrence 8, 169, 181–8
Murdoch News Corporation 103
music, use of 59–60, 83, 118–19, 127–8, 174

Nagra, Parminder 97
Nardini, Daniela 51
nationalism 111
naturalism 10–15, 24–6, 51, 83, 156–7, 164, 182
Nelson, Robin 1–2, 5, 23–33, 34, 50, 57, 169–71, 76, 79, 83, 89–90, 95, 176
Newton, Isaac 128

Ng, Vivian 145–6
Nichols, Bill 25, 188
Night and Day 32
Notting Hill Carnival 91, 93
NYPD Blue 76

The Office 25, 32, 183
open texts 19–20, 27
Oranges are Not the Only Fruit 27
Our Friends in the North 27, 29, 50–1
Ouseley, Herman 94

Paget, Derek 182, 185
Paglia, Camille 53
Pakistan 113
Paramount Television 114–15, 136
Park, Linda 130–1
Pearce, Lynne 161–4
Perlmutter, Tom 105
Petley, Julian 25, 183
Philips, Lesley 49
Phillips, Jonathan 82
Pieterse, J. 109
Pines, Jim 6, 66, 76–84
political correctness 8, 126, 141, 178, 182
postfeminism 44–56, 64, 125, 141–2
postmodern objectivity 109
postmodernity and postmodernism 2–4, 15–17, 21–32, 47, 56, 64, 74, 84, 90, 101, 118–27, 147–52, 155–7, 169–71, 176, 188–9; *see also* feminism: postmodern
poststructuralism 12, 25, 47, 70–1, 140
Potter, Dennis 50
The Practice 53, 57–8
Prime Suspect 41, 66, 78–81
Probyn, Elspeth 41, 43, 45

producerly texts 19–21, 116
Puri, Om 97

Quarshie, Hugh 184
queer 7, 73, 88, 170;
 as academic theory 143–7;
 in public sphere 139–42;
 and reading of texts 148
Queer as Folk 1, 7–8, 107, 138–9, 153–68, 172, 174, 180
Queer Nation 140

race, concept of 67
racism 6, 50, 66–70, 74–94, 110, 121–3, 135, 145, 184, 187
Ramsey, Fiona 83
Rassool, Naz 74
Raven, Charlotte 183–4
readerly texts 19–20
realism 6, 10–17, 21–6, 31, 51, 66, 73, 78–9, 83–4, 121, 147, 156–7, 183
reality television 24
Redhead, Mark 184
relativism 17, 28, 30, 64, 74, 89, 108–9, 147, 169–71, 188
'resistant readings' 106, 148
Richards, Thomas 116–20, 124, 134, 150
Richardson, Kay 32, 104, 152
Roberts, Robin 115–17, 122–3
Robertson, R. 103
Robins, K. 102
Roddenberry, Gene 113, 115, 118
Roof, Judith 74, 147, 157
Roots 69
Rushdie, Salman 96
Russia 106, 113, 128
Ryan, Jeri 131–2
Rye, Renny 50, 53

Said, Edward 131
Salmon, Hilary 95

Sandford, Jeremy 10
Sapara, Ade 80, 82
Second Generation 96–7
Secret and Lies 184
Sedgwick, Eve Kosofsky 143
Sen, Jon 96–7
September 11th 2001
    attacks 101, 110–11
Sex and the City 49, 64
Sex Traffic 64–5
sexism 79, 88–9
Shaft 92
Shakespeare, William 96–7
Shalit, Ruth 54–5
Shattuc, Jane 152
Shepard, Vonda 59
Shindler, Nicola 154, 156
Shohat, E. 75
Silent Witness 1
Simpson, Christopher 97
Sinfield, Alan 74–5
situation comedies ('sit-
    coms') 77–8, 152
Six Feet Under 32
Skelton, Charles 175
Skinner, Claire 48
Skirrow, Gillian 78–9
Smith, Courtney Thorne 55
Smith, Zadie 96
Soap 57
soap opera 13, 25, 31–2, 42–3,
    57–8, 90–1, 94, 104, 139,
    160, 172, 177, 181
socialism 9–10, 22–3, 27–8,
    46
The Sopranos 32
South Africa 107
Spaced 32
Sparks, Hal 160
Spence, Luise 12
Spice Girls 44, 52
Spigel, L. 34
Spronk, Barbara 101, 111

Stacey, Jackie 99–100, 102,
    161–4
Stam, Robert 12, 75
Star Trek 7, 100, 111–36,
    149–51
Star Wars 127, 184
Starr, Freddie 80, 83
Steinam, Gloria 34
stereotypes on television 76, 148,
    168, 175–6
Stirling, Richard 151
Stone, Oliver 31
Stonewall 154
Stratton, J. 150–1
Stratton, Paul 127–8
Straubhuar, Joseph 104
Street, J. 105
Strummer, Corinna 106
subjectivity 2, 7, 13–16, 20–3,
    31, 33, 74, 117
Supply and Demand 66, 80–95
Sawhney, Nitin 96

tabloid press 79, 154
Taylor, Africa 155
television, influence of 102–3
Thatcher, Margaret 46, 52
Thelma and Louise 166
Thirtysomething 45
Tikaram, Ramon 82
Til Death Us Do Part 77
Time magazine 34, 53–4
Tipping the Velvet 138, 147,
    150–1
Titanic 160
Trial and Retribution 79–80
Trineer, Connor 130
Turner, Tina 60
Twin Peaks 29–33, 59, 152,
    176–7
Two Golden Balls 48–50

Ulysses 133

Vahimagi, T. 176
Varney, Rebeca 172
Viacom Inc. 103, 114, 136
Vietnam War 125

Walker, Eamon 80–1, 89
Walter, Natasha 40, 44, 46
Waters, Sarah 138
Watney, Simon 142–3
Wayne, Mike 79
Wedderburn, Clive 91
Weldon, Fay 50–3
What the Folk 168
Whatling, C. 149–51
White, Barry 60
'white gaze' 85–6, 90
White Teeth 96

Widows 41, 78–80, 84
Wild Palms 31
Will and Grace 152
Williams, Raymond 10
Winterson, Jeanette 27
Wong, Benedict 82
Woods, Chris 142
World Trade Organisation 100
Wright, Elizabeth 10
writerly texts 19–20

Xena: Warrior Princess 149
The X-Files 1, 27, 31–2

Young, Lola 13, 67–70, 73–5, 79
Young, Shelagh 43–6
youth television 179–80